INVISIBLE LIMP

Debra Mak

First Edition

NEWMAN SPRINGS PUBLISHING
320 Broad Street
Red Bank, NJ 07701

First originally published by Newman Springs Publishing 2023

ISBN 978-1-68498-717-7 (Paperback)
ISBN 978-1-68498-718-4 (Digital)

Printed in the United States of America

The book is dedicated to my deceased son, Lance,
and his two children, Juliana and Ethan.

CONTENTS

PREFACE

To write this book, I used decades of journaling. I've written to you with my best memory of each event. The real and raw truth is what my readers deserve. I gave it in every sentence.

To preserve the anonymity of some of the individuals in this book, I've changed names of several. For the majority, real names are released with their permission.

ACKNOWLEDGMENTS

I OWE THE GREATEST DEBT TO the two people who invested their souls in this book. They read to edit multiple drafts that took years of their life to give birth to my book with heroic persistence. There is no language for human beings like Lorene D'Adam and Michael Stevens. Lorene was bold enough to make her critical points at critical moments. We broke down every barrier and finished strong. You were my best teacher. Michael, who laughed and cried with me through every chapter, thank you for always offering more Berea water and caring for me like a *brother*.

Without their confidence, the limp would still be invisible. You both helped me through every hard stretch. I'm forever grateful for your gift of time, trust, and faith in me. I'm so proud of how this anxious, bumpy road took us through thousands of hours and six years of hard work. Heroes have guts. You are both my heroes.

Special thanks to your spouses, Oliver and Carol, who gave up personal time with you to work on this book. Good heavens, have I not said, "Hallelujah. We did the labor and delivered this baby. You both have shepherded me through"?

Special thanks to my pro editor Sue Fiztmaurice, who taught me to show not tell, how to cut my sentences in half, and clearly showed me about the business of being a writer.

Deep gratitude to my readers Darlene Slusar, you have soul-expanding power; Kim Welch Lemon, thank you for not making giving up on me an option; Patty Penkava, Donna Goldsberry, Robbin Ricci, Lynette Mycias, you are such a river of blessings; William Brindier, *oh how we laughed*; Linda Bayliss; Carol Nagie; Marvin Nore; Karri Peifer; Christine Seitz. So many of you believed in my story before it became a book. You continued to believe in me through the long process of publishing. Most of you ushered me to the end. Some of you are lifelong friends. You kept me moving forward during the worst of times.

A deep bow to my dear friend Joan Simko. You are the woman who swells my heart. Thank you for coming and staying. My world is better with you in it. Always in all ways, Joan, I will remember your many gifts.

To my brother David, who is the one who traveled through this entire story for a lifetime. I love you, D. Willie Mak. You are still the one who makes me laugh out loud. We always found our way back to our roots…*together*.

To my other adopted brother Jeffrey Nore, thank you for always saying *yes*.

To Penny Friedman and her husband, Ron, whose spirits rose again and again as the most highly evolved humans who offered undying support. *I grew with you.*

To my mentors and supporters Sheila Hicks, Shayla Holtkamp, Rubi Gemmel, Debbra Huntsman Draudt, Lesa Little, Jeanne Mettler Doody, Becky Setliff, Arthur Batson, Jeffrey Trent Kaylor, Dr. Arthur Wernick, Colleen Drespling, Jeff Woods, Dr. Kimberly Rogers, Dr. Aaron Steccar, Bob Davis, Holly Conklin, you are all personal champions at different stages of my life. Thank you for your personal care, presence, and wisdoms.

To my two best friends Carla Currie and Renee Kumar, you are the mother I never had, my sisters I always dreamed of, my guardian angels on my shoulders who supported me for over twenty-five years during multiple traumas. No one understands my anxiety like the two of you. No one has given me the strength to be open about mental illness, addiction, and grief. You love me unconditionally. Thank you for the many moments and miracles. God bless *us*.

My deepest admiration goes to every reader who took a piece of this book and became aware of the power within. You traveled with me to grow more resilient. *I hope you heal.*

I can't end without giving thanks to my Facebook community. There are thousands of you I've never met. Your grace, humor, and support are not accidental. Without all of you, this book would not exist.

My debt to my "favorite stranger" on the planet, Flap. You believed in me when I stopped believing in myself. You picked me up from the bathroom floor. You supported my insanity, grief, anger, and many moods. You are the most selfless, gentle soul I have ever known.

Lastly, to my family. My book was not written for my children, grandchildren, niece, nephew. Please understand my story is for those stuck in deep suffering. I've always been the black sheep and lived differently than so many of you. I have touched each one of you, given a big piece of myself to each one of you in darkest times when the only energy I had was spent on you. It is my hope that our family may find peace. You are so individually and deeply loved by me.

Most writers only dream of having the love and support during their first book as all of you have given so freely. Thank you, universe, for aligning me with these human beings who brought this book from the beginning to publishing. I have never felt so much love and support from humanity. *It reclaimed my life.*

Chapter 1

SHATTERED

2011

MY SON IS DEAD. I'M sitting in the front row of a chapel in Orlando, Florida. My father is by my side with one hand on his Bible and the other on my rapidly bouncing right leg. My son Ryan, six feet four with brown hair and almond come-hither eyes, is a few feet in front of us in a closed red cedar casket. Close by are two large ivory candles and a photo display of Ryan. There's god-awful music playing. Ryan would have chosen Dave Matthews or Jim Croce. The smell of heavily scented flowers hanging in the air is reminiscent of Grandmother Maki's Avon perfume.

Guests approach the casket, pause, and bow their heads. They smile at the photos then greet and hug me. Many are crying. They all get the same response: "Thank you for coming. I really appreciate it." No one knows what to say.

I'm not feeling the "celebration of life" yet. If one more person tells me my son is in better place or that everything happens for a reason, I might scream, "His better place is here with his seven-year-old Forest and his two-year-old Rose!" My eyes shift to the right to

Forest, who is leaning into his mother. My heart hurts for everyone in our family.

I can't pray for strength. I'm angry with God and life and myself for not saving him. Ryan died from an intracerebral hemorrhage. He was on life support three days. My eyes stare at the casket. I want to open it, crawl inside, and see if there might be something—anything—I could do to bring him back to life.

Rain drums on the roof. The heavens are crying on Ryan's behalf. When I close my eyes, I can see a four-year-old boy in the front yard, joyously splashing in the puddles. I hear his contagious laugh. I see him track in through the front door, his face and clothes covered in muddy grime. I'm so glad I never stopped him. For a moment, I feel a calming effect as if his spirit is passing through the earth. It feels like the rain is grace, and I'm in a vessel between life right now and wherever death took Ryan.

People are filing in. Ryan's father looks drained, sorrowful. Carol, Ryan's older sister, is totally shut down. Brock, his younger brother, is crying. He lost more than a brother. Brock and Ryan were best friends for thirty years. The anxiety of this day chokes me.

The priest enters through a back door as people find their seats. Suddenly, my heart is racing. My face is hot, and I can't breathe. I exit the main hall, find a restroom, and close the door for a few moments of solitude. I talk out loud to Ryan, "What happened? How can you be dead? You are expecting too much from me today. I can't do this."

I pace and dial his cell phone to hear his voice, but I'm not soothed. It all happened so fast. One night he calls, invites me to see a movie, and the next night, he's in a coma. If it weren't for my other two children, I would call a cab, bolt, and check into a hospital until someone told me this was not happening. I lean against the bathroom wall, wondering how I will survive the next two hours. How do I go from hugging my six-foot-four son to holding a bag of ashes from an 1,800-degree cremation chamber?

I need to splash cold water on my neck. With one jittery finger, I draw circles around my face on the mirror and say, "Get yourself together." I slap both sides of my face—left cheek, right cheek, left cheek, right cheek. I drink handfuls of water. I need gloss. There are smudges of black mascara under my eyes. Dammit, I need to hurry and pee. My face needs more blush. My legs obediently carry me back to my chair, and I pull it a few inches closer to the casket.

I don't hear many of the words of the seven speakers. Dad starts with his fundamentalist prayer. My son-in-law Max is emotional when he reads the letter Forest wrote to his father. Ryan's sister-in-law Stacy reads a letter from Brock. Close friends, a cousin, and a coworker try to evoke smiles and laughter sharing memories of Ryan. I'm failing as an attendee of my own son's memorial service. Nothing sounds funny. *I want out of here right now.*

The priest uses words I've heard my whole life: "We are gathered here to celebrate that Ryan is now with God the Father." He looks right at me. "May you find comfort in knowing you will meet your son again in heaven."

Yada yada. Please! I don't know if heaven even exists. He speaks too long, and his words do not console me. If Jesus is watching me now, He's pissed.

I am the last to speak. It's my turn to express the divine power Ryan had on my life. The Holy Spirit must be with me at the podium because my voice does not shake. My words are clear. I look directly at his two children and say, "Your father was my Mr. Funny Man." Then I look around the room and say, "Ryan was the glue in our family. He was born with happy genes. He was a master of saying the unsayable. His comedic brilliance attracted a diverse circle of friends spanning all ages and backgrounds. Ryan was a leader. People knew when he walked in the door. My son did not know judgment. He accepted everyone exactly as they were and helped those less fortunate. Ryan had a magical energy that we will all miss. My son took a piece of me with him. I don't know how to survive without him. All I know is that Ryan was at peace with himself and the God of his understanding at the time of his death. For that, I'm grateful."

I ask everyone to please stand for a moment of silence. The tears of the men and women standing before me tell me Ryan mattered. I close with, "Thank you all for coming. Take time for each other and those you love. We are not promised a new morning. I know in my heart that Ryan's soul will be ever present. May God bless Rose and Forest, and may God bless us all. Peace be with you."

There are no balloons or doves to release at the close of the service. There is only strained chitchat. My heart feels cracked into two pieces—one half with Ryan, the other here, barely alive. The point of life is staying alive long enough to become your highest self. This all feels like a mistake that Ryan would die. A friend hands me a cup of water that feels like an act of grace for my miserable self. I gulped it down all at once.

I'm relieved that the service is over but anxious about what is next. I don't know anyone who has lost an adult child. Life has been hour by hour and suddenly flashes back to the intensive care unit a few days ago when I stood by with nine other family members watching Ryan's vital signs on a maze of medical equipment. We all waited and prayed for a miracle that did not happen. All I heard was the steady beep like that of a big city truck backing up. And then in a blink, the sound changed. Everything changed. All that was created in thirty-three years of life was reduced to one prolonged *beeeeeeeeeeeeeeeeeeeeeeeep.*

This is the darkest of all darkness. Is there anything worse for a mother? No, nothing.

Part 1

THE '70S

Chapter 2

COLOR MY WORLD

Forty years earlier

I WONDER IF ANYONE ELSE CARES how bright and blue the sky is or how far it stretches into the night. I've always been hypnotized by the vast space in the sky. My awareness expands as that space with a million stars draws me in. As far back as I can remember, my heart spoke to the clouds, the moon, and the stars. How many are there? How far away? Do they have meaning? My spirit swells in the majestic moments the universe presents. The sky is an old friend letting me know there is so much out there to learn and absorb in our evolutionary process.

It's a scorching hot July afternoon in 1971. My high school sweetheart and I are at Cedar Point amusement park in Sandusky, Ohio, going around and around on the giant Ferris wheel. My long hair is the color of summer-baked mud, and it blows wildly. We each have one hand on the gondola with our other hands laced together. My head rests on his chest. His neck smells like musk. Being with him feels like where I need to be.

We fell in love quickly and fully. Mason claims it was love at first sight four years ago at a ninth-grade house party. When he saw me walk into the room, he told his best friend, "I'm going to marry that girl!"

Mason was a star football player who was on the debate team and the honor roll. He looks like Donnie Osmond, so incredibly smart and a gentle nature.

I was the opposite. I was the girl who wanted to be your best friend the first time we met. High school was academically challenging, and I barely graduated. I could not focus. Being a majorette, busting out my dance moves and being one of the cool girls with the cool clothes and the cool friends ranked higher for me. After twelve years of religious restrictions, my parents moved to Berea, Ohio, and my brother and I were energized with new freedoms.

The next time I saw Mason was in gym class. We were learning how to square-dance. It was boy picks girl, and Mason picked me. Two weeks later, we broke off our other relationships and started meeting at *Spudnuts* doughnut shop on Front Street. That's where we really fell in love, that first young love you never forget. He wooed me with an old-fashioned style and with kissing that stopped my world. We both felt the exhilarating joy of a first love.

The cycle of the Ferris wheel is a reminder of the ups and downs in life and of the power of pauses. We broke up once when my parents caught us meeting in the middle of the night in our laundry room. My unspoken insecurities were real when Mason left for Indiana University on a full football scholarship. I had doubts about a long-distance relationship. We broke up for a week or so over this but understood true love doesn't mean you never break up. It made us realize that we sometimes need to separate to understand how much we belong together. Our love was like a raging fire that could not be tamed. We stayed in touch on pay phones and writing letters.

I work full-time at Cleveland Hopkins Airport and dream about a real career. I failed every college entrance exam and failed math in high school. Oh, yeah, I failed my swimming class too. I wish I were following the well-worn college path my friends are travelling. My creative energy was used twirling batons, dancing, and how I dress. Something more needs to happen with a career now that I need to financially support myself.

The Ferris wheel slows down. I smell funnel cakes and see children below eating pink clouds of spun sugar. Our gondola love nest stops at the top, and I feel anxious remembering how my brother would rock the seat when we were kids. Mason rubs my back. "I want to marry you."

"Are you serious?" I ask.

"Yes, I want us to get married."

There is no ring, but I say yes to this gig immediately. I'm sure a Ferris wheel proposal would be more romantic in Paris with a rock on my finger, but we adore each other. I convince myself that regardless of time, place, or the absence of a ring, there is no wrong proposal when it comes from the right person.

Our engagement dinner consists of sausage hoagies with the works and a Coke chaser. We sit next to each other stuffing ourselves. With all that grease, there will be intestinal trauma, but I'm in a love bubble, entrusting the rest of my life to a football player who secretly writes poetry and hides it under his bed. As we leave the amusement park, I get a piggyback ride to the car.

On the ride home I badger Mason with wedding plans. "I don't care if we can't afford a honeymoon as long as I can get the perfect dress. The wedding will be New Year's Eve 1973 with fairy lights, rose petals, and a full bar to keep the mood lively."

Regardless of what comes out of my mouth, Mason nods. But then he plays our song, Chicago's "Colour My World." Listening to the lyrics puts an end to my rattling on about plans. I want the marriage to be what matters, not just the wedding. We are holding hands that will hold the hands of our children that will hold the hands of their children that will hold our hands. The marriage will be a miraculous thing that will stand the test of time. I know this feeling will only grow from here. I'm marrying the person who is my holy instant thought all day long.

We stop to get homemade ice cream in a one-of-a-kind country store. The sun is sinking behind the trees. This is real love, baby. What a soul-smashingly beautiful day.

Chapter 3

A CRIMINAL ATTACK

IT'S A DARKER-THAN-NORMAL NIGHT SKY as I walk zombielike to my car after a long workday. It's in a now nearly empty parking lot, though in the distance, the rental car business is still open. I locate my keys in my handbag and consider whether to stop for food on the way home because I never took a lunch break. Just as I open my car door, I am grabbed from behind and shoved into the back seat of my car.

I scream, but it barely escapes me as he presses a knife against my neck, and I choke on my own breath. I'm powerless. My assailant is twice my size. He forces me onto my back and tells me to stay down. I get a look at his pulpy face. He glowers at me, still holding the knife to my throat. "You scream, you move, you make one sound and I kill you. These are my rules, bitch. One word and you die. One word, one move—do you get it?"

His speech is guttural. There are lights all around, and I'm hoping one person saw this and I will hear a police car any minute.

He gets in the car, pushes the driver's seat back, and closes the door. I'm trapped in the back seat of my own car. He starts the car and floors the accelerator. When he suddenly brakes, I roll forward. He floors it again and I slam back against the seat. Back and forth, back and forth. I am thrown around by his erratic driving. I've never known this fear before. I'm confused, disoriented, and I'm shaking uncontrollably. To be honest, I don't ever remember seeing this man.

Please, God, please, please, please, help me. Stop this. Please, God, help me, I keep praying. If there is a God, please hear me now.

He mumbles in spurts under his breath as if there's a short circuit between his thoughts and his words. Much of what he says makes no sense. He turns around every minute or two to look at me for a few seconds. Who is this man? What does he want from me? Why was he waiting for me? Panicky thoughts fill my head. What if he rapes me? What if he kills me? What if he kills me slowly? He's twice my size. There's no fighting back to defend myself. My eyes stay glued to his knife.

He turns the radio dial from station to station then off and on and the windows go down and up. He stops the car, pulls out a cigarette, turns around, and points the knife at my throat. He just looks, then he lights the cigarette and speeds off again. "What do you want from me. I can get you money if you just stop the car and talk to me. You can keep the car," I add.

He turns an ear toward me and seems to be listening, so I continue. "I promise I won't tell anyone anything. Please, just stop the car. I'm not the person you think I am. Please stop the car! I promise you I won't—"

He brakes hard, and I fly forward. He turns around and *bam*, slaps me hard across the face, screaming, "You stupid cunt! Stupid, stupid, stupid cunt! How stupid are you? Didn't I tell you not to talk? Didn't I? Listen to me, bitch. You talk again, you die. One more chance. One more. I will do surgery on you right here in this car if you say one more stupid word. No screaming. No talking. Do you understand what I'm telling you?"

I block my face with my arms and bob my head up and down. I'm cornered, completely trapped and under his control. My only hope for survival is submission. I can't make a mistake. My bladder is too full, and I feel urine flowing out. I'm too scared to even move. There's no talking to this man. If I don't obey his orders, I could die.

He drives on. I can't be sure for how long. When the car comes to a complete stop, he lights another cigarette and jumps out of the car. He yanks me out of the car into an upright position and throws his cigarette on the ground. He covers my mouth with his hand. The knife two inches from my throat. He forces me toward the entrance of an abandoned building. I glance at his face up close. It looks wolfish with eyes the color of bloody toilet water.

Inside, there is cracked linoleum, rusting metal, smells of sewage and rotting wood—fit for rodents and roaches, not for humans. He pushes down a hall with stale air and through a door. He bolts the door closed and ties my wrists behind me with a rope to a metal bed. A street light gleams through two windows. Dust and mold are everywhere. The room reeks of urine and smoke. He lights several candles and then a cigarette.

There is a chair and a large table scattered with empty bottles, ashtrays, cigarettes, Burger King bags, toilet paper, a magazine, a screwdriver, a Bible, a flashlight, and a belt. Next to the bed, there is a nightstand with another flashlight. Does he live here? On the wall, there's a world map and a painting of Jesus. I don't see a phone, clock, or any weapons as my eyes dart over every inch of the surroundings in preparation for whatever cat-and-mouse game is about to begin. The duct tape he uses does not cover my entire mouth but makes it difficult to breathe, and the lump in my throat, which feels like a giant pill is stuck there, makes it difficult to swallow. I'm not making a sound.

He sits quietly, drinking beer after beer. Then he turns to me and smiles. "Uh, do ya wanna beer, bitch?"

I shake my head. He laughs then sings and talks loudly enough that if anyone is anywhere near this room, they will hear him. "You are one crazy bitch and liar. You know you wanna beer, don't you? Jesus Christ, bitch! Drink a beer with me. It'll calm you down."

He laughs again and I hear the *tchkfzzz* of a beer can opening. He pours it over my head, pure entertainment for him. I hear it again as another can is opened. He pours that one all over me and takes a swig of alcohol out of a bottle. It looks like whiskey.

I'm losing oxygen. Extremely light-headed, but I must keep focused because he's completely unpredictable.

He starts dancing all around me. He removes the duct tape and brings the knife to my face, saying, "You know how the rules go. You only broke them twice. If you scream, you die. If you talk, you die."

As if to make his point he kicks me in the ribs. With an explosive laugh, he says, "How are you feeling now, Debbie Maki?"

Softly, with tears, I ask, "How do you know me?"

He kneels by me and spits in my face. I recoil as it slides down my cheek. "That wasn't the question," he says, and he walks back to the chair, setting the knife on the table.

With a smirk, he tells me where I live, where I work, and where I've been in the last month. He knows my parents' names and where they work. He tells me he will kill them too if I cause trouble. He knows my schedule. He tells me the name of the club where he saw me a couple of months ago and describes some of the people I was with. In two years, I've only been to a club twice. I've never seen this man before *ever!* He's a brainsick brute drinking, laughing, singing, walking, smiling, talking…more drinking.

He comes over to me with his whiskey as close as he can get. He strokes my face, my hair, and my neck. Then he sits next to me and rocks me back and forth, saying, "Poor baby. Poor baby bitch. It's been a hard day for my baby. I'm sorry, sweetheart. You are my baby now. You belong to me."

He drinks intermittently then continues rocking us back and forth, looking at me, repeating, "My poor baby. Let me rock you." This is pain on my ribs.

Eventually, he goes back to his chair, although by now, he can hardly stand. The whiskey bottle looks empty; he throws it at me. It misses and lands by the door. He opens another one and lights a cigarette. He opens the Bible and stares at it. He's not reading it, just turning pages. He's so drunk that he falls off the chair then climbs back up and staggers over to me. "A dumb bitch like you ain't probably afraid of the devil. I ain't fraid of no devil."

He opens my mouth and sticks his finger down my throat until I gag. Then he loses his balance and needs his hand to catch himself. He's losing control over his body.

I need to escape. The door is so close, and the knife is on the table. If I could break free from the bed, I'd outrun him. He's close to passing out, so I say under my breath, "Have another drink." He hears it.

His next slap is so hard, the room becomes a blur, but I hear him say, "I'm going to kick your crazy ass for telling me what to do. No bitch tells a man what to do."

With a cigarette in his mouth, he unties me, throws me on the bed, and rips off my clothes. He starts to rape me, but his erection fails. He reaches for a swig of booze and tries again. He spits on me. I want to throw up. He keeps at it as he says, "We start with sexy driving. Then sexy fighting. Now sexy rape. Then comes sexy dead."

This continues for one or who knows, maybe three hours. I've lost track of time. My mind is on high alert, but my body is exhausted. Finally, he ties me to the bed again, no duct tape, and staggers back to the chair, but this time, the ropes don't seem as tight.

Now he's emotional. "My mama is dead. So is my sister and my cousin. I never knew my daddy." He starts crying.

"I'm so sorry," I say. "That's horrible. Really, I mean it. I'm so sorry."

He looks at me like a normal person would, so I continue. "That's a sad way to live. If you're sad, I can help you. No one needs to know. I can just take you somewhere and help you. Why don't we leave here so I can help you?"

"Do you think if I kill you, God will let me into heaven when I die?"

He asks as he picks up the knife and points it at me. Is this it? Am I going to be stabbed to death? How many times will he stab me? How long will it take? I feel my heart racing again. Instead, he puts the knife down and opens another bottle. He lays his head on the table and cries. I wrestle with the rope behind me, watching him every second.

"Where do you want me to put your body after I kill you, Lake Erie or Coe Lake by your mother?"

He knocks several things from the table onto the floor, including the knife. It's now closer to me than to him. He slumps off the chair onto the floor. His eyes are open, watching me. I continue to loosen the ropes while trying to figure out my best move. Do I make a run for it? He seems too drunk to stand. I'm almost free of the bed, but if he notices, I'm dead.

I'm dizzy, and I'm trembling again. I'm finally untied, but I keep my hands behind me. I'm worried that I will pass out before he does. He sees the knife and moves toward it. I jump up with both feet and one hand off the floor. I reach for my purse and clothes and *move to the door.*

"You stupid bitch!" he screams, then he falls trying to get to his feet.

I unbolt the door and throw it open. Run. Run. Run. Down the steps. Faster. Faster. It hurts to move. I make it down one floor. I hear him bellowing, yet I don't understand his words. Run. Run. Run. Two steps at a time. Run. Run. My body is on fire. He's still yelling, but I can't see him. I hurl the front door open. I'm naked on the street, and I don't dare stop. I glance behind me, and now I see him stumbling down the stairs. I scream for help. I jump in my car and look for the keys in my purse. They're not there. Fuck! Where are the keys? In the room? I'm shaking so violently that the steering wheel is shaking. The keys are still in the ignition! Thank You, God!

I start the car and floor it. I'm free! I'm in a crazed state, hardly capable of driving, *but I'm free!* I have no idea where I am or where to go as I gasp, and I drive, and I scream out the window. I only need one person to hear me. I stop to throw up and lay my head on the steering wheel, feeling the power of survival but only briefly because he may be chasing me. I'm weak and disoriented. I drive through red lights and stop signs, bouncing off curbs. I hear horns. It's black outside.

I see a man walking down the street. "Help me! Please help me! A man is trying to kill me!"

He takes off down an alley, not wanting anything to do with me.

The adrenaline that has flooded my body over the past several hours is exhausting me now and impairing my thinking. I throw my clothes on and notice that my shoes never came off.

I'm lost. I'm driving until I find a highway sign and follow it. I think about finding the police, yet I couldn't tell them where to find him. He'd come after me again. The next time, he'd kill me and my family. I head for the Berea exit. I want to stop and get help, but I'm still paralyzed with fear. I'm afraid of everyone on the road. Is he in one of these cars? I need to go home. I need to call my fiancé. I need someone to tell me what to do because I can't make decisions.

Should I go to the hospital? Yes, the emergency room. They'll know what to do. Southwest General Hospital in Berea. But will they call the police? Is calling the police a good idea?

I need Mason. I need my mom. I need to go home. What if he's waiting there? I can't go anywhere in Berea. I should call the police. No, I'd better not. I can't go home while it's dark. I need to stop and breathe. I can't breathe.

I notice a pack of his cigarettes on the passenger seat, and I chuck it out the window.

It takes at least an hour to know where I am. I'm afraid to park my car in the driveway. What if he's waiting for me? Dad is already at work. Mom is surprised to see me walk in the front door. When I walk up the stairs, I pass out. My brother is there, and she lies to him, "She had a bad day at work with her boss."

She walks me to her bedroom so I can lie down. I tell her the whole story, every detail. She paces, cries, and screams. She calls my father at work and tells him to come home. She keeps asking me questions. Mom is afraid of reporting the rapist to the police. She believes what I believe because she had noticed a man who fit the description driving past our house in a red car, sometimes more than once a day. "Oh, dear God, that must have been him," she says.

I call Mason. He comes home, and I'm afraid to tell him everything because he could die. Everyone is terrified. No one is coming up with answers. Everyone is afraid of making the wrong decision.

We agree not to say a word to anyone, or the entire family might be killed. I call my employer and quit my job.

The more I talk to Mason, the more I feel I can trust him. We sit in his basement, and all I could say is, "I was raped." The attack shocks my nervous system into complete silence. I'm afraid that if my fiancé finds out what happened, it will end our relationship.

My parents tell me to get the hell out of Ohio. Mason is back in school, and when I call him, I tell him, "I'm coming to Bloomington this weekend. I want to get married."

He does not stop me, and we elope and move into a small trailer off campus in Indiana. As soon as possible, my parents move to a different home. There are no rape crisis centers, no hotlines, no books, no women therapists. I stop talking to my friends and family. My mother doesn't want to speak to me about it. Only God can hear the details.

The trailer is my cave. I know it's time to find a job, but it's impossible for me to go anywhere alone. I'm depressed and hate being with anyone but my husband. I believe everything that happened is my fault, which is why I can't tell the police. It's my fault for not looking at the parking lot close enough to see danger—my fucking fault. Everyone knows that. I dressed wrong, went to the wrong places, hung out with the wrong people, and didn't watch out for myself. I was stupid. He knew it. He knew I was a stupid girl who would keep her mouth shut. I'm living a life in shock...every damn day.

Mason is my everything. I know he is a safe haven, and I do whatever he says while losing more of myself each day. I never feel okay, and he knows it. He tells me I am not the same person he fell in love with. He wants that girl back. I focus on pleasing him because without him, I doubt I will survive. He gets me a job interview working for some doctors. I'm hired, but everyone must notice that something is weirdly wrong with me.

Every detail of that night is stored in my memory. Flashbacks take up all the space in my head. In my thoughts, I'm raped over and over again. My parents treat me like nothing happened and are in denial. No one else knows. Now the monster lives inside me. I often think about killing myself, but I don't share those thoughts with anyone. I'm too stupid and fucked-up to ever accomplish it anyway.

I fool the world. I act like I can work, buy groceries, answer the phone, stay married, sit at the family Thanksgiving table, and laugh at all the family jokes. I convince other people that I care about them, while I don't even care about myself. I remember birthdays and call people when they're sick. I get along with my coworkers. I'm an actress. I became one that night. I show up in my world pretending I'm Debbie. I fool everyone, but I can't fool my soul.

I want out of this body. I'm stuck in the rape room in my head. I hear him, and he won't shut up. His words are getting louder and louder. I survived, but it feels like I'm buried alive.

Chapter 4

MUSIC IS MY DRUG

SOME PEOPLE ARE AFRAID OF cockroaches or snakes. Others are rattled when the stock market plunges. Men freak me out—all men, except my husband. Mason is patient, and I feel lucky that I'm safe and loved by this beautiful man.

The attack feels too freakish to discuss with him. I don't want the images in my head to be in his, too, because I'm convinced the marriage would probably end. I work hard to strengthen the marriage, and I crumble with any inkling of not making him happy. I feel sexually dead, but Mason will not feel it. It's almost like I'm disconnected from my body. Before the assault, my sex drive was full-blooded, but since then, it's nonexistent. In my heart, I feel the love for my husband, but I can no longer feel it sexually. The depression I feel is real. The only way to sustain these feelings is to create an imaginary world, a different identity. All day long, I'm someone else, somewhere else, acting like everything I feel is normal. Otherwise, my insides will explode.

A monster steals ten hours of my life, and I'm instantly a version of myself I hate. If I had to pick one word to describe myself, it would be *worthless*. Everyone I meet is better than me. My self-esteem is gone. The blame game feels real. Why, if I did nothing wrong, do

I feel so worthless? I try to convince myself that I'll be okay again someday. How or when this will happen is a mystery. The entire mental and sexual assault is who *I am now*.

I am now a victim who suffers in complete silence with the fear my attacker will show up in every parking lot. I believe everything he said, and this life is nothing but a dream. I'm longing for that girl before the attack to come back. My husband knows something is wrong with me.

Coworkers ask, "Are you okay? You're not all here."

I tell them nothing is wrong, but I don't sleep well, and showing up for work on time is hard. I'd rather lie on the couch all day with our new dog. Then comes the verbal warning that I may be fired, so I kick it up a couple of notches, drink strong coffee, arrive early, smile, and kiss ass to save myself. Percocet helps. There is a supply of it at work, and when the lab tech leaves for lunch, I take it from the lab.

With the money I make, we can afford to rent a charming little place with a fenced backyard. Mason buys a motorcycle. He's still a student, so I'm the breadwinner in the family, but he'll work summer jobs until football practice starts. We are not struggling financially. On the outside, we appear to be doing well. Rape has turned me into someone I'm not.

During the months following the attack, my mother writes letters, calls every week, and visits. Gradually, she is more able to talk with me about what happened. Our conversations are private and offer temporary relief, but she wants me to remain silent to protect everyone until she finds the right help for me. I listen and trust her every word. She's the only who talks to me about what actually happened. How am I coping? How is my marriage? Am I functioning? I lie to her and tell her I'm fine. I can't talk about what I don't understand but crave her questions.

Working out in the gym becomes an obsession. I'm there daily, sculpting my body. Breaking a sweat gets me out of my head. Driving my Ford convertible with the top down and listening to loud music for an hour or two help. Mason, Percocet, Mom, exercise, driving, and music are what stop me from killing myself.

Mason and I start selling Amway. We are taking this gig seriously and recruit our parents. It means working nights and weekends in addition to my full-time job, but it gets me out of my mental penitentiary. He finds a sponsor. We all click and subscribe wholeheartedly to self-help books and attend a motivational seminar in the mountain town of Gatlinburg, Tennessee. We host large meetings at which Mason does the selling, and I demonstrate how products work. I believe I will become a positive person again if I hang out with only positive people, read only positive books, talk positively, and think positively.

Wrong. It doesn't happen. I'm in deep shit. The beast in me wins.

Then one evening, as we are leaving for one of our Amway meetings, my father calls and says, "Debbie, your mother is in the hospital. Her breast cancer is back. They are doing surgery tomorrow. She didn't want to worry you, so she asked me not to call."

"Wait. What? Mom is in the hospital? Her cancer is back? Which hospital?"

"Southwest General. But please don't call her. I'll call you tomorrow right after her surgery."

My parents have lost their minds waiting to tell me. Mason and I scrap our meetings, pack the car, and take off for Cleveland.

I'm not afraid of cancer, but when it spreads to her lymph nodes and chest wall and chemo begins at the Cleveland Clinic, Mason and I ditch life in Indiana and move back to Cleveland. When she needs full-time support, we move into their condominium, where I'm the caregiver of everyone while Mason and Dad both work full-time.

Mom's job is to get better. She has many close friends who knock at our door every day. I'm far less social since the attack, and there are times when I send people away. It's frustrating that the only person I could talk to about my rape is now sick. I can't burden her with my problems. My social anxiety increases to a level where I don't want to even talk to anyone on the phone. What requires me to speak is constantly interrupted by my paranoia. I can't focus without Percocet, and there's no way to get it prescribed. My next drug is sugar.

It's 1975, and the side effects of chemotherapy are unmerciful. Mom eats, throws up, eats again, and throws up again. She can't sleep. The day all her beautiful blond hair falls to the bathroom floor, we cry together quietly as I collect it and gently place it in the wastebasket. Then we hurry out to find her a suitable wig. We are both becoming skilled at suffering in silence.

During this same time, I discover a lump in my right breast. I'm only twenty-two. The tumor is removed at the Cleveland Clinic. Time crawls, and the men of the house consume a couple drinks. The pathology report brings the good news that it is benign. Thank you, sweet Jesus.

I try hard to wear that positive mask, but fear and hopelessness have taken up permanent residence. My head is still in *that* room with *that* animal. Dad insists Mason and I attend Rex Humbard's Cathedral of Tomorrow, but it will take more than an evangelist to cure me. The only part I like about it is when we go to brunch afterward. My father wants my husband to be saved. All I know is this whole *saving* thing Dad is obsessed about should be used on saving his daughter and wife. Church sucks right now. Rape and cancer have created a religious rebellion with "on again, off again" relationship with God. Our relationship is twisted.

My senses are heightened but not in a pleasant way. I smell filth, and I feel the yuck and crud all over me from that night, so I often shower and bathe twice a day. Hot water helps. The lights in the bathroom are turned off. I don't like looking at my body or my face. I refuse to be in family pictures. When in front of a mirror, I quickly turn away because that person scares me. I don't recognize her. I'm not *her*.

I start journaling, which turns out to be a painful pleasure that helps. I write daily when no one is watching. Within months, I have several notebooks full. I hide them in a suitcase. I can focus when I write, but I can't read. Mason is an avid reader. I watch him devour books and wish I could pick up even one and finish it.

It's springtime, and Cleveland has a floral vibe. My period is a week late. Stress can do that, so I'm not concerned. When a month passes without a trace of blood, I see my OB. Hooray! I'm pregnant.

This news is like a big breath of fresh air for our entire family. It's the first grandchild on both sides.

Mom and I share happy thoughts, and she shop's immediately for girl stuff. At Higbee's department store, she buys pink dresses with matching hats, pink blankets, pink onesies—pink everything. When I show her outfits for a boy, she puts them back, saying, "It's a girl. I know you're having a girl."

Her joy brings relief. Baby shopping cheers up her cancer. Within a couple of weeks, a few of her friend's schedule baby showers.

During the early weeks of my pregnancy, Mom takes care of my barfing while I take care of hers. I crave canned green beans. It's not an easy first trimester. While new life grows inside of me, I'm preoccupied with cancer cells growing inside of Mom. I see fear in her crystal-blue eyes every day. She wants to be here to spend time with her grandchild and to watch me raise my child. The baby is her spirit force to beat the cancer.

I can't fail as a mother. The flashbacks I wake up with, the shame I feel—I need a professional to talk this through with me before I subject a child to my anxiety. I do things like start the washing machine and forget to add the clothes. I unload the dishwasher, putting away dishes that were never washed. At the grocery store, if a man even looks at me, I abandon my cart and hurry home. My body feels detached even while pregnant When anxiety surges forward, I consume sugar and pace. Pacing helps me manage depression. The faster I walk, the calmer my mind feels. I pace—often—every single day.

My anxiety affects my breathing enough to see a cardiologist. A heart monitor comes home with me. I'm having panic attacks that lower my oxygen and cause breathing problems. I'm told I must learn how to control my anxiety. When the doctor asks, "Why are you so stressed? Is it your mother's cancer?" I answer, "Yes." I don't want to tell him about my attack. I can't speak the whole truth. I'm certain the giant wolf who did this to me doesn't have breathing problems. Being attacked and not speaking about it creates another layer of internal chaos.

It's August 1975, and it's blazing hot. Mom is waterlogging the geraniums in the courtyard. She loves the smell of the fresh minty flowers. Suddenly, she throws down the hose, grabs a tissue from her pocket, and with the force of someone vomiting, coughs up massive amounts of blood. She screams, "Get your father!"

Dad holds on to her as blood drips all over his shirt. They're both crying. I can feel their hearts shatter in unison as he walks her back to the bedroom. He asks me to call her oncologist and then closes their bedroom door. Mom is admitted to the Cleveland Clinic the next morning for tests. She spends the night there.

As she settles into her hospital room, she asks me to get her markers and a poster board. She draws heart-shaped flowers, a pink rose, cute baby faces, and in the center, she writes, "I'm going to be a grandmother. I know it's a GIRL."

The nurses congratulate her in advance. She will be a grandmother in just three months. Mom has turned fear into art.

Once Mom is resting comfortably, Dad and I go out to grab a bite to eat, but beforehand, we meet her oncologist in the corridor. Mom's results are in, and he asks us to come to his office. Dad and I sit side by side, anxiously waiting while the doctor stalls, removes his glasses, taps a pen on his desk, and avoids eye contact. He shifts through papers, taps again, looks at us with eyes that say it all. His voice is flat. "Carol has terminal lung cancer."

Dad is silent and hangs his head. I'm angry. I stand up and start pacing. I sit back down because I can't catch my breath.

"Bill, I'm going to do everything I can to make her comfortable," the doctor says.

My father can't believe it. He's afraid and starts crying, "Not my Carol. No, please, not her, not yet. She's been so sick the last few weeks, but I never thought I would lose her. I don't want to lose my wife."

"I'm sorry, Bill."

I'm back on my feet, pacing. Dad says, "Sit down. Please sit down."

We hold on to each other for a couple of minutes until we hear, "Carol will need full-time medical care. It might be better if she could go somewhere."

I jump up and get almost nose to nose with the doctor. "I'm her caregiver."

He answers, "But you're pregnant. She will require twenty-four-hour medical attention as her condition worsens." He does not say how long she has, and we don't ask.

I raise my voice, "You are telling us to drop her off somewhere and let people who don't know my mom take care of her while she's dying? That's not how our family works. Get me an appointment with someone who can give me a full breakdown of what I need to do to take care of my dying mother!"

The doctor arranges for me to meet with a nurse the following morning when I will learn to give injections using oranges. A hospital bed, oxygen, and medications are ordered. He tells us he will give Mom the sad news, but I say, "No. No, you're not talking to her. We will handle everything. Thank you."

Dad and I walk to a vending machine and drink a soda. We spend ten minutes talking over the best way to tell her the diagnosis, and then we walk into her room. She never asks how long she has. Mom expects to live long enough to meet her grandchild. "I will go to the hospital by ambulance if necessary to see my first grandchild."

*****

Today is a mistake. Mom tries but can't make it through my last baby shower. So many extended family members she cares about are present, but she is too weak to sit up. When she needs to lie down in a bedroom, I decide to leave the shower. She cries in the back seat of the car where she needs to lie down. She has no strength to move. I pull over to fix the pillow and pull her head up to help her get more oxygen. I hate this day.

*****

It's a glorious day in October, my favorite month. The baby is due in six weeks. Brilliantly colored leaves crunch underfoot while others swirl and blow away in their final dance. The clouds overlap each other, and the smell of burning wood is in the air.

I'm walking alone. Mom's optimism is gone. She can't stand up to walk to the bathroom. When she tries to walk from the bedroom to the kitchen, it takes a half hour. She's angry that I bought chocolate Tootsie Rolls instead of multiflavored. There's not enough ice in her glass of water or enough breading on her pork chops. The oxygen tank by her bed at maximum flow does not provide enough air for her to breathe. The only comfort I can give her is to lie down next to her and place her hand on my belly. She waits until there's movement and smiles at me with tears in her eyes. There's no time limit for how long I will stay with her like this because it calms her, which calms me. My forty-seven-year-old mother looks ninety-seven. For her birthday, I buy her a winter coat to wear to the hospital when the baby is born. The coat boosts her confidence that she will be here for the birth.

*****

It's a Sunday evening. I'm ready for stillness. My nineteen-year-old brother David comes through the door from Kent State University with a look of sad despair on his face. The bond my brother has with his mother is holy. He's her favorite child. I've known it all my life.

My father says, "Debbie, why don't you and Mason spend a couple of hours with Mason's parents and take a break?"

I have not left my mother for three weeks, but Mason, David, and my father insist we join Mason's family for their homemade spaghetti dinner. Just as dinner starts, the phone rings. Mason's father hands the phone to me. It's my dad. "Debbie, we are at the hospital. Please get here right away. Your mother was brought here by ambulance."

Mason and I rush to the hospital. My mother is dead on arrival. I'm nine months pregnant, and my mother is dead. There is a chair, and I collapse into it. A nurse approaches, "Would you like to see your mother? Your father and brother are with her."

"No, I don't want to see my dead mother."

My brother and father walk toward me, and we cling to each other, feeling the profound absence of someone we loved dearly. Dad wants to say a prayer, but I object, "Please don't, not now. I'm not in the mood for a prayer."

Dad listens, and we head for home.

This will make an atheist out of me. Pray about what? How my life was stolen at age twenty? How my mother is dead just days, maybe hours away from meeting her first grandchild? *God is a liar!* I feel soul sick with no idea where the hell life is taking me now.

On the way home, Dad explains to me that one of Mom's last requests was that I would not be present when she passed away. That's why I was rushed out of the house.

We bury her a week later, and a large gathering of friends brings a generous luncheon to a Lutheran church. It's not long afterward that I feel my first contraction. My daughter is born with a cone-shaped head after twenty-nine hours of labor. She weighs seven pounds, nine ounces. We name her after my mother—Carol.

Not long after I'm released from the hospital, my baby and I drive straight to the cemetery, where the flowers are still fresh on the grave. We sit on the cold ground, and I introduce Carol to my mother with tears falling down my cheeks. "Mom, look at us. You were right! It's a girl! You have a granddaughter! I named her after you, Mom. Can you hear me?"

I look up at the sky. I feel the breeze on my neck, and yell, "Mom, do you hear me? DO YOU HEAR ME?"

I quietly reflect on the last several months. My daughter will never meet my mother. I'm mothering motherless at age twenty-three. Emotions are swirling around. There is no peace here. I need to leave.

The first months of my daughter's life are challenging as I am suspended between grief and joy. I miss my mom so much, I ache. I rock Carol all night long to soft music while the house is asleep. The right song is literally like a drug. It calms me.

Carol and I go to the cemetery again. It feels like my mom, Carol, and I are the only souls here. It's a bright sunny morning with birds soaring high. Carol is snug in one of Mom's pink blankets, and her face is buried in my neck. I notice the headstones of others who died even younger than forty-seven. We sit down at Mom's grave, and I speak to her, wondering if she can see or hear me.

Growing up, I was taught that when we die, we go to heaven or hell, and the only way we get to heaven is if we are saved and accept Jesus Christ as our Savior. I imagine those who believe this tend not to grieve as much. At twenty-three years old—after sexual assault and the loss of my young mother—my faith is gone. It's a crooked path. I don't know if I will ever enter a church again. Sitting at this grave, imagining her frigid bones below me, does not lessen my pain. Carol and I stand and walk back to the car. It feels better not to come here, but instead to hold sacred space inwardly for her. Mom has a home there.

When I put Carol back in the car, I kiss her hands and cheeks. She is my girl. I'm her mother. We have many years ahead of us. I look up at the sky and say, "We love you, Mom," then I cry all the way home because my daughter will never get to spend one hour of her life with my mother. My daughter is perfect. Carol is my lifeline. She is the number one reason I must seek help. Carol, Carol—my girl—she is brand-new life in my life.

Chapter 5

ROACHES LOVE THE DARK

IT'S BEEN FOUR AND A half years. Rape crisis centers are scarce. Qualified therapists are even more so. Images flash incessantly through my mind. Energy-blocking chatter lives in my head. My mind is a torture chamber with no exit door.

Someone I love is watching me, though. Being a good mother requires calm and patience and a few bites of chocolate each day. I need to be emotionally healthier. I want to be an exceptional mom, and I want Carol to rise higher than her mother. I pray each day without fail that my daughter will have a better life than mine.

Carol and I go to the library every week. She loves the "story hour." I check out children's books, mothering books, self-help books, and spiritual books. We read all her books, but mine are returned unread. Journaling privately is my self-help. I think her favorite time with her father is reading books. When they rock, he sings "Dream a Little Dream of Me" (Mama Cass).

It's a dull November evening. My baby and I are out for a walk. I sit for a moment by a tree. She sucks her thumb, and I marvel at this little one asleep in her stroller. Gently, I stroke the curls that frame her sweet face. I made this kid.

I hear the songs of nearby birds and watch them chase each other. As streetlights blink on, I talk to the sky. There's no one else to talk to; my friends are all estranged. Nature is a safe haven where I privately have a good cry. I think about Mom and wonder what happens to someone when they die. If there is a God in our world, it is that force that allows me to carry on, to rise above the trauma, and raise this miracle Carol. I absolutely love having a daughter.

Life is moving fast. I'm five months pregnant. Dad is getting married to a woman he met just six months ago in a country club bar. Her name is Joan, and she has no children. David and I give Dad our blessings even though it seems too soon. My father is not wired for single life.

My parents shared a happy marriage. They rarely argued, and my brother and I grew up in a home where we understood what it meant to really love and enjoy a partner. David is struggling with the loss of our mother. He talks to me about his pain. He is only nineteen years old. Our relationship has grown since our mother died. We are talking, real talk, for the first time. My brother is becoming my best friend.

Mason accepts a straight-commission sales job. It requires a whirlwind move to Toledo. He believes he'll make a grand a week. He'll be on the road five or six nights a week. I support my husband's business decisions. He's disciplined with a solid work ethic.

The house we're renting is a Colonial with a basement, three bedrooms, two bathrooms, a huge kitchen, family room, living room, and a great backyard for what will soon to be our two kids. I'm enjoying this new setup, at least until the surprise knock at our door. It's the property manager. "I hate to give you bad news when you're pregnant and have a little one, but the rental company must ask you to leave."

"What? We've only been here for a couple of months."

"It's obvious you are not able to afford the house. We are willing to work with you. We have a less expensive town house available."

"You will work with us? This is all a mistake. My husband won't call until tonight. He will take care of this. He travels on his job. Please give me time to speak to him."

"I'm afraid it's nonnegotiable. You need to vacate immediately. Call me tomorrow morning if you wish to avoid eviction so that we can complete the paperwork for your move to the town house." As she walks out the door, she adds, "Your daughter is so cute. She really loves that peanut butter and banana sandwich."

I slam the door behind her. *Holy Shit! We are getting kicked out!*

When Mason telephones, he becomes angry. We rarely fight about anything, except money. He's working long days into long evenings, so I dare not be mad about anything. His straight-commission job is not producing the big bucks. There's nothing to do but start packing.

Our next residence, the sight-unseen town house, turns out to be infested with cockroaches. They're everywhere. And if this many are visible on the floor, counter tops, stairs, in the bathroom, crawling up the fridge, and all over the stove, then hundreds more are here. One crawls into my hair, and I see one on Carol's leg. Another dive-bombs into my cleavage. I have a fourteen-month-old toddler. I'm seven months pregnant. We can't live in a roach-infested rental. My days are spent spraying, stomping, wiping, and scrubbing. I inspect Carol constantly to make sure there are no roaches on her, but what happens when I fall asleep?

Mason has our car, so I push Carol in the stroller to a nearby mall each morning to get out of the house. We walk around, looking at things we cannot afford to buy. We eat lunch in the food court. The mall becomes my daughter's playground...every day.

Everyone else's life seems to be moving forward, but we're riding this bicycle backward. This stress could drive a mother to sell crack. I imagine a phone conversation with my best friend Carol from high school. She's a nurse and happily married. "How's everything, Deb?"

"I'm a frothing lunatic. I hate myself and where we live. I'm about to have two children under the age of sixteen months, and I spend half my life killing roaches. Mason travels a lot, and my check to J. C. Penney for a shower curtain bounced."

No, I absolutely refuse to speak to healthy humans. No sane person will understand my life or want to be a part of it. I'm ashamed—tired of problems, of making excuses, of feeling neurotic, of being afraid of everything, of feeling isolated, of existing. I'm a mother, wife, and rape victim. My mind thinks and talks too fast to avoid the cerebral ways I relive my attack.

Yet Mason and I are still okay. There's an abundance of love in our home despite my misery because I hide it well. We make a plan. When the baby comes, the four of us will live in motels on the road until we have enough money for a decent place to live. I get it. I go with it.

It's March 29, 1977. Carol is asleep, so I take a bath with the lights off. It's a tranquil oasis for my mentally misunderstood self. The roaches are having a party on the side of the bathtub. They're part of the family now. No matter how many I kill, another hundred show up. Roaches love the dark, so there must be a gang of them hanging out with me tonight. *Bless their hearts.*

My eyes close while my body sinks deep into the hot water. I'm dreaming of becoming a psychologist and paying the water bill on time. I wonder where I would be today if I were not a victim of sexual violence. Suddenly, there's pressure in my stomach so tight, I can't sit up. Oh, and here comes more pressure.

"Whoa, baby, slow down," I say out loud. These contractions are so intense, they feel like electric shocks. It's nearly impossible to get out of the tub. Mason is driving home from Detroit, so I have no way to contact him. By the time I lie down in bed, the contractions are even closer together.

I phone Mason's parents. They are on their way to take care of Carol but will not arrive for at least two hours. I call Christine. Our husbands work together, and she is my backup. She arrives in twenty minutes. I really need an ambulance because the contractions are less than two minutes apart with each lasting a full minute. Christine kindly asks the next-door neighbor to help me down the steps and into her car.

I'm in the front seat of a gold Cadillac Coupe DeVille. My labor is fast and intense. Christine is shouting, "Breathe! Deep breaths! I'm serious, Debra! Breathe!"

I'm gasping for breath between contractions. She doesn't shut up. "Are you pushing that baby?"

"No! The baby is pushing me!"

"Bullshit! Stop pushing! Don't you have that baby on my front seat!"

A gush of warm fluid flows over the front seat. "Shit!" screams Christine. "You keep that baby in you! Stop pushing and breathe!" She presses the gas a little harder, darting in and out of traffic.

"Just drive!" I yell. "And shut up!"

We careen, tires screeching, and bump into the ER curb where a wheelchair awaits. Christine yells some more. "She needs a stretcher! She can't walk! The baby is coming!"

In seconds, I'm on a gurney with people all around me firing questions. "What's your full name? Who's your doctor? Are you married? Where's your husband? What's your date of birth?"

My answers are full-throated, growling-bear impersonations.

It's a speedy delivery with only two hours between the first contraction and our second baby's birth. Just as Mason hurries through the door, out comes an almost-nine-pound beet red screeching baby boy. This baby at five minutes old is stretching and flailing and looking all around. When he kicks off his blanket, I know my baby boy has a spark. We are delighted with the arrival of Ryan, my second miracle.

Mason lives at the hospital with his new son for the next few days. Literally every emotion a wife can feel for her husband as I watched him hold his son was all wrapped up into one. *Mason was falling in love with his little guy…fast!*

Spring arrives as flowers push through the earth. With roach world in the rearview mirror, Mason and I begin a new chapter living in welfare motels with dumpster aromas, Burger King dinners, and middle-of-the-night shenanigans. I'm really trying not to say anything crazy about this life while I spiral down deep and dark inwardly with anxiety…all day long.

Carol clutches her Raggedy Ann doll, colors, enjoys books, and turns a bed into her playground. The nightstand is her toy chest. She plays well all day while Ryan projectile vomits. His six-week checkup is in some random emergency room. I'm not sure why he throws up after every feeding and has a rash all over his face.

When Mason's sales are good, we find a motel with a pool so Carol can swim. We live on fast food that Mason brings home. Carol loves picking weed bouquets that she calls Mommy's flowers. She pretends to read the Bible out loud. She's never bored.

My mind feels like a box of rocks. At other times, it bucks like a wild horse. Never before did I watch soap operas. Now I do. Carol and I tune into Ryan's *Hope* and *General Hospital* every damn weekday to kill time. Our walks outside consist of laps around the parking lot. We watch an endless stream of people getting off and on buses, and before you know it, it's time for Ryan to eat and vomit again. We miss our daily walk to the mall to eat our carcinogenic hot dogs. We move from place to place, depending on cash flow. Clearly, this plan is failing. It's a mistake, and don't we all make mistakes when we are young? I blow it off because I'm stuck.

The four of us end up in Mason's parents' basement. We are fortunate to be welcome, and my children are happy. They have grandparents, an uncle, and two aunts who adore them. There are healthy meals and cookies and a backyard with a pool. Aunt Sherry becomes Carol's favorite person on the planet. We file bankruptcy and get food stamps.

My mother-in-law, Josie, and I sit in lawn chairs in the backyard, watching the family splash around in the pool. She knows about my rape, but we have never discussed it. We sip the Hungarian tea I brewed and chat about jobs for Mason. She supports my idea that if Mason loves sales, he should find a job in an essential industry. I suggest the medical field. Our family would have good benefits. We need health insurance. Mason is smart. He's worked since he was ten years old. He's going to find his way. Josie asks, "What about you? Are you going to work?"

"Not now, not with two babies. I can't leave them, not for a single day."

I'm hoping that answer will lead to a deeper conversation. Instead, Josie goes inside and brings out homemade banana cake slices for each of us. Her heart is as big as a sunflower, but I doubt she and I will ever talk about rape. I miss my mother.

I'm suddenly uncomfortable and need to take a bath to unpretzel my brain. The lights are off as I sink into the water. I just need twenty minutes to myself. A steamy hot bath in a dark room calms my mind. It has the same effect as music. It blocks out the knife, duct tape, smells, slaps, and screams. I breathe into the moment and bless myself for surviving one more day and for being the best mother I know how to be.

I had higher expectations of myself. My friends all have college educations and careers. It really bothers me that I don't make my own money and that I depend on Mason so much. Josie's question about working made me think twice about working. She worked all her life with four children. I can't control this feeling that something bad will happen if I work outside the home. Besides, I'm one of the rare mothers who's actually not miserable being a stay-at-home mom.

I add more hot water and try to forget about everything for two more minutes. The sexual violence did damage, but the forced silence is almost worse than the assault, so the logical way to free myself from the flashbacks and the anxiety would be to find the right therapist who will help me by talking it through.

I'm not ready to get out of the tub. When I open my eyes, there are ghostly shadows of my attacker. God…what I want to do—what I really need to do—is allow myself to completely fall apart. *Or have I?*

Chapter 6

HOME TO MY ROOTS

HOSANNA IN THE HIGHEST, I sing to you! Mason is employed with a medical company doing work he loves. He'll have a steady income with benefits, so we're moving to my birthplace, Youngstown, Ohio.

Grandfather Anderson has consented to share his home with a two-year-old, an eight-month-old, two adults, and a cocker spaniel. He's my mother's father, and he came to Youngstown from Stockholm, Sweden. He is the most introverted man I know. He lost his wife and his two daughters to cancer. He keeps everything in the house exactly as it was when Grandma died. Her toothbrush is still in the bathroom sixteen years later.

He has a strict routine and doesn't break it. His days are spent doing crossword puzzles, studying the dictionary, working in his rose garden, and reading the Youngstown *Vindicator* from start to finish. He sits on the porch at night and feeds the raccoons that come up from the ravine across the street before having his one cup of Sanka instant coffee and four gingersnaps. He goes to bed at ten o'clock every night, and he smells like Old Spice every morning. He never misses Lawrence Welk on Saturday nights or church services Sunday morning at St. Paul's Lutheran Church. Most of all, Grandpa appreciates my homemade suppers and teaches me how to beat him at Scrabble.

There are countless reasons why I love going back to my roots. My cousin Sharon is number one. As children, we were like sisters. She was my favorite playmate. We were called the "giggling cousins" because we could not stop laughing during prayers, yet we never got into trouble for it. Our children are the same ages. We spend a few days together each week. Her love and laughter are contagious. Carol and I adore her, and for the first time in five years, I find myself laughing out loud again.

I won't be sharing my rape with Sharon, though. She would fall apart, so not talking about it lets me breathe a little easier around her. My connection with her is almost soothing. She is a distraction to my nervous system that let me know my brain is on fire. Sharon feels like a lifelong sense of some kind of identity that I lost the night I was raped.

The trauma is a fact of life. I act like I'm in control but constantly think I have no control. I'm doing what everyone needs and wants while I have no real understanding of my own needs and wants. I feel the depth of my roots on Hopewell Drive where I grew up, but I'm not the same person I used to be. I'm beginning to think I will never be free of the trauma I have experienced. Even though I can laugh again, I feel detached and uncomfortable. I need to get help.

*****

I'm relieved. Mason and I are finally going to an appointment with a psychiatrist. I hope to find some answers. In less than twenty minutes, the doctor concludes, "You have been dealing with anxiety for too long without treatment. I'm going to start you on lithium and Valium. You'll need monthly labs for the first year. We'll monitor how you're doing and adjust accordingly. Do you drink alcohol?"

I give Mason a "Why are we here?" look as I answer the doctor, "No, I don't drink."

He asks Mason, "Does your wife drink?"

"My wife does not drink alcohol," Mason replies.

When I ask about the side effects, he hands me a pamphlet and two prescriptions. "Make an appointment to see me in a month."

I stuff the papers in my purse. "I have two young children. I'm a rape victim. I need to talk. I'm not taking medication." My face and neck are hot. "It took me five years to walk through your door, and this is it: two prescriptions?"

"You need medication for your level of anxiety."

I have the urge to pick up the nearest lamp and throw it across the room. "You'll never see me again!" I slam the door.

Mason walked out before my rant and is sitting in the car playing ZZ Top. I hang my head out the window to let the wind cool my face. I'm distraught enough to dismiss the idea of therapy for months. Mason and I don't discuss a single word of this appointment.

We start attending my childhood church Evangel Baptist. My other grandparents, Helen and Steve Maki, attend this church. It's healing to be in the same pew with them again. On my dad's side of the family, my relatives are strict Baptists. They are honest, good people, and we get along well. If they knew what happened to me, they would ask me to pray about it and turn it over to God. I am not convinced God hears my prayers. There's no one in my family I trust with this. If there is a God who is answering prayers, I think he or she is paying attention to the famous people—you know, like Diana Ross and Goldie Hawn.

My Hungarian grandparents are my favorite people. They play gospel music, and Grandpa feeds the birds toast every morning. They live just two miles from us, and I see them a couple of times a week. They share stories of escaping poverty in Hungary and of the Great Depression. My grandmother beheaded chickens in the third grade to help the family survive. She owned two pairs of shoes and one dress. She dropped out of school in third grade and made all her own toys. A piece of fruit was her Christmas present. Those stories are filled with wisdom, irony, and humor.

As we all sit at the dining room table eating good food made from scratch and listening to their stories, we cry with laughter. My grandparents have ironed hankies they use to dab the tears in their eyes from laughing so hard. Thank God for my grandfather, who is the reason our family has a sense of humor. He once pulled me aside and said, "Do not let anyone or any situation in your life ever take away your sense of humor. If you lose your humor, your spirit will die."

When he offers a job helping him sell tombstones to widows, of course I accept. I get to hang out with him and earn a little money. When he and I are alone on the front porch, he will take out a piece of paper with a poem he wrote and allow me to read it if I promise not to tell Grandma. He and I have other secrets, including the bottle of whiskey I found in his basement. Drinking alcohol is against their religion, but I swear no one in the family will know if he takes a shot or two after his shower in the basement. This man is the best adult in my life right now.

Carol is two and a half years old and finally masters potty training if I let her hold a Twinkie while she pees. It's her rules, not mine. Ryan has asthma.

I make a bold move by signing up for a psychology course at Youngstown State University. My dream of becoming a psychologist is real, even though I need one. Mason supports this idea and drives me to campus the first night. I won't drive there alone. In the classroom, I feel the stare of another student, a guy. When it's time to leave, he follows me and asks, "Hey, what's your name?"

I take off running, but I hear him say, "What's your problem? I was only trying to talk to you."

I keep running, thinking he's going to grab me, rape me, and kill me. I don't look back until I find Mason. I'm out of breath when I jump into the car and begin searching for a song on the radio. I'm in a full-blown panic attack with both kids in the back seat. I quit school day one.

The next day, I start making phone calls to find a therapist who works with victims of sexual assault. When I find someone who sounds qualified, we arrange to meet. He takes a full history and asks how the sexual assault has affected my life. He listens enough that I go back a second time and then a third. It feels good to have someone take the time to hear what I need to say. On the fourth visit, he says, "I would like for you to participate in a television show where a few women will be speaking out about rape. I think your story is needs to be told, and it will help other victims." He explains that my face would be shielded, and my name would not be used.

"How can I help others when I need help myself?" I ask.

"We have been talking, and I think you're doing better."

I would love to help others someday, but he has completely misjudged my progress. I'm not anywhere close to being able to speak on television about something that still terrifies me. Nobody gets it. I need to talk to my brother about this.

I flee from his office, driving my car in the pounding rain. The wipers are going full speed, and I am counting my breaths like a Zen master. One, two, three—I need more breaths because if I don't calm down, I'm going to drive this car off a bridge. I stop for a Coke at a 7-Eleven. I'm addicted to it. Abba is turned up on the radio, and I take a drive. I can't pick up my children in this condition.

An hour later, the storm has passed. When I stop to pick up Ryan and Carol, my cousin asks, "Did the doctor say everything is okay?" Sharon thinks I went to an OB-GYN appointment.

"Yes, I'm fine."

On the way home, I blast the music to drown out the noise in my head; otherwise, my head might explode. Carol yells, "Mommy! My ears hurt!"

Ryan is smiling, kicking his feet, and seems to love the music cranked up high. I take them for a pony ride set up next to a Dairy Queen, and my sanity returns. My children are my only lifeline. I can't lose my marriage.

*****

It's a pure-white winter day. Ryan is wheezing badly. He squirms on my lap and won't let me put him down. He can't eat, sleep, play, or laugh. His breathing speeds up. "Mason! We need to go to the ER right now!"

As Mason packs a bag, Ryan's lips turn blue, and he grows limp in my arms. I hold him close as his chest continues a rapid seesaw motion.

My baby boy is admitted immediately. He's strapped down in an oxygen tent that covers the entire crib. There are tubes and IVs, and I'm not allowed to hold him. When he cries, I can only rub his foot and talk to him—no picking him up and no removing him from the oxygen tent for any reason. His condition is life-threatening. He's restless and scared.

Mason and I work out a routine so I can run home once a day, shower, and then run back to the hospital, where I spend the night. Carol stays with Mason's aunt Kathryn. The doctors are doing everything they can to accelerate healing, yet a week has passed with no improvement in Ryan's condition.

I've stared out hundreds of windows in the last five years while thinking about my life. How many times will I look up at the stars for answers? I will not survive the loss of this baby, not a chance. I wonder what I'm doing wrong and why horrible things keep happening. How long can I hold on to this rope with one hand if it keeps slipping? I'm emotionally exhausted. I'm twenty-five, but I feel so old. The avoidance and escape of my reality shuts me down until my nervous system explodes.

At last, Ryan's cough improves, and the wheezing stops. The doctor says, "We're going to observe him for a couple of days. Nothing changes. He still needs to be in the tent, but we can take the straps off now and let him move around in bed. I think your little guy is going to be fine."

When the tent is finally unzipped, Ryan jumps to me, laughing. We swing around in circles with his little legs wrapped around my waist, and I kiss his cheeks, his forehead, and his nose. He yells, "Mama, out! Mama, me out!" We are ecstatic laughing and crying tears of joy.

For the next several days, I do nothing but play with my children. This close call scared the devil out of me. My focus must be on getting emotionally stronger and finding the right therapist to help me achieve that. My children need a mother who is not traumatized every day of her life.

Ryan is tested for allergies. He has nineteen. His allergies are causing the asthma attacks. The follow-up care is strict. The list of dos and don'ts is two pages long. His bedsheets and blankets must be changed daily. The house must be dusted and vacuumed daily. We cannot have a dog. He needs medications and is required to go for injections and breathing treatments twice a week.

Now that he's feeling better, Ryan decides his name is Tony. He tells everyone at the doctor's office he is not Ryan anymore. Ryan attracts women in the elevators. When we walk into the office, he goes straight back to the nurse and gets his shot. No waiting room for Tony.

A mini-emergency happens the morning Ryan has a doctor's appointment. We can't get into our station wagon. The locks are jammed. Fortunately, the driver's side window is down, but nothing I do will open any door. A locksmith informs me the repair will cost more than the car is worth. He gives me the name of another tradesman who might have a better solution, but the other guy's assessment is the same. My car has no working doors. We have to climb in and out of the window. I push Carol through the window then Ryan. They jump around like it has suddenly become an indoor playground. They watch me crawl in. I'm not laughing. They can't stop laughing. Now they are wrestling in the back of the wagon.

I'm not parking this nutty car with these loony toddlers laughing at me anywhere we can be seen. I find an isolated spot to make sure no one sees us. I crawl out first while my goofy angels refuse to come to the window so I can pull them out. I yell, "Carol, why are you not listening to me?"

She laughs and says, "I want to listen to you, Mommy. Can we get a cookie at the mall?"

"We are not at the mall, Carol. Ryan needs his shot. Get over here right now."

Ryan yells, "My name is Tony!"

Basadafadadoododoo! I make up words to avoid using profanity, and my kids think it's hilarious. Carol laughs. "Give us a cookie and we'll come out."

We're going to be late. She wins. I have vanilla wafers in my bag. She sees the box. I carry Ryan and hold Carol's hand and yell at them all the way to the entrance of the doctor's office. When it's time to get back into the car, the whole party starts all over again. We function like this for months. Mason needs our good car for work, and another car payment is not in the budget.

Mommy's car needs to be dropped off in a field somewhere so she can blow it up and watch it turn to fuck dust. Then she deserves a vacation somewhere besides a tent in the woods.

My brother saves me when he moves to Phoenix and gives me our mother's car. It's a green Vega with over one hundred thousand miles, but the doors open and close. The kids squawk every time they must ride in the Vega. They liked the other car better since it came with a cookie and Mommy outbursts they found funny.

Anaïs Nin warns that anxiety can kill love. I read it five times, and it confirms that I need to find another therapist. At night, after they have had their baths and we snuggle together with a book, I kiss my kids' juicy cheeks. A hundred times a day, I kiss their faces. A tear falls when I think about how much love I have for these two children.

When I find a job to distract my anxiety, I hire a woman. Her name is Birdie. The first week when Carol is crying with an ear infection, I quit the job. The best thing about my life is being their mother. Having a son and a daughter gives me a reason to keep fighting. I'm not going to lose this fight. I'm going to win it for them.

The whole job thing is no longer a priority. My job is to get well and raise these children higher than myself. One that is most essential is that both turn out to be good people. My son and daughter soothe the place in my heart that is terrified of my inner life. When I go too low, I find truth. The fact is all I care about is my two children. There's no other reason.

Chapter 7

POOTER AND GOAT

A NEW ADVENTURE IS ABOUT TO begin. I'm pregnant. The little darling is a statistical anomaly since I have an IUD. My little sprout must really want to be in our family. After the baby's birth, my tubes will be tied. Three babies in four-and-a-half years *is* this mama's uterus limit. Although the baby's gender doesn't matter, I secretly hope Ryan is blessed with a baby brother.

Mason has been promoted to district sales manager. We both hope this marks the end of our financial challenges. His job takes us back to the Cleveland area, close to the royal blue waters of Lake Erie in Bay Village. We have rented a cozy bungalow with a backyard and a basement on East Oakland Road.

I feel my children's exuberance as I watch them jump and clap at the sight of our new home, and I promise them a sandbox and a swing set. I'm excited about growing my first garden. The neighborhood is teeming with toddlers, so mine will have plenty of playmates.

On moving day, Carol shows up with a clothes basket full of daffodils. She picked all of them from the next-door neighbor's yard. "Look, Mommy, I have a present for you."

Luckily our new neighbor has a sense of humor. We make her a huge bouquet, and I ask Carol to apologize. Kindly, the neighbor accepts, "Oh, honey, it's okay. You're too cute to get mad at. What's your name?"

She answers, "Carol," then she hides behind me the moment she feels the mistake.

I'm so proud of Mason. I stood by him as we learned how to lose and begin again. At age twenty-seven, he already knows failure is only for those who quit. He's a smart, honest businessman on his way up the corporate ladder. The worst is behind us now. I know it and feel it, so I start looking for another therapist to help me deal with this feeling of being split off from myself.

Mason's parents, Bob and Josie, celebrate our return and invite us to Sunday dinners. Bob has a passion for cooking and is a natural talent. He makes everything from tasty soups to the best barbecue chicken I've ever tasted. He decides the meal he will create, and it's fun when Mason's three siblings are all around the table. Josie dotes on the children and keeps pots of coffee brewing. Afterward, we sit at the kitchen table for at least two hours while Bob smokes and does most of the talking. Ryan loves all the commotion, and Carol loves Aunt Sherry. When Carol hands Grandpa her doll, he says, "That's an ugly baby," then he throws the doll back at her, and she has a big belly laugh. She throws the doll back to him, and the game repeats for a few rounds until Josie stops it.

My children will grow up knowing and enjoying their grandparents. It's an extra layer of support, especially since my mother is no longer here. Ryan and Carol love coming here. They don't need any other kind of entertainment. All they need is Grandma Josie's house, which comes with laughs, homemade desserts, a different set of rules, and playing with Grandpa's garden hose.

Money is no longer as tight. I can pay someone to cut my hair. Mason affords better suits and ties, which he needs me to choose for him. The kids have very special birthday celebrations. The day of their birth is the most important holiday to me, so my kids wake up to balloons every color of the rainbow. They have a candle in their breakfast doughnut and one gift. Then comes an all-day celebration that includes a memorable birthday party.

My mood is a little lighter but still stuck. Magazines are in the budget, so I subscribe to *Psychology Today*. The writers seem irrational and overhyped. They seem to think my trauma is my responsibility to heal. This makes no sense to me. A stranger shows up in my life, robbing me of peace and making me question whether I will ever find justice, and it's my responsibility? The first magazine gets torn up and thrown in the trash. Maybe I'm not ready for the psychology of anything. Maybe I'm still trapped in that room. I'm certain it's going to take more than just me to work through this. I need the right person who, so far, seems as elusive as a butterfly.

I'm still praying for the miracle that I will at some point look myself in a mirror and know the woman looking back at me. I hate my own reflection. She's not me. Something is lost inwardly. A part of me feels dead, and I still refuse to be in photos. I refuse to look in the mirror. I refuse to give up believing I will find myself again.

Our third child is born on November 2, 1979, and he's flawless, my third miracle. Mama's love times three tiny little humans equal something unquantifiable. Mason wants to name his second son Brock. We can't agree on a name. Two days after he's born, the nursery staff puts *Sylvester* on his bassinet identification card since Mason and I can't agree. Carol and Ryan come to visit their baby brother, and Carol falls in love the very first minute. She calls him *Pooter*. Our son is named Brock Robert. His middle name is after his grandfather.

Mason and I have the whole shebang: bills paid on time, home sweet home, and three beautiful children. He holds my hand more now and gives it an I-love-you squeeze. There is a fresh feeling of intimacy in our marriage that felt lost since the rape. Our marriage is on the upside of life. Thank you, God.

My new addiction is running. One mile becomes two, and within three months, I'm running five miles a day. Running wins back a feeling of power that I had lost. It makes me feel alive. It beats nibbling all day on gross amounts of carbs. My weight after three back-to-back pregnancies is down to 120 pounds. My dress size is a five. At night when the kids are asleep, I do jumping jacks, sit-ups, squats, and lunges. I work out the upper body. I want to condition enough to start running marathons in a few months.

I make an appointment with my first female therapist who works out of the offices in the Great Northern Mall. She and I and begin the arduous process of describing my attack and the trauma that came with it. She understands how I'm still held captive. She does not talk much, but she listens, and I see her every week. One day, she asks what my long-term goals are and why being a mother is not enough. I tell her, "I want to be a psychologist."

She suddenly turns away to hide her look of disbelief. She takes a sip of her coffee, turns back, makes eye contact again, smiles, and says, "Why don't we work on *smaller* goals?"

"Why?" I ask, glaring.

"You still have so much anxiety, and you have three children to raise. I'm afraid ten years in school might be unrealistic. Remember, you had a difficult time working a full-time job without Percocet. When you talk to me, I hear so much self-hatred. The weight of all these bizarre thoughts and behaviors needs to be dealt with."

"What's your idea of starting small?" I ask.

"Why not start out selling Avon?"

"Oh, yeah, this is helpful. Thank you. Here I am again with another cocoa-puffs psychologist. How would you feel after losing eight years of your sanity to another person's insanity if you were told to sell Avon when you finally found the courage to talk about it? This is your opinion of me?"

"One of the major pieces of the recovery puzzle is to provide a realistic assessment. I'm here to help you become whole again."

I grab my purse and yell, "Screw you! Your parents paid for your college education while I was stuck in a room fighting for the parts of me that a stranger killed off. I'm here to get those parts back. I came here for support, but I'm not talking to someone who doesn't think me capable of more than selling Avon. My ass has worked five hundred times harder than yours. Your mother is raising your children while you work. My mother is dead."

I slam the door, and I hear a picture fall off the wall. I leave in tears and find the first McDonald's for a Coke. Michael Jackson music blasts while I roll down the window, yelling to the street, "I'm a survivor! When will you understand that, world?" Then I blast the music louder.

The woods are my place of worship, so I go there to soothe my bruised spirit. There's an internal torment that came after this sexual violence. I believe every horrible thing anyone says about me. Now I'm convinced I will never accomplish anything more than being a good mother and selling Avon.

I walk fast then break into a jog that accelerates into a sprint. Blood circulates to my brain, and I stop to think. Problems float around in my head all day, yet nothing is more intoxicating than my home filled with healthy, happy children. If I'm doing anything right seven years after my attack, it's that I can play and sing and laugh with all three of them all day long. One baby on the breast, the other on my hip, and Carol holds my hand. We go out every day. The daily dose of happiness keeps me from crashing and putting a gun to my head.

It's Labor Day 1980, our last hurrah of the summer. The empty sky stretches out for infinity, and our whole family gathers for a barbecue at Sherry's house. We feast on hot dogs and burgers, homemade potato salad, baked beans, pickles, and numerous desserts. Ryan climbs trees. Carol shadows her favorite person, cheerful Aunt Sherry. Brock stays on my hip all day. His separation anxiety is right on schedule at ten months old. The men play basketball.

Later, Josie says, "I'm off this Friday. Can Carol spend the night on Thursday?"

I answer, "Sure!"

We make plans to drop her off Thursday night and then head home after a perfect day. Almost perfect: Robin wasn't there.

Robin is Mason's younger sister. She graduated from high school this past June. She's a breathtaking beauty with freckles, green eyes, and artfully messy long coal-black, hair. She recently broke up with her boyfriend of three years. Mark was a high school dropout and an unemployed bricklayer. The first time I met Mark, I was nervous because I noticed a knife in his boot. He claimed he carried it because he was handy. That knife was only one of the reasons I never allowed him to be alone with my children. I would not trust him with a porch cat. There was something wrong with him that reminded me of my rapist.

After Robin broke up with Mark, he abducted her, dragging her by the hair down the railroad tracks to an empty greenhouse. He threatened to kill her. Robin escaped when Mark fell asleep.

Mason's father called the police, but the police did nothing. In fact, they discouraged Robin from pressing charges because Mark has enlisted in the army and will be leaving soon. Mark's mother stated, "Mark is intelligent, and he's a good boy. He is in love with Robin."

I'm convinced Mark belongs under close supervision in a psychiatric facility. He seems mentally ill and needs help. The incident was written off as a lovers' breakup conflict. Mark has been deemed safe. The cockeyed optimism of the police and their minimization of Robin's potential danger make my insides boil.

The police did advise Bob and Josie to be on high alert and to refuse all contact with Mark. Despite this, Mark makes harassing phone calls to their home, causing Bob to keep a baseball bat under his bed.

I don't think Mark is going anywhere without Robin, making me worried enough to call a lawyer for legal advice. He tells me there is nothing I can do. I hope I'm wrong about Mark, but I worry about Robin. We all count the days until the day Mark ships out.

It's Friday, September 12, 1980, and our monkey house is rockin' and rollin' at six o'clock in the morning. Carol has an ear infection, which prevented her from going to Grandma Josie's for an overnight last night. Our home smells like fresh-brewed coffee and French toast. Mason has been hobbling on crutches all week. He hurt his foot playing basketball on Labor Day. Brock and Carol climb into his lap as he watches the morning news. Ryan, my gifted procrastinator, is still potty training and causes chaos when I lock myself in the bathroom. He says, "Mommy, get out. I need something."

Carol jumps off Mason's lap and tries to help Ryan get a piece of French toast. She says, "Don't give any to Pooter, or you will get in trouble."

Ryan says, "His name is not Pooter. It's Goat."

I hear them both start laughing as Carol runs back to her daddy's lap. My toddlers are giving their baby brother a nickname. Brock is a hit in our family. He's a near perfect baby if he's on my lap or hip…and adorable. He has my mother's Swedish genes.

Holding his nose, Ryan looks at me while I pour a cup of coffee. He says, "The doggie pooped behind the couch. It smells. Can you clean it up?"

I answer, "Ryan! We don't have a dog."

He grabs a banana, laughs, and jumps into Mason's lap. "Don't be mad at the doggie."

Now all four of them are laughing while I clean up what Ryan did behind the couch. Carol thinks everything Ryan says and does is funny. Mason has a hard time being serious around the antics of our family's Mr. Funny Man. This is a game to Ryan, but I'm no longer playing it. He is potty trained everywhere but at home. I take him to the couch.

"No more M&Ms for you. No more Superman underwear. If you're not going to be a big boy at home, Mommy is putting you back in diapers. This is not funny for me. Look at me please, Ryan!"

"My name is not Ryan. It's Tony." He looks at me with those shining brown eyes and that irresistible smile. I give up!

As I pour my third cup of coffee, the telephone rings. It's too early for the phone to ring. I yell to Mason, "I've got it, babe." I hurry off to answer the bedroom telephone. "Hello."

"Hello, this is the Berea police," a male voice says. "Have I reached the home of Mason?"

"Yes. This is his wife. Why are you calling?"

"I need to speak to Mason," he says.

"My husband is on crutches. Can you please tell me why you're calling?"

There's a brief pause. Then he answers, "I'm sorry to inform you that his father, Robert, has been shot."

Part 2

THE '80S

Chapter 8

ONLY GOD KNOWS WHY

"MASON! GET OVER TO YOUR parents' house! Your dad has been shot!"

Mason rockets up, spilling the kids from his lap, punches open the front door with one crutch, and hobbles to the car. "That motherfucker shot my dad!"

We both know who did this. Carol and I follow him outside. "Drive carefully," I call after him. "I'll be there as soon as I can find someone to watch the kids."

He flies off down the street. Carol asks, "Why is Daddy mad? What happened at Grandma's house?"

I lead her back inside. "Don't worry. Please help Mommy pack Brock's bag."

A couple of neighbors hear the disturbance and come over. "Family emergency," I say without elaborating. I ask them to watch the kids for a few minutes while I quickly make some phone calls.

My dad will be at the house in a half hour. He offers to keep Brock after driving me to Bob and Josie's. Carol's playmate's mom, Sylvia, shows up to take Carol and Ryan. Carol asks, "When will you be back?" Carol never asks that question when going to a friend's house.

"I will call you as soon as I know, okay, honey?"

"Don't forget, Mommy."

I blow her a kiss. I'm standing in the front yard still in my nightgown, and my father will be here any minute. Brock is screaming in his crib while I take a fast shower and get dressed.

Brock and I jump into Dad's car fifteen minutes later. My father doesn't stop asking questions. I've already told him everything I know. "Dad, please, all I know is Bob was shot. I don't know anything else."

Suddenly, I remember Carol was scheduled to spend the night at their house last night. "Thank God for ear infections," I say. "We cancelled Carol's overnight at Grandma's last night. She would have been at their house!"

My dad drives below the speed limit with his left foot on the brake. I beg him, "Please go a little faster. I need to get there."

As we turn onto Walnut Drive in Berea, my father hits the brakes and makes a full stop. "Oh my god, Debbie! This looks really bad." There are ambulances, police cars, media, and clusters of neighbors—so many people. Yellow-and-black crime tape surrounds the house.

"Jesus Christ!" I yell. "Don't drive down there, Dad. Brock doesn't need to see any of this. I'll call you as soon as I know anything." I scramble out of Dad's car, kiss my baby on the cheek, saying "I love you," and begin sprinting toward the house.

Mason is on the sidewalk, being interviewed by the media, so I search for Josie, Matt, and Robin as I approach the house. Two police officers block me and say, "Ma'am, you can't go in there."

"I'm Deborah, Mason's wife. Bob is my father-in-law. Where is my husband's family?"

I'm escorted into the next-door neighbor's house. "Stay inside this house with the family, please."

The first faces I see are Matt and Sherry, who are sitting close together on a couch, with tears streaming, seemingly unstoppable. There are at least fifty people in the house, including Father Garrity, the priest of St. Mary's Catholic Church in Berea. When I don't see Josie, I assume she's with Bob at the hospital, but where is Robin?

Mason walks in and collapses into me. He is more composed than his siblings. Father Garrity quickly joins us to explain.

Early this morning, before seven, Mark Henley was hiding in the bushes in front of the house, waiting for Matt, Mason's fourteen-year-old brother, to leave for school. He knew the family routine. As Matt left, Mark forced his way through the door and told Matt, "Run! Go on, Matt! Run!"

Matt ran next door to Bob and Karen Carroll's house. The Carrolls called the police immediately. Once Mark enters the house, he locked the door and went upstairs. It's likely no one inside heard him. They were still in bed. He crept into the bedroom and fired his shotgun, first at Josie. *Bang!* She died instantly. Neighbors heard the shot. Mark took aim again and hit Bob's shoulder, which he could have survived. Neighbors heard him shriek. The next shot was to his chest. *Bang!* Sirens were heard within three to four minutes.

Mark then locked himself in Robin's bedroom. Two more shots were fired. Robin had no chance to escape. With the final shot, Mark took his own life.

I scream when I hear all three family members are dead. I remember the baseball bat Bob had kept under his bed to protect them. Could anything have protected them or us from this tragedy?

Five minutes, four people dead. The coffee pot was still brewing when the police arrived. Bob and Josie were forty-eight years old. Robin was eighteen. Lt. Peter Verbeke calls it the *grisliest crime in the history of Berea, Ohio.*

The day's events are heart-stopping. All eyes are on Matt, a freshman in high school. He is not talking, just staring at the walls. The missing family dog, all of ten pounds, reappears, trembling but alive.

Bystanders are asked to disperse. Family members go to Sherry's house, which is in the same neighborhood. Well-meaning people come and go. Many are dropping off food.

I suggest to Mason, "I need to figure out what to do with our kids. They can't be part of any of this. I'll go back home to make arrangements for them."

Mason agrees. His aunt Kathryn, Bob's only sibling, has arrived from Sharon, Pennsylvania. Mason's focus is on her. Mason and I kiss goodbye.

My father and Joan agree to keep Brock for as long as necessary, so my father returns to pick up clothes, diapers, and toys. Youngstown relatives come to take Ryan and Carol. Ryan thinks he's going on a vacation. Carol knows something has happened. Mason wants them to know their grandparents and aunt died, but I don't know how or when to try explaining this to the children. The only thing I know for certain is that they can't be with us right now. They're too young. That funeral would traumatize Carol. Besides that, my heart should give full attention to Mason, Sherry, and Matthew.

It has been a long time since I worried about my husband. He's unfailingly a rock, but he's also a human being, and this might break him. I fear it could break all of us.

I phone my brother in Phoenix. He won't be able to fly home. I'm not sure why, but I think it's financial. We talk for two hours. It's days like this when I miss my mother the most.

Mason refuses to look at the news on television or in the paper. The story bursts out all over the media. The front page of the Cleveland *Plain Dealer* reads,

> Jilted Suitor Takes Revenge. Kills 3, in Berea and Himself. Next page: Was Love a Lethal Catalyst in Berea Slayings?

There's a photo of Mason in front of his parents' house with a headline: "Berea Killer was Burdened with Problems." Yes, he was! And when he finally unburdened himself, he slaughtered our family.

In the succeeding days, my role is to focus on the minutiae. We make arrangements with Baker Funeral home: three caskets, three sprays of flowers: father, mother, sister.

We plan the funeral mass at St. Mary's with Father Garrity. We need eighteen pallbearers. Each parent had a small life insurance policy, enough to cover funeral costs. At the funeral, Father Garrity speaks directly to our family, preaching forgiveness and mercy. His eyes are on the five of us the entire time. It's like we are the only human beings in the church. He speaks about our feelings of emptiness and pain. He seems to understand our suffering and delivers a beautiful eulogy.

The air is empty, but the sun is warm as we ride in a limousine following a police escort and three hearses to Lake View Cemetery. Everyone has crashed. Shock has frozen our emotions to keep our hearts beating. It works like anesthesia. The limo smells like hot leather and cigars.

On the ride to the cemetery, I stare out the window, thinking of Labor Day, the last time we were all together. Mason's parents were fun people. I don't have one bad memory of them. We were free at their home to say and do whatever we pleased. Tears fall when I realize my children have now lost three grandparents.

After the burial, I ask the limo driver to crank up some tunes. Michael Jackson's "Rock with You" breaks through the silence, and for the first time in a week, we're together, making eye contact, flashing the briefest of smiles, tapping our feet, connecting.

The obligatory gathering at Sherry's house is exhausting. People say stupid things, laugh too loud, and act weird because they are either in too much pain or trying hard to escape it. I want to go home. I miss my children, and I need to rest my spirit.

Sherry, Patrick, Mason, and I meet for breakfast the following day then speak with the lawyer. Mason, the eldest, is the executor of the estate. There are hours of paperwork to do. The notorious crime-scene house will likely sit unsold for years. We all concur that Matt is the one who needs stability, so Mason and I agree to take care of Matt. He needs to stay in the same school and be close to friends. The house is thoroughly cleaned by trauma-scene specialists. They remove all the furniture, sanitize the entire house, install new carpeting, and apply fresh paint. Then the downstairs is remodeled for Matt to have his own space.

Matt stays with Sherry while the work is completed. Once we are moved, I contact the school counselor for an appointment to discuss Matt's grieving process. He suffers silently. I worry about him every minute.

Everything I was doing for myself toward healing stops. Taking care of everyone else becomes my number one priority. The running stops. Therapy stops. Over time, I gain fifty pounds.

My writing increases. Carol starts writing with me. At five years old, she reads at the second-grade level. Throughout the past year, I've taught my daughter to read and write. My children make the transition well. Mason and I grow quieter toward each other. He works long hours. Music plays all day in the house. Sherry stops by almost every day, and our relationship grows stronger.

I'm twenty-eight. Two very violent crimes have had a direct effect on my anxiety. The adults in my family have become detached actors in the wake of multiple murders. Life has meaning, and so does death. I've lost too many, myself included. I have no prayers after enduring this level of violence. My writing is my escape, my therapy. My three children are a reminder that my life matters. They are my world, my only reason.

Chapter 9

ANGELS ON EARTH

I'M THIRTY YEARS OLD TODAY. Mason and I are celebrating at the Akron mall. Yep, the famous Akron mall, where no passports are needed. We spend the night here right at the mall. This is somewhere between bizarre and totally okay. I'm acting like this kind of getaway is normal. At least the food court has pizza and ice cream. This is definitely a five-star mall experience. There's no place I'd rather be for my birthday, marking the start of a new decade, than at a *fucking* mall.

Life moves forward, ready or not. Mason, Sherry, Matt, and I each grieve privately. I'm walking, not running. I'm not sleeping. I've never had a weight problem before. I do now, and I'm addicted to sugar. It bothers me, but the untreated traumas I have lived through keep me in a "fight, flight, or freeze" energy all day long. I crave caffeine, carbs, and sugar. Food is my new drug. I'm on the way to being a hundred pounds overweight. There's a psychic death that comes with my silence.

Sherry gave birth to her first child, Joshua. She will move heaven and earth for her baby boy. She is a larger-than-life mother. We spend a great deal of time together. Brock and Joshua become buddies almost immediately. I'm glad our children will grow up beside one another.

Matt comes and goes. He's really a good kid who acts normally, but I feel his pain.

Mason deals with grief by reading books during long baths. We make him a tray out of wood that fits perfectly across the tub, where he can set his mug of coffee and his book. He will stay there for two hours. I serve him dinner on a tray while he sits in a recliner, watching television for the night. We don't talk about rape, we don't talk about murder, and we certainly don't talk about our grief. Actually, we don't really talk much at all. Our conversations are all about his work or the children. Our sex life is almost gone. Despite how bad life feels right now, Mason continues to do well at work. My addiction is food while my husband copes with life by becoming a workaholic.

My heart hurts when I see the faces of Matt, Sherry, and Mason. I don't know if peace can be found after this amount of tragedy. All the memories are silences that keep a soul hollow and numb. Murder and rape often leave victims with speechless horror. All of this sucks for all of us. Every single one of us have a lot of healing to do. Mine is the loss of identity after rape, loss of a mother, now loss of my husband's mother, father, sister. I'm only twenty-eight years old.

My new friend down the street has three children the same ages as mine. We each had our daughters first and then two sons. Kay becomes a fast friend, and she gains my unwavering trust. She is calm. I'm never calm. She is entertained by my wit and sarcasm. I have not had a close friend since high school. We have that high-speed verbal communication where nothing is lost. She holds me accountable and offers support like no other woman ever has.

Between Kay and Father Garrity, I feel blessed to have two people who make me feel I have something more to offer the world than three happy children. Kay listens to my dreams. Father Garrity and I meet for consultations. I love him so much; he turns me into a Catholic. Mason and I become members of St. Mary's Church. My hope is church will strengthen our family. We have all three children baptized and decide to take our marriage vows at St. Mary's.

Carol makes her first communion and breaks her arm playing football with the neighborhood boys. My *girl* does not complain about the pain until later that night. Off to the ER we go, and I bring her a piece of her white cake she never ate on her special day.

It's Friday night. The kids and I are hanging out at Kay's. Her husband is working, and Mason is hanging loose with solitude. We let the kiddos play indoors and out. They play well together with few problems. They are a version of *The Brady Bunch* kids in the neighborhood, a mix of six personalities that all get along. The only one who causes trouble is Ryan.

Kay offers me a cold beer. I've never drunk a beer. In my entire adult life; I've had fewer than eight alcoholic beverages. The first beer dulls my mental and emotional pain, so I drink another. Kay grabs one and asks, "What happened to you?"

I take several more sips while pondering where she's going with this question.

She adds, nonchalantly, "I'm not talking about what happened to your in-laws. Something else happened to you."

My throat tightens. "How do you know that?"

Kay stands up and says, "The very first time I met you in Karen's kitchen, I noticed half of your mind was somewhere else. Between your body language and the red blotches, I saw all over your neck, I could see something else was seriously wrong."

She is looking straight into my heart with her blue eyes, and I'm tempted to tell her it's none of her business, except I trust her, and I'm feeling the buzz of Budweiser. So I begin, "I was raped. It was more than sexual rape. There was a lot of mental abuse." I drink another beer and continue.

Kay drinks beer, smokes cigarettes, listens intently for hours without judging. I pace and talk. The more I talk, the more I pace, the more I drink. The more I drink, the more I let the trapped silences come out of me. I feel safe at this kitchen table with my misery and fears.

This is the kind of therapy I have been longing for since I escaped that room almost ten years ago. Finally, my miracle comes. I've found someone who actually listens and hears me.

I've lost count of how many beers I've hammered down. The kids are all scattered on the family room floor asleep. Daddy will be watching the children Saturday while Mommy goes to bed with her first hangover. I'm dehydrated. My head is throbbing, and my stomach is angry, but with every single breath, I exhale relief. My two best friends are now Kay Malone and Bud Weiser.

My baby Brock keeps falling down the steps and running into walls. At first, we thought his effort to keep up with Ryan, his favorite person, was causing his falls. Brock is a happy toddler, and Ryan and he are constant companions. He follows his brother everywhere. Today, he does not see the steps and goes flying, hurting his shoulder. I make an appointment with the pediatrician, who sends us to an eye doctor. My decision is to take my little guy straight to the Cleveland Clinic.

After extensive tests, the diagnosis is total blindness of the right eye. He was born with it, and the nerves behind the eye are dead. There's no surgery or treatment. My son is going to live his life with one eye. His only restrictions are that he will never fly a plane or serve in the military, and he is encouraged not to play baseball. At three years old, he's already riding a bicycle with no training wheels. I'm not treating him like he has a disability. Brock is the most athletic of my three. He's not going to stop, and I refuse to make him think anything is wrong.

On the way home, I buy him a new pair of shoes. He loves shoes more than toys. Then we stop at Ukrop's to pick up what he needs for his favorite dessert: strawberry shortcake. With this news, I can't stop from kissing his adorable face. It's another heartbreak that really sucks.

My kids transport me to a pain-free alternate universe. Writing while chewing on red licorice is how I cope at the end of the day. I try selling Avon to the neighbors, but it's not my thing, so my career with Avon lasts three weeks. Kay inspires me to begin therapy again, a better choice than getting drunk. She is becoming my hero. Actually, *she is my hero.*

Matt is sixteen, so I teach him how to drive. He also gets a huge birthday party, but I can't find a lifeline for this young man. My family is not the family he grew up with. He wants that family back, and it shows every time I try to include him in whatever we're doing. It's obvious on Christmas morning when twenty gifts under the tree don't excite him. I'm only fourteen years older than Matt. I don't know how to parent a teenager. It's hard because I feel he hates being here with us. I would hate being in his shoes, and I slip into them often to keep him at least feeling safe. He really never talks much about his family, and he gives me no problems.

It's summer 1982, and I love having the kids home all day. Carol loves to feed the ducks in the morning. Ryan wants to go to the park. Brock wants what Ryan wants. Working mothers complain about not having enough time with their children. Nonworking mothers complain that staying home is harder than working. If there is a benefit from tragedy, it's the way it enables you to appreciate simple things others take for granted. I can swing at the park with one of my kids on my lap and sing Karen Carpenter songs out loud. People think it's wacky that I get high off this stuff. I'm fortunate to have a husband who makes enough money that I can be home in the beginning years with my three children. My heart needs this time with them.

We make up our own play at home. The living room turns into a motor home. The family room is a boat. The kitchen table is a tent. The front door is a soccer goal. Carol, at six years old, locks herself in the bathroom and takes all the deodorant bottles, toothpaste, and soap and plays independently while talking to herself for an entire afternoon. I'm the one who forces her to play with friends. At seven years old, Carol is obsessed with the movie *Annie*. She asks me if her second-grade class could create an *Annie* play for school. I'm a hell-yes kind of mom, and three times a week, ten seven-year-olds move the living room furniture into the dining room, and we practice, learn all the lines, and this gig is a huge hit at Parknoll Elementary School. The things I do for love—my kids. Oh my god, how much I love being their mother.

Mason is ready to leave Cleveland. He thinks the change would help heal our tragedies. For months, we toss around the idea of moving to a different state. I worry about Matt and Sherry, who have lost too many family members.

The last person I want to move away from is Kay. She is my first best friend in adult life. If there are angels on earth, she is mine. No one can handle me or my anxiety like she can. Kay's energy brings me contentment. I'm in a blue funk over the possibility of losing her. Mason accepts a job in Richmond, Virginia, as the director of sales and marketing for General Medical. He will be traveling overnight a lot again, but the move offers a new beginning and a higher income.

Mason and I spend three days in Richmond looking for a home, which we find nestled in the woods of Brandermill with nature trails, swimming pools, and a country club where I will never belong. Country club folks won't know how to handle me. There's a golf course for Mason and great schools for the kids. My favorite room is the master bedroom because it has an unfinished room attached that can be my writing space. I fall in love with Richmond on day one. I will miss Kay's friendship every day, but she promises we will stay in touch, and I believe her.

The best part of moving day is when Michael, a young boy, rides his bike right up through our front yard to introduce himself. He lives a few houses down. I listen on the front porch as he talks nonstop about Richmond history and current events. He's gregarious and seemingly unaware of his superintelligence. As he leaves, he invites me to meet his mother, father, and Mary Kelsey, the family caregiver. Michael's mother is bedridden with multiple sclerosis.

I tell him, "I would love to meet everyone, especially your mother."

"She loves when people read to her."

"I will make a point of stopping by once we're settled."

Michael shows up every day. He and Carol are the same age and the same grade in school. He is her first friend on Stoney Ridge Trail.

Michael's mother, Susan, struggles to form words, making her difficult to understand. She has spasms and lacks muscle control. Her brain function is compromised. I worry for her eight-year-old boy. Thank God Michael has Mary Kelsey, who loves him like her own son.

My emotional pain is different from Susan's. How hard it must be for her to not have the health and strength to take care of her son, yet her attitude is so much better than mine. I learn a valuable lesson from a new friend. Real strength is an inside job. She holds her ground with compassion. She shows no pity on the life she's been dealt. Her strength inspires me.

Susan was an English teacher until her illness took control. She loves poetry We begin reading her favorite poets: Frost, Longfellow, Shakespeare, and Whitman. I read to her every week. Too few months later, I'm asked to read a poem at her memorial service. Michael is always welcome in our home as if he is part of our family. He's easy to love.

My husband is driven, still works long hours, and travels frequently. He is learning high-level management skills and continues to be successful. Demands on me keep getting tougher. There's no feeling of accomplishment for ironing his shirts or packing his suitcase for overnight travel. Most of the time, I feel like a single mom. My role is to be everything for everyone, and I do it well. I am addicted to the adrenaline rush of go, go, go! My potted plants, husband, and three children are thriving, so at least I'm doing something right, but taking care of myself is low on the long list of priorities. I'm gaining more weight.

On the surface, our marriage looks okay. We hold hands when walking, kiss hello and goodbye, sleep in the same bed, and Mason never forgets Valentine's Day, Mother's Day, or my birthday, but our relationship is slowly dying. It's only a matter of time. My unresolved problems seem to accompany me no matter where I go. The fantasy of a new beginning is simply that, a fantasy. When my breathing problems worsen and my inner demons talk to me all day, I make another attempt at therapy. The next therapist suggests that we retraumatize me, a perilous tactic. I ask her, "Have you personally experienced sexual violence?"

She shakes her head.

"Then how in the hell am I going to trust you?" I ask her. "How will you know *what* to retraumatize? What kind of game is this for you?" I grab my purse and then the doorknob. "Find another guinea pig. I'm not sure you understand anything I've told you." I slam the door and run to my car.

As another attempt at therapy fails—or am I failing at therapy?—I wonder if I'm beyond help. The anxiety attacks and breathing issues tell me I need another cardiologist. I can't catch a breath unless I lean on something, bend over, and breathe deeply. Almost immediately, my breathing becomes shallow again. This goes on for days or sometimes weeks. It's uncomfortable.

Mason agrees I need another cardiology evaluation. Turns out nothing is wrong with my heart. The doctor confirms panic attacks are lowering my oxygen. Once again, I refuse medication, and I remind the doctor that I'm not a heart patient. I'm a raging rape victim. I'm a bloody mess, and there's no drug for inner rage. I stop at Martha's bakery, get two dozen cookies, and eat half before I'm home. I take long walks every day, and when I feel no control over my thoughts, I binge on sugar, then I switch to salt. Food calms my anxiety long enough to feel I can function.

Virginia is known for its goldilocks climate—not too hot and not too cold—with relief from the Blue Ridge Mountains. There's nothing I miss about the subzero climate in Cleveland, but I do miss Sherry and Kay. One month, my phone bill is almost a thousand dollars. Mason can't know about this, so I skip a mortgage payment to keep the phone turned on. The mortgage will get caught up with our tax refund.

While taking a shower, I notice my lymph nodes are swollen. There's a lump in my upper right back that a doctor never removed. He said it was benign. This won't be convenient for anyone, but I'm going to the Cleveland Clinic. My breasts feel hard, and I'm scared. Sherry flies in and takes care of the children while Mason and I drive to Cleveland.

After a full examination by my mother's surgeon, there is an uneasy look on his face. He says, "I'm worried about your family history. You started having tumors at a young age, and the Anderson family genes seem to have a higher-than-average risk for breast cancer. I want you to consider a double mastectomy to prevent it."

This sounds out of the ordinary and derails my conversational groove.

He continues, "I know it's a lot to think about, but there's a good chance you will get breast cancer early like your mother. She was diagnosed at thirty-four the first time. You're thirty-three. Think about it."

"So you think I may have a genetic predisposition to breast cancer?"

He replies, "Yes."

A couple of minutes pass...*bingo!* "Let's do this. I don't need to think about it. How soon can we schedule it?"

He tells me, "You're brave. I will be right back."

I am brave, but I'm also a mother. Having my breasts cut off is not a traumatic event when compared to dying of breast cancer in my thirties. Watching my mother die from this disease put it all in perspective. I'm more terrified of cancer than most women.

The doctor returns. "Since you came all the way from Richmond, I was able to schedule this for next Wednesday. You will be admitted Tuesday evening. My assistant will provide you with further instructions. Do you have a place to stay for two weeks? You can't go home until I remove the tubes."

"Yes," I say. "I have a place to stay."

"You made this decision quickly. Do you need more time?" he asks.

"No. I appreciate you working me into the schedule so fast."

He leaves again briefly while I pace with my hands behind my head. I don't need Mason's approval. I don't need anyone's opinion. I'm doing this. There's no data on anyone having this done for preventative reasons, but it makes perfect sense. My decision is coming straight from the heart. When my doctor comes back and we discuss reconstruction, his eyes are as hard as stones when I say, "I'm not having reconstructive surgery. My children were nursed, and if a man needs my breasts to get his dick hard, he's not my kind of man."

Kay is in the waiting room. "What the hell?" She is surprised that my situation warrants a double mastectomy, but without delay, she supports me.

My husband is fine with it, provided he can get back to work in a week. Kay arranges to take care of me until the tubes are removed.

The rest of the family thinks I've lost my mind. They tell me I'm crazy, paranoid, selfish, and that we all die from something. It's a smart life-or-death decision, and yet no one supports me but Kay and Mason.

I'm admitted on Tuesday evening. Kay and Mason will come early in the morning before I go to surgery. Wednesday morning, when the patient transporter comes and no one has arrived, he says, "I need to take you now. Pre-op is ready."

So I go into major surgery alone. My mother comes into my heart, and I say the Serenity Prayer to myself. I can hear her telling me, "You are making the right decision. I'm so proud of you." Mom would have spent the night with me and validated my courage.

Prep nurses check my vitals and attach IVs. I'm given medication to relax me. An elderly lady next to me is having knee surgery, and I tell her my story. "Keep looking up. That's the secret of life. Be deliriously happy with the choices you make or get out," she says.

They move me from the gurney to a table in a brightly lit room. Everything shines. It's freezing in here and smells like disinfectant. Humans in blue scrubs move around with purpose. A nurse checks my wristband and asks, "What's your name? What kind of surgery are you having today?"

My doctor arrives. It's time to get the party started. He asks how I'm feeling. I answer, "That depends on how you're feeling. Did you get enough sleep? Did you have sex last night? If you didn't, I really don't want you to proceed."

There's soft laughter in the room as he answers, "I'm sure I slept better than you. Do you have any questions?"

I answer, "No. Let's get this over with."

Next is the anesthesiologist, the man who will knock me out with no guarantee I will wake up. People sometimes die in these rooms. "Count backward from ten to one," he says.

Screw the counting. My thoughts are with my three children. I'm out in seconds.

In the recovery room, I accuse the whole family of being soulless. Mason is with me. Nurses are floating and shape-shifting. I want to go to a Madonna concert. I'm weighed the next morning, and I'm pissed to learn that without breasts, my weight has dropped only two and a half pounds, no huge loss.

Mason quickly returns to Richmond to get back to work. Kay signs on as my number one caregiver. She even comes back to Richmond while I recover. We talk about everything, including our damaged marriages. She admits that hers is over too. We both married young. Mason and I are not surviving our tragedies. We've been married fifteen years. We are both equally unhappy.

Mason and I do not argue. He's not abusive. He's the hardest-working man I know. He keeps working longer hours, sleeping more, and spending more time reading in the bathtub. He's an honest man, but we are coexisting in this marriage for the sake of the three children who rarely see him. Mason is a workaholic since his parents and sister died. We live in two different worlds. He doesn't understand mine, and I don't understand his. Nothing ever changes. We no longer sleep in the same bed. I'm on the couch. The only thing worse than a loveless marriage is staying in one. I need and want a divorce.

Kay and I take long walks. When I talk, she listens without interrupting or judging. She's an angel who truly wants me to heal in this life. She and I met a few months ago and checked into a hotel. We spent three days talking about my rape. We smoked, we drank a little, and I poured a liter of coke over my head with this new feeling of human connection. Someone is actually listening to everything that happened that night and trying to understand it. There was a type of traumatic neurosis to me where I spent my life pleasing everyone in order to not feel a direct threat on any level.

There were different body languages that were uncovered. One is how I need to hold a pillow while sitting and cover my vagina. Another was how I picked the top of my head until it bled, how I was trapped between escaping into a fantasy mindset to a total shutdown, how addicted I was to sugar and felt safe being seventy pounds overweight. The whole experience was like a walking dream.

A part of me left that room and there was shining new light. Every color was brighter. I could smell the air. It was deeply bizarre with equal parts of me being lost and found. We celebrated this new feeling of my "inner light" back on by eating at Pizza Hut. Kay reminds me, "This is not the time to worry about sausage on your pizza. Eat whatever you want until you start feeling better about yourself, then lose the weight."

There must be more to life than being born, surviving tragedies, getting married, raising children, and dying. When Kay returns home, I'm able to drive again. On the back roads, I stop and stare at the continuously morphing clouds. My emotions float away through the expansiveness of nature. As I pull into my driveway, I feel I can be more than a rape victim, more than a wife and mother. I'm a writer in search of answers. On this day, at this moment, I decide to write a book.

I rearrange furniture to make space for my first writing desk. I sit down and joyously start typing words on an old Royal typewriter. It's 1986, and I have begun. I begin by telling myself that writing this book is my new marriage partner.

Chapter 10

PRECIOUS LADY LIBERTY

I GAZE OUT THE WINDOW OVER my first cup of coffee as a deer runs through our yard. Nature places me in a trance long enough to feel empty. My children are eating breakfast before school. Logan, our golden retriever, is eager to come inside to slurp up any Cheerios dropped on the floor. "Ryan! You're stupid!" Carol yells.

"Hey, what's going on here?" I ask.

Three-year-old Brock is crying. Ryan is smiling. Carol is furious. She grabs Brock's cereal bowl, throws the contents into the sink, and brings Brock a fresh bowl. "Ryan sprayed Windex in Brock's cereal, Mom!"

"Ryan, sit on the couch, please." I have exactly fifteen minutes before we leave to explain to my dark angel why we never put cleaning products in food. "You could have made your baby brother really sick. Ryan, do you know what the three most important rules are?" And on and on and on I lecture him.

His eyes sparkle even when he's in serious trouble. "There's more than three, Mommy."

"Not right now. For you, there are only three."

My threatening stare makes him grab a magazine and cover his face. I take the magazine away and toss it to the floor.

"Look at me. The three rules are: be kind, be kind, be kind."

"I know, Mommy. I know because you told me about being kind before."

"Do you understand that? Do you think being kind to your only brother is important? Being kind is how we treat each other. What you did was unkind, so there will be a consequence when you get home from school. Sit right there until it's time to leave," I say.

"Be kind, Mommy," Ryan replies.

I give up.

I savor a few more sips of coffee before the kids grab their backpacks and we head out the door. Ryan runs ahead and yells, "Shotgun!"

Every day, I remember how I almost lost Ryan. We get over our bad experiences fast. I'm not a mother who needs to dwell on the negative. I'm not a fan of punishment since it doesn't work for me. If I send them to their rooms for an hour, I'm back upstairs in fifteen minutes setting them free. Instead, I lecture them at length. They hate it. Carol has been lectured maybe once. Ryan is my jam-packed-with-action child with no filter. He will do anything for a laugh. Brock strives for perfection and cannot ever be accused of doing anything wrong. Poor little guy might need therapy as an adult. Nah, maybe he will learn to love his imperfections.

Today, I'm taking the bold step of meeting with a divorce lawyer to find out what's involved. While driving there, I remember how our love died. Tragedies killed our marriage, beginning with the rape. The fire we used to spark just by looking at each other is not even a dull flicker now. This is not the right example for our children. A healthy marriage is a deep and loving friendship. Mason and I barely talk. We barely listen to each other. We barely exist.

I've been dying inside over the past fifteen years. Mason doesn't see it, feel it, or deal with it because of my fear of his reaction. All of the dysfunction is my fault. Everything is my fault, and I deal with it by disappearing in my car with music. Divorcing him will set him free from my problems and allow him to marry someone else. My traumatized brain can't love any man.

I've learned two things about marriage through therapy. First, a woman who hates herself cannot be loved, and second, some marriages grow closer during tragedy while others fall apart. I wonder if Mason and I really loved each other at all. Maybe I just *needed* him, and he *needed* me. Maybe we were both codependent. Maybe this, maybe that—all I know is we stay together for the children. Right or wrong, it feels wrong, and I know I'm the one who needs to take action.

I believe the divorce will be healthier for my body, mind, and spirit. If I get a second chance at life, I want to find a soul partner who understands my dark, twisted self as well as all the tiny, beautiful things. But you can't love yourself without respect first. I have enough emotional intelligence to know I'm a shitty marriage partner. I'm stuck and miserable. It feels like a trap, and one of us has to speak up and do something about a failed marriage.

The attorney is charging five hundred dollars to process our divorce, provided it is consensual. I want full custody of my kids, child support, and shared profits from our house. I don't want alimony. Legally, I could get it, and my attorney advises me to, but it's a matter of pride. I need to support myself financially, and I don't anticipate much difficulty doing that. Being dependent on Mason's money has come at its own cost. Mason has no respect for me. Not only have I screwed up his credit, he comes in contact with independent women breadwinners. My priority is to find the right therapist so I can gain full control of my life no matter how difficult it may become. I miss the person who had dreams...and believed they happened.

The Commonwealth of Virginia demands a one-year separation when dependent children are involved. Today, the divorce papers officially will be filed. I'm not saying anything to Mason until I have the confirmation in hand.

I have an electrified feeling of relief as I walk out the door without one damn tear. I've made the right decision. The until-death-do-us-part vow is not realistic for all of us. Today, I'm facing the reality that our marriage has been dead for years, too many years. It's not his fault or mine. We drifted so far away from the feelings that sustain marriage that we can't find our way back. God knows we both tried. We were in love in high school. Rape killed me and my marriage. I'm to blame for all the ways trauma made me break. I'm the problem.

While driving, I drink a tall Budweiser. Barnes & Noble has five books I want on how to manage life after a divorce, so I buy them. My collection of books is large enough to fill a bookshelf. None of them ever get read. My mind races, making it hard to focus. This has been a challenge my entire life, which is why I almost failed as a senior in high school. Still, I love books, and I hope my anxiety that spirals into more anxiety will one day end when I find the right therapist.

One beer is not enough. My next stop is Lucky's, where I buy a six-pack of Budweiser. The kids are treated to fast food. After homework and showers, I lock the bedroom door. With beer on ice in the wastebasket, I chill with a Bee Gees CD. Kay answers the phone, and we talk for two hours. My Christlike friend never cuts me off. If I need to talk for hours, she listens. Fifteen minutes of the conversation involves my divorce. The rest is rape talk. She encourages me to keep searching until I find a therapist who can fucking talk about *rape!*

Seven beers are not enough, so I drive to get more. Boozing it up with music relaxes me and allows what feels like a higher cognitive function. I start to believe I could become an author one day, then I black out.

It's Christmas Eve. The driveway and porch are lined with luminarias. A six-feet-tall Frosty the Snowman stands outside our front door. Inside, the scent of cinnamon and pine mixed with aromas fill the air. The live tree is covered with homemade ornaments and strands of popcorn and cranberries my kids made. For the first time in eight years, my father and Joan are here for a week. My brother David is here from San Francisco, and everyone's spirits are high. We all attend Christmas Eve Mass at St. Edwards.

My fifty-something stepmom brings eight Cabbage Patch dolls with her. They all have names, outfits, and spread all over the bedroom. I'm intrigued by the mental challenges of others since I have so many myself. However, I'm not taking that neighborhood walk with her, and neither is Carol. She asks, "Why did Grandma want her dolls here for Christmas, Mom? It's weird."

David is the kids' favorite uncle. He has taken charge of the kitchen since he's a professional chef at the St. Francis Hotel, where he prepares large banquets for hundreds of people from all over the world. Dinner is a slow feast of crab legs, prime rib, and double-stuffed potatoes. Ryan helps with everything as Uncle David teaches him to cook. We have salad, spaghetti squash baked with honey, hard crusted bread, and several options for dessert. Candles flicker at the table, where my children know they must remain until everyone is finished eating.

David's career is a huge success, and my father loves reminding me of how well David is doing compared to me. He doesn't even commend my mothering. The insane humor that bounces from one person to the next creates a carnival of laughter. I'm bracing for the moment my feelings will get hurt. My family does not understand me. Someone will get drunk and remember my screwups and make a fool out of me. It happens every time we get together, and it sickens me. Shit happens when a family slides under the influence of alcohol.

David is wrestling with all three kids, so I get the camera. Their little heads are caught in his headlock.

Carol leaves the match and opens her favorite lemon cookies that my grandmother Maki sends her every year for Christmas. She grabs a book and searches for some solitude. Mason pours a scotch on the rocks, lights a cigar, and steps out onto the screened-in porch. I look at him, knowing this will be our last Christmas together.

The kids and I have a Christmas Eve bedtime ritual. We sit in a circle. The dog nudges his way into the center of the circle. The children and I hold lit candles. I turn the lights out, and we go around the circle, each saying what we are thankful for. Carol begins, "I'm thankful for my dog, my friends, and cookies."

Ryan: "I'm thankful that Uncle David is here this year."

Brock: "I'm thankful for Santa and Jesus."

Me: "I'm thankful that I spend every day with all three of you. You are my best Christmas gifts."

I remind them that the real point of Christmas is to celebrate the birth of Jesus. I say a short prayer. All three keep their eyes on me, and our spirits are joined. They don't ask questions. They listen. It's the best part of Christmas Eve for me. It's a reminder of the beauty of birth.

Once the house is silent, I sink into the couch with some egg-nog. The tree sparkles, and the fire flickers. The stockings are full of tiny wrapped presents. I count all the gifts one more time to be sure each child has the same amount. Christmas morning always comes with too many presents. My husband does not know how many thousands of dollars I spend on this holiday.

I don't know why Christmas triggers every emotion. I miss people at the same time I feel pure joy in the ones still here. There's sadness, yet at the core, there are all the Falalalalas.

It's three in the morning, and I'm still wide awake. The tradition at our house requires the children to wait upstairs until Mason and I are downstairs. When they hear the jingle bells ring, six feet come running down the stairs.

Leftovers from Christmas, some years, are packed in the car and some years are taken to the homeless shelter. I want my children to understand that the holidays can be difficult for many people, that just because some people are poor does not mean they are less worthy. I want them to enjoy experiences with people from different backgrounds. In my life, I've experienced both sides—dark and light, rich and poor, fat and skinny, happy and miserable. The harsh judgment I've dealt with on the dark side feels criminal. I feel it from my own father.

*****

Weeks pass, and the divorce papers are ready. Mason doesn't understand why I'm inviting him out to dinner, but he consents. It's been two years since we had a date night out or dined out alone. We meet at a Mexican restaurant at seven o'clock. He orders a margarita, and I drink ice tea. I can feel my pulse in my throat. I wonder what his first reaction will be. "I filed for a divorce," I say.

"When?"

"A few weeks ago. I have the papers."

"Okay." He orders another margarita. We devour a basket of chips and salsa. He looks untroubled. "How are you going to survive financially?"

"I will figure it out."

Still no anger, shock, or sadness. He looks relieved.

I continue, "I've thought about this for a long time. We both know our marriage is not salvageable."

We order dinner. He makes no attempt to change my mind. We agree there's no reason to tell the kids until right before he moves out. He looks at the divorce papers then hands them back to me. "We can discuss all the financial details later."

As we leave, he gives me a hug. There's no hesitation, no "Are you sure?" On the drive home, I realize my intuition is right. *We both want the hell out.*

The next morning, I call Kay to tell her my news. I find out that she is considering leaving her husband and moving to Richmond. I'm overjoyed with the idea of having my best friend close by again. A few months later, she and I pack up a twenty-four-foot U-Haul and take turns driving it 483 miles. Our six children take turns riding—two in the truck, four in the car. She moves into her own apartment and starts working at Bath and Biscuit, a dog grooming shop.

*****

Mason and Kay have become buddies. She could use a less expensive place to live with her kids. Mason favors the idea of her family moving in with ours before he makes his exit. He may doubt my ability to make it financially. All I know is her moving in seems like a smart idea for all.

Most of the neighbors stop talking to us when they see the new arrangement—three adults, six children, and chronic head lice that migrate from one kid to the next and even to the adults…and dogs and cats that keep getting run over by cars. I find a job taking care of two little girls, Brittany and Lindsey. That affords us six months of head lice treatments, taco nights, and more books.

Our divorce has been final for months, yet Mason hasn't moved out. Finally, we sit all three children on the couch and tell them Mommy and Daddy are divorced and that Daddy will soon be moving. We talk for an hour about how life will be. No one appears upset, except Ryan. Mason hugs him and says, "You will always be my best friend."

The end of our marriage is messy, but the kids are spared. There is only a hollow feeling, and there are no tears when Mason drives away on New Year's Day. I'm not angry, sad, or confused. All I know is venturing into the unknown with no education, no work experience feels frightening.

There will be no stepfather. I'm not healthy enough to date anyone. I make a promise to myself not to date anyone until the kids are raised. My focus is on getting a good job and keeping the family unit tight. It's not about me. This is all about making sure my three children continue to thrive.

Kay begins working the night shift in the emergency room at a hospital. I find a job in the deli at Ukrops grocery store, making less than eight bucks an hour. At the end of the night, I reek of bologna and cheese. On day one, the manager tells me I'm too slow and that if I eat one piece of cheese, I'll be fired. I can already feel an exit coming. How long can anyone be expected to slice bologna and kiss ass?

Nothing inspires me about a job where I have to repeatedly ask, "How can I help you? You need it cut thick? Thin? Would you like a sample? Thank you for shopping with us. Please come back again." The ladies with the big diamonds on their hands who ask for one third of a pound of salami need to find another clerk. This job is not creative, I hate wearing a uniform, and my paycheck is less than five hundred dollars a month. Sponge bathing the meat cutter triggers rape flashbacks. Before I finish training, I want out.

I need another therapist. I find Ann, who would be a lovely lady to have Sunday brunch with instead. After several sessions of talking about everything but rape, she tells me, "You have great communication skills. Why are you not using them?"

I explain that I am writing. When I ask her if we could spend a few sessions discussing my rape and my low self-esteem, she suggests I turn my focus to selling real estate. Her solution to sexual violence is selling houses? No...frigging...way. Why the fuck are therapists so removed from having real discussions about rape? Is it because of the stigma around this crime, or do I sound hopeless? Am I too stupid for a real career? Yeah, that's it. They all know I'm stupid.

She's the only therapist who quits me before I can quit her. She walks me out, saying, "It was nice to meet you, but there's really nothing more for us to talk about. Good luck to you, Debra."

After a three-mile walk, I arrive home, fix dinner for six kids, and then start writing. Writing has a powerful effect on my anxiety. Hours feel like minutes. I even start writing a book about me in the third person. My name in the book is Leah. The first sentence of the book is, "Leah is not sleeping naked tonight." I spend weeks writing out the entire rape scene and hide the pages under the mattress. *No one will ever be allowed to read it.*

Job number two is waitressing at the Dairy Bar from six to noon, six days a week. I can cuss here among the staff and wear my bohemian clothes. I make good money. It's not magic. I'm the cute and chatty server who builds a brand-new customer base. I am making a difference in the world. Everyone loves milkshakes and needs those extravaganza omelets with ham chunks. I love the fast pace and meeting new people. I connect better with strangers than friends.

The owner gives me all the assholes—the party of six crammed into one booth who wolfs down their food then ask for a manager to cut their tab in half because their meal sucked. Then they walk out without leaving a tip. Were these humans criticized too much in their childhood? If customers cross the line with my level of service, I remind them how fortunate they are to not have a malignant tumor. The owner asks, "Would you please stop saying that?"

"No, I won't stop. My energy is growing your business, and I will say whatever I please."

Today, I get a call that my children's father is moving almost nine hundred miles away to Orlando, Florida. I'm shocked by his decision, but Mason is smart and wants to start his own medical company. He promises me the child support will keep coming. I believe him and also know there's no stopping him. Mason has wanted to be a millionaire since the days of Amway selling. There's a burning desire in this man to be wealthy. One day, I know he will make it.

I feel sorry for Ryan, who takes this news the hardest. He gets a little more attention from me for a few months. I'm proud of how the kids handle this. My three children are doing great. Carol is my overachiever. Ryan is a free-spirited social climber. Brock is a rising-star athlete. The boys love their mama and show it. Carol is less demonstrative. She knows something is not right with me on the inside. I watch her pay attention to my many moods.

My daughter sees that I'm different from the mothers of her friends. I'm not sure she likes the difference. "Mom, why are you dedicating a song to yourself on the radio? Don't you think that's a bit strange?"

At first Carol is amused. I'm dialing a radio station to request "One Moment in Time" by Whitney Houston to be dedicated to me. I have not been drinking. I have just decided this is my song. Carol grows more concerned. "It's not normal for anyone to dedicate a song to themself. How will you feel if someone you know hears this?"

I keep dialing.

"Mom, stop dialing the phone. Why do you need to do this?"

I can't explain why. The song plays ending the discussion. What seems disturbing to my daughter is not the least bit strange to me. When I'm moving with total abandon to Stevie Nicks's music in the kitchen, all three of my kids stop, stare, and wonder. My boys laugh. Carol studies my behavior.

There's never enough money to survive. The water is shut off one week. The car insurance is past due. My car breaks down, and there's no money to fix it. Kay finds a sales job selling for the Yellow Pages, and life gets easier financially. My stress is spilling over onto hers. We both feel the financial consequences of divorce.

My new friend Mary was a concert pianist for the Richmond Symphony. Now she has lupus and teaches piano at home. Her son and Ryan are soccer buddies. She loves long country road outings as much as I do. The only difference is she drinks and drives and listens to classical music and NPR while I beg her to find soul music or Bon Jovi. I'm attracted to artsy women who are less domesticated.

Mary spends time with her animals and children and is one of the most creative souls I've met. She takes me to find books about how to write a book. I can actually read them. I will read a page twice, but at least I'm reading books, which is progress. Mary doesn't do laundry because Mary simply doesn't do laundry. She pays someone else to do it. She invites me to the Unitarian Universalist Church. It's all spiritual energy, and I dig it.

Her friend Mark is a cellist. He comes to church barefoot. He flirts with me, and we click immediately. The three of us go to concerts, museums, church, and coffee shops. Mark does not drink alcohol, and our connection ends abruptly when I show up drunk at one of his performances at a church, pretending to be the conductor. Mary explains that he also felt less compatible when I told him my favorite book was *The Bell Jar* by Sylvia Plath.

I'll admit it: I'm not healthy. Eleven therapists have tried, and I'm on a hunt for number twelve. Finding the right therapist is like trying to find the right husband. Luckily for me, Kay and I did find a dive bar called Al's. It's easy to spot because there is an eight-foot Statue of Liberty next to the front entrance. Everyone here seems depressed with lots of problems. I love this place. The guys buy us beers. I never go without Kay, and we don't show up that often, but the urge to be there is growing stronger. I think about the bar all the time.

We go straight there after I realize I've alienated Mark. The next morning, I wake up with the eight-foot Statue of Liberty in bed next to me. My leg is wrapped around her. I have no recollection of how it got here. I do recall dancing by the jukebox in one of my goddess dresses.

Kay says, "You passed out at the bar after acting out the diner scene from *When Harry Met Sally*. Al let you buy the statue, and it was on the front porch. We bought it the next day. I'm not sure how you brought it upstairs. We have to stop going there, Deb. Something bad always happens to you."

My hangover lasts two days, keeping me home from work. Since the first Budweiser in Kay's kitchen, I've gotten drunk every time I picked up the first drink. Now I'm blacking out. It feels like a force is taking over my entire being. I drink the first beer to relax…then the second. Three beers become five, which become eight. I can't stop. It's the only way I know to escape my pain. Alcohol takes me into a mental state where my dream of actually doing something with my life feels possible. It makes me feel like I will actually become someone until I drink eight beers and tell anyone sitting next to me my life challenges. They don't listen to me. I end up hearing their problems and trying to fix them.

When I take a long bath after a night of drinking, I feel the filth again. There must be something wrong with my nervous system. No matter how much I pray or write, I keep making bad things happen, and I don't understand why. I need to find a way to stop drinking.

When I look in the mirror, I want to know a good person is looking back. My own nakedness scares me. My body is ugly, and I hide it with layers of clothes, mostly black. I'm still running as far away from that room, that night, that girl, that insane person. The running is in my head. There has to be someone who can help me bury that woman to give her back a life. I don't recognize her. All I know is *I hate her!*

Part 3

THE ’90S

Chapter 11

HOW COFFEE CHANGES MY WORLD

WAVES OF ANXIETY WASH OVER me. My friendship with Kay may be over. Casual friends come and go, but she's the most loyal friend I've had. She knows everything about me. I'm truly afraid to live without her, but I need to learn how to manage my anger without directing it toward her. The beast in me unconsciously shows up. It's not controllable until I act on it. Then comes the regrets. It's a horrible way to exist. I need help. "There's a dark cloud that follows you everywhere," she says.

After a ten-year friendship, she's wary of my mood swings. It's not her fault. My mood can change from one hour to the next. Her children don't like me. They may even hate me. It is certain they don't want to live here anymore. I'm wrecking this friendship with my unresolved problems. While others move forward in their lives, I'm immobilized in my traumatic experiences where I can still smell my rapist, see my mother's dead body, the memory lingering of the wreckage of our family from the murders of family members. I'm losing this fight.

A few months later, Kay moves out. This feels worse than my divorce. She finds a small house that's only a mile away. The boundaries are set. It feels like punishment for not being able to heal. Thankfully, she and I are still friends, and we talk often, but Kay is a social being. She will make many new friends that soon enough she won't have time for me. I feel it coming. There's no apology I can offer her for being so messed up. There's a point at which apologies mean nothing. Losing this friendship is life-changing. It feels worse than losing my mother. She's the only one who really, really tried to help me. I'm scared to be this alone.

Why is there such mystery surrounding my madness? Why do therapists refuse to allow me to talk through the details of rape, murder, cancer? I swear, I will never confide in another friend again because the outcome will be another loss. The only solution is to continue the search for a professional who has the right energy to deal with me. All I need is one freakin' person. How can this be so damn difficult?

I drive without a destination. If I end up two hundred miles away, it's fine. The fresh air slows my mind down long enough to feel the sadness of losing my only real friend. I'm a horrible person, a horrible friend, a horrible writer. I'm not a horrible mother.

The front door lock is broken and does not get fixed. This is the first time I'm the only adult in my home since I was raped. Anyone can walk through the front door. At night, I put chairs in front of it. Now that Kay is gone when anything breaks, it stays broken. When a doorknob falls off, I take the whole door off and throw it in the garage. Our home is nothing but a crappy shelter. The kids laugh, but Brock and Carol are too embarrassed to invite friends here anymore. Ryan doesn't care. His friends still show up.

Mary tries to help by recommending another therapist that she likes. Before I go into the session, I buy cigarettes even though I'm not a smoker. I pray this lady has a little intuition and is unafraid of real talk about sexual assault. She takes notes constantly, adjusts her glittery glasses, and burns sandalwood incense.

It's hard enough wading back into past trauma with a stranger, but my eyes keep glancing at her hairy legs, jarring my thought process. I'm distracted by that hair on her legs.

"When you think of colors, Debra, what color do you see first?"

Dear God, get me out of here. I've already paid the copay so I answer, "Black."

She squirms a little. "Do you see any other colors? Maybe purple?"

Where is she going with this color bullshit. "Nope, all I see is black."

"Are you suicidal right now, Debra?"

"*No.* I am the single mother of three children. Why do colors matter? I'm here because of extreme anxiety that causes breathing problems. I'm emotionally unstable, and you start out wanting to talk about colors?"

"Colors are a way for me to see how dark your thoughts are."

"Holy crap! Tell me how I can get the images of rape out of my head."

She grabs a water bottle and says, "We are going to begin by doing some writing exercises. Are you familiar with journaling, putting your thoughts and feelings into words? Let's also practice some deep breathing and meditation. How much time do you spend reading? Have you read *You Can Heal Your Life* by Louise Hay?"

My heart sinks. "I'm done now. Thank you for your time." I walk to my car, see my keys locked inside, walk back inside to call a locksmith.

I understand why victims of rape or any sexual violence can become alcoholics and drug addicts, why they may become suicidal. No wonder their relationships often fail. We live in a culture in which getting to the root of these traumas is difficult, sometimes impossible. One of the first questions is, "Why did you not report the rape to the police?" as if reporting the assault would have enabled me to overcome all the negative residual effects. I feel stupid when I answer with how extreme my fear was and that I thought being silent was the only way to survive.

I felt powerless. I lived with the daily fear that my rapist might show up in any parking lot I parked in and that he could attack me again, but this time, I would die. I am guilty of nothing, yet this is a crime for which victims are often made to feel guilty immediately and can suffer a second type of assault in a courtroom. When our culture stigmatizes the victim, wrongly accuses her (or him) of being at fault or minimizes the crime, it prevents hundreds of other victims from reporting or getting help. Kay helped me understand I did nothing wrong. I walked to my car after work. That's all I did. *I walked to my car!*

With forty dollars in my checking account, I quit two jobs and collapse. Within a week, I land a job with the Richmond Symphony scheduled for five nights and Saturdays. I'm also hired on the spot at MCV Hospital to work five days a week as a morning barista. Sundays are my days off. I'm working sixty-two hours a week. This is not a victory. It's survival.

Life can be harder on the children of any single mother, especially if she is without a career. Ryan deals with it better than his siblings. He's the one who doesn't mind duct tape on his soccer shoes or fewer clothes. He starts working at the age of twelve to earn enough money to go to the mall with his friends. People give him odd jobs because they see how poor we are. He wants his bedroom painted forest green. It's something I want to do for him for being such a soldier during these hard times, but I have no idea when I can afford the paint. He and I share an honest rock-solid relationship.

I'm energized by working in a diverse culture, serving coffee to smart people. My negative energy elevates to positive as my inner extrovert comes back to life. I love the job. People like me, talk to me, and want me to make their drinks. I'm the braless hippie chic with a free spirit who makes sure the doctors, nurses, and visitors get their perfect caffeine buzz. My skirts are long with vibrant colors, and I curl my hair every day.

A Russian anesthesiologist has a crush on me. I'm the only one allowed to make his venti half-caf-half-skinny latte with extra froth. He leans up against the wall and watches me work while he drinks. One day he says, "I can tell your family came to America on a boat.

You're very Eastern European looking. It shows up in how you dress and work."

He invites me to dinner several times, but I decline. My dark side will destroy his attraction. He has no idea how different I am in real life. He doesn't seem like the kind of guy who enjoys dive bars. He keeps asking, and I keep refusing.

After a few months of working at the coffee kiosk, one of the owners wants to meet with me. "We are impressed with your work. We are also worried there is some theft going on. Everyone seems to really love you and the good energy you bring to our business. I would like to offer you a promotion."

My knees are bouncing herky-jerky, "Tell me more."

Ken explains, "We want to promote you to regional manager of all the Richmond locations. It would require you to wear a pager 24-7 since we operate seven days a week. The job entails making daily deposits and maintaining a coffee inventory. You would do all the ordering, hiring, training, and terminations. Since all three owners live out of town, the position would involve a lot of multitasking and more hours. My concern is that you have no management experience. The stress level is high. I'm not sure you want all this responsibility."

If Ken knew my life story, he would not worry about whether I can handle stress. With a smile, I respond, "I'm a single mother. No one multitasks more than a single mother who works two jobs. I'm an expert at multitasking. I've longed for a chance like this. There are changes that need to be made. I see them, and I will fix them. Some people need to go, especially the ones who smell like pot or show up late for work every day. There will be strict policies in place. I'm comfortable with responsibility, and I want to grow your business."

When I systematically list all the changes I would make, he asks, "Where did you get all of this business knowledge?"

"My ex-husband is a successful businessman. I learned from him. He discussed all of his business with me."

"Congratulations, Debra." Ken smiles and shakes my hand. "You have one hundred percent support from me and the hospital administration. They all speak highly of you."

Wow, do I feel alive right now! I am going to be a manager! I'll finally have a respectable title. The increase in salary means I can quit my second job. Fresh squirts of happy tears burst out. This job offer represses some trauma since I will be working seven days a week doing something I love. The other benefit is there will be no time to drink. When my pager goes off, I'm expected to find a pay phone and call immediately.

In the first year, we open two new Richmond locations. I manage five locations, and my staff is growing. My pager goes off day and night. Between the owners and the employee's, I stop at a pay phone at least thirty times a day. I'm a problem solver, and the questions come at me constantly.

> Debra, some guy stole our biscotti's. Can you get to the Nelson Clinic right now?
>
> Hi, Debra, I'm sorry but I'm throwing up. Please send someone to relieve me soon.
>
> Debra, my period started, and blood is showing through my pants. I need to go home.
>
> Debra, where is the Ethiopian coffee? You told St. Mary's it would be here today.
>
> Debra, am I allowed to study on the job if we're not too busy?
>
> Debra, someone stole the morning deposit out of the register. It wasn't locked.
>
> Debra, is it okay if I give this surgeon a free triple-shot espresso? He's been in the OR all night.
>
> Debra, you need to be in Williamsburg tomorrow by noon.

> Debra, the espresso machine is broken. Get over here now!

I get pulled from one location to another, and I love the pace. There's no time to think. The stress of this job is easier than the stress I had before taking it. I have implemented a three-strikes-and-you're-out policy, and it works. As it turns out, I'm a good leader. There are days when I don't know if I can handle everything, but somehow, I do exactly what needs done.

My children are on their own too much. They look out for each other and have friends who are like family. They are responsible because I planted those seeds in them in the years I spent as a full-time mother. Carol and Ryan are in high school. Brock is in middle school. All three play sports. Carol and Ryan have part-time jobs to pay for their own clothes. They all make good grades and do their own laundry. Ryan finds a new job every three weeks while Carol and Brock stay in the same job. I'm so proud of them, and I make sure to have one good conversation with each one every day. Carol and I sit on her bed at midnight and talk. We don't have dinner together, but the fridge has food, and they manage well.

I'm full of guilt that I can't get to their games. Whenever possible, I drive to one field, make sure Ryan sees me, then drive to where Brock is playing and wave hello before hurrying back to work. My day starts at six in the morning and ends after midnight. I'm living on four to five hours of sleep. My energy has never felt better. *My rapist is not following me everywhere.*

All three owners have a huge celebration with a live band in one of Richmond's breweries. I'm given a bonus and a "Manager of the Year" award. Everyone keeps offering me drinks that I'm smart enough to decline. When we have enough money to open our sixth location, the owners send me to the University of North Carolina to do the hiring, training, and the launch.

Eventually, I receive the go ahead to hire an assistant manager. I approach Kay, and she accepts. As months pass, the stress of being responsible for five locations takes its toll. My highs and lows become more extreme. I don't know why I'm suddenly a different person. I've maxed out eight credit cards and applied for three more. I can't keep up with home or car repairs. I borrow Mary's Honda until I can make the money to fix my own car.

After two years of working the job, Ken calls me into another meeting. He tosses me a red shirt with a logo and says, "What do you think?"

"I'm not wearing this."

He laughs. "We are all wearing it. The company is big enough now that we need everyone in uniforms with name tags."

"That's fine. I'm not wearing it."

He asks, "Why?"

"I hate uniforms. I never wear pants. If someone wants to know my name, I'll decide whether to tell them. You can't force me to wear this. I'm not a golfer."

He laughs again.

Snap! I'm choking on my words, feeling like I'm going to cry. I throw the shirt back at him and ask, "Why wasn't I a part of this decision? I made all of this money for you." I stand up, arms flying, cussing to myself. I tell him, "No one controls me. No one tells me what to wear. I'm not wearing this shirt."

The crying starts, and Ken looks nervous. I'm embarrassed to be crying. I tell him I need water and will be right back. I have no intention of coming back. Suddenly, I'm crying like a toddler and running, running, running past the administration office, past my staff, running to the escalator, running out the door. I start yelling, "I can't do this. I can't do this." I can't breathe, yet I keep running. I even kick a garbage can, still yelling, "I can't do this." I sprint through the parking garage and floor the gas pedal, but I hit a curb, which blows out a tire.

My pager rings, and when I finally call the Williamsburg office back, I'm told, "You are suspended until further notice."

Snap! I drive to Kinko's and send a letter of resignation. *Snap!* I get drunk.

*****

As much as they will allow, I spend the following week with my children. I talk with Mary about my reaction at work. She absolves me of my guilt by telling me that working seventy hours a week was too much. She helps me fix the car, and we hang out, drink, and talk for a few days.

For a month, I don't work. I stay on the couch when the kids are at school. I'm on my own island and need to figure out how to make money.

During the month, my favorite person on the planet dies. The kids and I take off for Youngstown, Ohio. My grandfather Maki's words come back to me: "When you see a cardinal, it's a reminder that you were loved. Think about those who are no longer here, but don't be sad. Think about the love you shared, nothing else."

For his memorial service, I write a poem titled "Wings of Crimson." It is about the impact his peace, humor, and poetry have on my life. It is said that we love those who influence us the most. His influence is one of the reasons I'm still alive. I loved him more than my own father. I grieve for months after his death.

*****

Sergio's Pizza hires me to wait tables, and so does Oscar's retirement community. One job is six nights a week. The other is six days a week. I have work tomorrow, and yet I'm on my sixth beer at TGI Friday's happy hour. Driving home like this would not be smart. Home is a few miles away. How am I going to hide my condition from the kids? Ryan's friends are all drinking. He can't see me drunk.

Mary picks me up. I leave the car in the parking lot, pretend to be sick, and go straight to my bedroom. The kids cannot know about my drinking.

In the morning, I call off both jobs for the day because I need to write. There's a connection between how I lost myself in that filthy room, how I lost a good job, and how I binge drink. My moods go from high energy to no energy, from believing I could be an author to thinking I will eventually have to kill myself to escape this pain. I don't understand why it's always one extreme or the other. Why am

I on a dizzying road that leads to ruined relationships and self-sabotage? For eleven hours, all I do is write. Writing helps me see that I'm not a screwup. I'm really a good person in search of answers and the meaning of my life.

On an early Saturday morning, I'm speeding to an ortho office. Brock broke his leg playing soccer. All I feel is guilt. I should have been there. He'll be in a full cast for eight weeks. I hate seeing him in pain. He can't go to school, and he can't even watch TV because ours broke three years ago. He has sixty-five dollars, so I take it to buy materials to keep him occupied while confined. He is puzzled by my choices.

Our financial situation has never been worse. It's not extreme poverty because we have shelter. The oven and dishwasher don't work. When we flush the upstairs toilet, water drips down through the kitchen ceiling. The hole in the ceiling is six feet long. The foundation of the house has shifted, causing a crack in the fireplace big enough for critters to come in. The kitchen and downstairs bathroom floors are worn through and need to be replaced. Every piece of furniture we have was someone else's discarded furniture. I've never owned a new car, and something costly is always breaking down on my used car. I cut my own hair and my kids' hair. One night, I borrow cereal for dinner. If the kids get twenty bucks from my brother for their birthdays, they spend it on shampoo or food. I'm not a poverty-proud woman.

Even though I feel like I'm failing my children, they don't appear to be struggling. They are cooperative, and they can see how hard I'm working. We need to sell the house. It would bring down my overhead and allow me to work only one full-time job. My teenage boys need a mother watching them. My daughter is already raised and is raising me.

There's an old sandy-colored couch up against my bedroom window where I watch the shades of night turn black. I'm lying here, holding on to my body pillow, staring into the sky. When I stop and become still and silent, I am *nobody going nowhere.*

It's calming to view the world without stepping into it. I'm safe in this space. My body and breathing are relaxed. It's almost three in the morning. I hear crickets sing. My shoulders are covered by the gray-and-white quilt I've slept with for a decade. I drift off for what seems like the briefest moment before hearing my kids moving about the house, getting ready for a new day. Brock knocks at the door. "Are you awake, Mom?"

"Yeah. Do you need something?"

"Can you make some over-easy eggs for breakfast."

I jump to my feet. We sit together while he eats the eggs and toast plus a pint of strawberries. He brings up the sixty-five dollars I owe him. He's fine with waiting for it but confused about why I brought home coloring books and crayons that he outgrew years ago. The truth is, I can't explain my thinking. Why would I buy a thirteen-year-old coloring books?

He walks out the door. "See ya later, Mom."

"I love you, Brock."

He doesn't respond.

One breath in, and one breath out. I call off work. I'm trusting the God within. My body and mind need a rest that releases years of sad, angry, confusing tears. There's no energy to think or move, write, or continue acting like I'm okay. I'm not okay. Something is wrong with me, and it feels like a force stronger than rape. I'm alive, and my heart still beats for my children. I dive deeper into my spirit with the same kind of faith I felt when I read the Bible, the same kind of spirit when I stood up at age ten at a Wednesday night prayer meeting and told the congregation that I would spend my adult life as an Ethiopian missionary. "The kingdom of God is within me."

I need that spiritual energy working in me right now. Where is she? What happened to that ten-year-old girl?

Chapter 12

BUSTED

WHO CARES IF I'M FORTY years old today? No one. I'm completely and undeniably alone. Why would any healthy human want to hang out with my bullshit positivity or my suffering? They wouldn't, and they don't.

I'm celebrating alone at Third Street Diner, a writer's hangout in downtown Richmond. There are eight barstools with ripped and worn upholstery. The servers are eclectic with blue hair, tattoos, and miniskirts with fishnets. I'm playing tunes on the jukebox, and after being sober for a few months, I order my first glass of zinfandel. I guzzle three glasses in forty minutes. I'm mildly buzzed and digging it. Zin is my new sweet and fuzzy Zen for this celebration.

"Throw bacon on my grilled cheese sandwich!" I yell to the cook. "It's my birthday."

He serves it without saying happy birthday. What a sack of joy.

There's a man sitting next to me who looks like he's in his fifties. He could be homeless. His personal hygiene needs attention. He has an overgrown beard, dirty fingernails, a ripped shirt, no socks, and holes in his shoes. His head hangs so low, it almost touches the bar. Before he even gestures, the bartender sets down beer after beer and a shot now and then. He must be a regular. After several minutes of silence, he lifts his head and asks, "Are you alone?"

I reply, "Yes. I'm hanging out until the music ends. There is no greater therapy than chilling awhile with music."

He's a bit creepy when he looks directly at me with his oily eyes, but he doesn't seem like a threat. Besides, there are no other barstools left. He mutters, "I hope I'm not bothering you…if you're trying to be a wallflower."

"It's okay. You aren't bothering me."

He extends his dirty hand, grinning like a devil, and says, "My name is Dick. What's yours?"

I answer, "Debra."

Dick tells me he was in Vietnam, and he has no family. He lives in the hotel across the street and starts drinking when he wakes up. Halfway through his sentences, he pauses, staring into space. Something is wrong with him. I feel genuine empathy as we continue our conversation.

"There's something different about a woman who comes into a bar alone."

I smile and answer him, "Oh, yeah, I'm different all right."

He thanks me for being his friend. It's more like a rent-a-friend connection in bars. I note his lethargy and listen to his pain while drinking more zin. "We all need a little help in life, Dick. I'm happy to listen."

He talks at length about his personal struggle with life after war. I'm interested in how trauma changed his life because Dick and I have some things in common. Soldiers of war and victims of sexual and psychological violence deal with lingering consequences. Other people, family included, don't understand our mental torture. Instead of standing up with us, they may even regard us as crazy. We're not crazy. The situation was crazy. Being treated as if we are crazy by loved ones or society can feel worse than the trauma itself and add to our mental punishment.

He and I survived different battles, but at least I shower, go to work, take care of my kids, sing, and speak in complete sentences. He inhabits a deeper, darker hole than mine, and he can't make his agony invisible the way I can.

Dick cries when he talks about how many heads and limbs he witnessed being blown off. "Everyone I killed was loved by someone—a father or a spouse or a brother. I caused those people so much grief because I killed someone they loved. Debra, I can't live with that in my head every damn day."

"I know. Ruminating thoughts are the bitch after trauma," I answer. I'm aware after hearing Dick's story that I could be him, stuck on a barstool. I could die right here, estranged from my own spirit to survive.

I catch the bartender's eye. He holds up the empty two-liter bottle of wine that I drank. I ask him to call a cab for me. Dick and I hug goodbye as he says, "Thank you for listening to me. You're a good woman. You must have gone through something too. Hope you come back."

None of my children are home. Carol and Ryan are still at work. Brock is at the library and has a ride home. They bought me a birthday cake and cards and left them on the table. I feel guilty about missing the moment. I leave them a note then crash into bed before they get home. I try hard not to let them see me when I've been drinking. It has happened a few times, and there's no worse feeling than my children mocking my behaviors that I don't even remember. Tomorrow morning, the alarm clock will go off, and the four of us will eat birthday cake for breakfast. I'll need a cab to get my car.

Our family life is nontraditional and flexible. It feels like my children and I are growing up together. Carol and Ryan know I'm troubled. Carol wants distance from me. Ryan wants to be closer. Brock is too young to understand. I protect him more than the other children.

When I spiral down too low, I look at their faces when they are asleep. They are the reason I'm still here. I'm so proud of all three of them. They are doing well despite my mental health challenges. They are responsible individuals with their own distinct personalities. I would fight with the fangs of a wolf if anyone dared to fuck with one of my kids.

My protector son Ryan is job hunting for me. He sees my exhaustion from working two waitressing jobs seven days a week. We are living on credit cards for bills and necessities. He recalls all too well the consequences of the last time we lived this way.

Ryan has a friend Jimmie the Hippie. His mother, Rubi, needs a personal assistant because she owns a computer business. Her husband, Skip, is in medical school, and they have a newly blended family of six kids ranging in age from six months to fifteen years. Ryan has convinced Rubi to consider me for the job. The job isn't one I would pursue, except I feel obligated to meet with Rubi since my son arranged the interview.

When I meet Rubi, we feel a connection within the first half hour. Rubi is deeply spiritual. She isn't judgmental. I feel only love from her. Even with the sharp contrast between her success in life and mine, she doesn't make me feel inferior. She's generous and willing to pay a lot of money for my services. She wants what I can give, and I accept her offer. This will be my first job with weekends and nights off in a few years. I will no longer need a second job.

The house is jam-packed with laughing, some crying, and so much love. The children—Hannah, Ellie, Andy, Kyle, Jimmy, and Ben—are each a holy gift to Rubi. Four of the children have lost a parent. I'm instantly attracted to her nurturing heart.

Our working relationship becomes personal. When Rubi is home, we start our mornings off with a pot of coffee and a chat. She is the model of inner peace and fearlessness. She sees right through my black veil, my layers of bullshit, my acting as if I'm okay. She rejects my talk of feeling unworthy, and she explores those feelings with me. She introduces me to Marianne Williamson's book *A Return to Love*, which inspires me to read *Energy Anatomy* by Caroline Myss.

Talks with Rubi are healing. She listens with intention and teaches me that being vulnerable is not a weakness and that it's never too late to pursue a calling. She knows I am writing, and she is the first to tell me, "There is great purpose in your story, and there are women who need to hear your story. You need to write the book. It will show you why you are here and why you survived so much tragedy. I feel a huge reward coming for you. Keep writing, Debra."

Rubi also points me toward a more spiritual path, making me consider life's bigger questions. Why are we here? What brings deep meaning to life? What exactly is a calling? How do I want to be remembered? I begin exploring spiritual writers. Religion has always been my garden of weeds, but I start attending the Cathedral of the Sacred Heart Catholic church. I feel like a survivor again, and I believe in my dream of telling my story. I regard the spiritual awakening I receive at Rubi's kitchen table as nothing short of a miracle.

I stop drinking and join Briarwood Rec Center. I'm exercising and losing a bunch of weight.

Rubi sees that her six-year-old Ellie does laundry better than I can. Thankfully, she appreciates how much love I give the children. I am not a woman who will ever develop hypertension over keeping a perfect home, but when the house is out of control, I know how to recruit four kids to assist me. We bring the house up to Rubi's standards in one hour, maybe two.

One early Sunday afternoon, I arrive home after running errands and find Ryan upstairs in my bedroom. At least thirty of my journals and my manuscript are open and spread all over the bed. "Oh my god, Ryan! What are you doing? Tell me you are not reading my writing!"

He leaps off the bed, runs down the stairs, and goes out the front door. I run after him yelling, "Get back here right now."

I lecture him on the front porch until my voice nearly fails. "This is infuriating. You obviously have no respect for my privacy. I've told all three of you to never read my writing."

He dares to jump in, "Jeez, Mom, chill out! You're saying the same thing over and over. Who is Leah in your book? In the first sentence when you say, 'Leah is not sleeping naked tonight,' is that you? Are you Leah? Is the title of your book 'Oceans of Acorn' or 'One Chipped Tooth'?"

He grins. I'm ready to wrestle this kid to the ground. "Can you make me a fried-egg-and-cheese sandwich while you lecture me?" he asks.

"Yes, I can," I answer forcefully.

He laughs and finds the ketchup. The lecture continues. He finishes his sandwich. "You stay in the kitchen until I'm done talking to you. You need to understand my writing has been personal to me for twenty years. Do not take this lightly. No one reads what I write. Do...not...ever...touch...my...writing...again."

He wants to meet his friends to play basketball and thinks I'm overreacting. As he walks toward the door, he turns around and says, "Mom, if you have been writing for twenty-ears, don't you think it's time someone reads it?" He jumps on his bike and yells, "You're a good writer! You should publish a book. Why don't you become an author?" Off he goes on his bike.

I slam the front door and cry. I'm embarrassed. He read details of my rape. After pacing around the house, I remind myself I almost lost Ryan. I never stay mad at him. He is also the one who watches me and constantly asks questions. I love this kid who approaches tough times with humor. He has the brain chemistry of a stand-up comic. I might love him too much. He has conquered the mother.

For the next few months, I struggle with writing. One minute, I'm convinced I'm a writer. The next minute, I'm certain I'm not. God, if you are nudging me toward a purpose, toward writing, please, God, help me bow my head. Help me put my story to good use. Then one tear falls, I put on my running shoes and head out to Brandermill nature trails. I feel the air and sun as I sweat and breathe hard, trying to shed self-doubt. I resolve to make writing my new lover.

*****

Rubi and Skip are taking off for a long weekend getaway. I agree to stay with the children, and she leaves a credit card. It's the first weekend in months that I'm unable to write, and I feel tense and perturbed. I pack the four younger kids into Rubi and Skip's van without their permission. We travel to Virginia Beach for the weekend. The kids are excited about the trip, and we play on the beach in the golden grains of sand to the music of the waves. The sunset is pink and orange from our hotel room balcony. The kids jump on the beds and eat junk food.

Hannah, the two-year-old, is the only one to return home without a severe sunburn. It was seventy degrees, and not once did I think of sunscreen. When Rubi and Skip arrive home, three of their six children are lying on blankets on the living room floor with painful skin and flu-like symptoms. This is, of course, unacceptable to the parents, and I have no explanation for my negligence. In fact, I wonder if the kids are safe at all with me now? Rubi and Skip are focused on the children, and I leave the house confused.

Something happens when I walk through my front door. It causes me to start running and keep running faster, as fast as I can up the steps, down the steps, through the kitchen, back up the steps, through each bedroom. I run in the garage and scream. The running doesn't stop for at least twenty minutes until I collapse on the bed, holding a Big Ben clock to my right ear to stop the noise and the screams in my head. *Ticktock, ticktock.* I take a deep breath. *Ticktock, ticktock.* More breathing. It takes an hour, but the sound finally slows my mind down. The negative energy exhausts me.

Rubi does not fire me, but I eventually quit. The disgrace drives me away from this beautiful family and from a job that paid me enough money to live comfortably without working two jobs. All I hear in my head for days is, "You stupid cunt." How many times am I going to screw up my life?

I shut down completely until Carol comes into my bedroom and says, "Mom, why are you not going to work? Are you sick? You have been in bed for three days. What's wrong with you?"

The fact that my daughter is witnessing my surrender to pain brings me to my feet. I answer her, "I don't have a job."

"Why? What happened?"

We sit outside on the porch, but I can't find the right words. We talk about what's going on with her in school. She resigns herself to the fact that her mother is unemployed again for the tenth time, yet I know she wishes she had a normal mother with a good job. All of her friends' mothers seem to be healthy women with lucrative careers. They have homes where the toilets work and the doors lock. I can't understand how I raised such a responsible daughter when I can't get my life in order. I feel bad for her. I feel bad for all my children. They deserve so much more than the life I'm giving them. They are teenagers now, and they see the difference between me and everyone else.

Shame is a painful feeling. It reduces me to a powerless state. All I know is how to love my kids, and I do it well. The rest of it is becoming a challenge because there is something seriously wrong with me. Once again, I need to find another job, and I need someone to help me figure this out.

The next morning, I drive to Swift Transportation. They are hiring long-distance truck drivers. The position includes a great salary and benefits. After two interviews in one afternoon, I'm hired and scheduled to go to Atlanta to get my commercial driver's license training. The manager lets me climb into the truck to get a feel for what it's like, and I'm glad to see there's room for me to write in the cab. The sucker weighs twenty-six thousand pounds. It's fifty-three feet long. I'm finally going to see our beautiful country.

It's a little on the wild side, but the thought of this is exhilarating. I can't wait to tell Kay. I pick up a twelve pack of beer and drive to her house. We down some beers as I tell her the details of my new job. Kay listens, but I notice her what-the-hell looks. I'm not here for her approval. I need a real job so I can get a real house.

Finally, she stops me. "Deb, seriously? Come on now. What the hell are you thinking? This is about the craziest job idea you could come up with. You know it is. Stop this crap. I'll give you three reasons why you've lost your mind today: Carol, Ryan, and Brock. Did you even think about your kids before you accepted this job? Are you taking them with you? Are you homeschooling them in the truck?"

I call my brother with the news since Kay doesn't like the idea. He says, "You're talking crazy. If you take that job, I will never speak to you again."

I'm on beer number five before it finally hits me. Something must have snapped in me to have even considered such a job. Why did it take hours and two people who know me well to bring me back to reality? Jesus Christ, what is wrong with me? (Stupid cunt.) I throw my head back and finish off my ninth beer.

I leave Kay's and drive straight to Lucky's for another six-pack. I continue to drink as I drive up and down the five-mile Brandermill parkway with the radio on and loud music pulsating in my brain It's getting dark. The kids will be home soon.

I need a song…right now. I need a song. I dial the car radio through the garble of choices. Ah, Mariah Carey singing "Hero." I roll down the window and put my arm out dancing my hand in the spring breeze. This song was made for me, so I blast it and sing along, "There's an answer if you look inside your soul." I'm feelin' it!

"Then a hero comes along…

"And you know you can survive." My voice is killin' it!

"You finally find the truth…

"And the hero is yoooоou."

I'm belching out trapped air and singing right up there with Mariah. I pop open another beer, feeling great, except for the high-pitched siren that cuts right through my song. In the rearview mirror, there are flashing blue lights coming up fast behind me. There must be an accident on the parkway since the cop is in a hurry.

This is some crazy shit! The closer he gets to me, the slower he drives. Holy crap! He wants me to pull over. I push beer cans under the seat while pulling out my driver's license and registration. He shines a bright light in my eyes, "Good evening, Ma'am."

I answer, "Good evening, sir. How are you?"

"Do you know why I stopped you?"

I'm shaking. "No. I'm two minutes from home and driving back to be with my kids. I'm a single mom."

"Where are you coming from tonight?"

I don't make eye contact. "My friend's house. She lives a few blocks away. You can call her. She'll tell you I was there."

He comes closer. "Did you drink alcohol at your friend's house?"

I choke on my words. "I don't know."

He takes a step back and says, "Think about it a minute. You should know. Have you been drinking tonight?"

I don't know how to answer him, so I say, "Why are you asking me so many questions? All I want to do is go home to my three children."

He answers, "I stopped you because you were driving nine miles per hour and crossing the line."

My head rests on the steering wheel. "I have a lot of problems. I'm okay to walk home. Please let me get to my children."

"I smell alcohol on you, and I see two beer cans on the floor. How many drinks did you have, three or four?"

Busted! "I've never been stopped by the police, and I don't know how to answer your questions."

He backs off and says, "Okay, relax. I'll be right back."

All hell is about to break lose. I frantically search for gum or mints in my purse. I'm strung out and want to go home. My driving record is perfect. I've never committed a crime. I need to tell him that and walk home. When I throw the car door open and start walking back to his police car, he yells, "Get back in your car right now, or I will lock you up!"

Pfffh! What is *his* problem? I return to my car and wait. Why is he acting like I did something so wrong? I'm a half mile from home. No one is hurt.

He comes back and asks me to step out of the car. "May I please go home now?"

"No. I'm doing a few sobriety tests."

The tests don't go well, and the handcuffs are on. "Am I under arrest?"

He smiles and says, "I'm taking you into custody to do a Breathalyzer test to see how much alcohol you drank tonight. The more you cooperate, the sooner you will be home."

On the twenty-minute drive to Chesterfield County Jail, I tell the officer, through choking sobs, my entire life story. He listens to every word. The handcuffs are removed at the station. I see just one other officer. They walk me toward the Breathalyzer machine, and I refuse to blow. "I've had breathing problems since I was raped. It's medically documented. I can't blow."

They look at one another. "Either blow, or you could do jail time and lose your license."

I inhale deeper than I ever have in my life and *blow the fuck* into their machine, then I start to tell the second officer my life story. He says, "We aren't putting her in a cell. Let her calm down for a while in the drunk tank."

"What the hell is a drunk tank?"

"The drunk tank is where drunk people go who have never broken the law." They tell me to think about how I got here.

I keep talking, "You guys see a lot of bad people. Do you know the difference between people who are talking bullshit and those of us that have dealt with too much bullshit for two decades?"

It doesn't matter what I say. I'm locked down in a filthy drunk tank half gagging from the smell of urine. This must be where messed-up rape victims end up while their rapists roam free in search of their next victims. Ten minutes pass and I yell, "How long do I have to stay in here?"

"It depends on your behavior. You're talking too much."

My mouth is totally shut now while I position myself in the center of the floor with my knees pulled up to my chest, head down, assuming the inner posture of a raging mongoose. Now and then, I scratch the top of my head, digging into it deeply enough that it bleeds. I'm the only damn drunk in the damn drunk tank. Maybe I seriously need to stop drinking. It feels like an hour has passed when the officer asks, "Debra, how are you feeling?"

I don't pick my head up. I yell, "Humiliated."

They tell me if there's anyone that can pick me up, I can go home. Kay answers the phone and arrives in thirty minutes. The cops preach about AA meetings. They believe I'm a good person with unresolved problems. I need help. No shit! They hand me paperwork with a court date and advise me to get a lawyer. I'm so emotional, I hug them and say, "I'm really sorry. I love you guys."

Kay gets me out of there. Our ride home is silent. She sees how upset I am and does not make me feel worse than I already do. She's my only real friend in life, and I've hurt her. Still, she shows up here. I think my screwups scare her as much as they scare me.

I need a lawyer. I need therapy. I need my children. I need a job. I need to get sober. I need a brain transplant.

There are moments when everything feels right, but then it all disintegrates. Kay is done. Our friendship is walking a thin line. I can't explain what I don't understand, but I don't blame Kay. I'm just the master of lugging around foul feelings and guilt.

I have no understanding of why bad things keep happening when I know I'm a good person. Being arrested will not kill me. Going to court won't either. What will kill me is if I cannot change the fact that I'm a hostage to fear. I am not simply that woman with the layers of filth and fear who drinks. The victim in me is in control, and she is a beast. Half the time, when I think about rape, I can't describe it. My words come out too slow or too fast. I'm seeking language large enough to heal me. Where is God? He needs to wake up this blackout girl from her big snooze of twenty-plus years.

Chapter 13

BABY STEPHEN

THE BLACK SHEEP OF THE family do things differently. I'm the designated driver of change in my family. I'm certain extended family members don't understand. How could they? I'm nothing like the girl they knew long ago who joined them in prayer at the start of a family gathering. It's understood on a deep level I will never feel normal emotions again. I'm permanently damaged.

No one in my family knows me better than my brother David. For many years after Mom died, we were best friends, but even that relationship drifted apart because he is really happy and I am not. My hope is that he and I will always stay connected, but too much scar tissue from my old wounds seems eventually to destroy all relationships. With or without everyone I grew to love and then lost, I need to find a way to some other identity. Besides a mother, I have no idea who I really am. I study a photo of myself at nine months old and I wonder if I knew then what I know now, would I have even chosen to be born?

The negative thinking is not helpful, so I drive to Dunkin' for my favorite brew and a bran muffin. I pick up a *Richmond Times-Dispatch* because it's time to search the want ads for a new job. My career as a professional nanny hit rock bottom. My sacred time with Rubi is over. It's a sick, sad feeling. She's a beautiful woman who helped me so much. I will never forget her.

Hanover County is opening a new regional facility and hiring correctional officers. The only requirements are a high school education, a clean criminal background check, and successful completion of their extensive hiring process. This is a good day. I can do this. The only obstacle is my recent arrest, but I will apply anyway because this job would be stable, include good benefits, and provide a decent retirement nest egg. A job like this would enable me to buy a different house. As I read more, I become curious to what I might learn about and from incarcerated people. I'm more curious now than ever about what feeds the criminal mind.

The phone interview is scheduled. I nail it. They are taking me to the next level, which involves meeting with five people, including sergeants, lieutenants, and the director of human resources. I'm not nervous. My life experiences make me a great fit for this kind of work. With eyes wide open and a normal heart rate, I complete the next step by answering questions such as…

> If two inmates were fighting and another one had a seizure, what would you do?
>
> How would you respond to an inmate with contraband?
>
> If you were armed during an inmate transport and the inmate escapes, what would you do?

The in-person interview lasts over an hour. I proceed to the next level, which includes a psychological and physical exam, authorization for a full background check, and a polygraph. The offer comes three weeks later, pending the results of the background check. Training begins in a few weeks.

My DUI charge could nix the whole thing. My court date is soon. I hope the charges are reduced so it does not interfere with my background check or my scheduled training at the academy. The Commonwealth of Virginia requires every officer to pass state requirements to keep the job.

My shift theoretically starts at 6:00 p.m. and ends at 6:00 a.m., but since I'm required to report thirty minutes early and stay thirty minutes after it's a thirteen-hour shift.

I'm on my way for a uniform fitting, and the kids and I stop at Ukrops for a celebration dinner. Carol is so excited, she calls her dad. He actually talks to me on the phone. "Congratulations! You have always wanted a career, and now you have one."

Mason and I rarely speak. It means a lot to me to hear his confidence in me.

*****

Today is St. Patrick's Day. Ryan suggests making green milkshakes. Carol and Brock join in the fun. The blender is roaring when I hear the phone ring. There is a voice that sounds like my brother screaming on the other end. He cries, "Stephen is gone! My son is gone, my baby!"

"Stephen is gone?" I answer. "What?"

David cries, "Stephen is gone."

The blender stops. All three of my children listen in. "What do you mean Stephen is gone? Where is he?"

David catches his breath and says, "We lost him a couple of hours ago. He's gone."

My brother wanted a family his entire life. He met Kathleen at work, and they gave birth to their first baby, Stephen, three and a half months ago. Having a son was David's dream come true. The baby stopped breathing at the babysitter's home and died of sudden infant death syndrome. Their precious infant, put down for a nap, somehow slipped right out of this life. Unimaginable.

I don't know what to say to my brother, who is barely able to speak. All I know is my children, and I need to figure out a way to be with them in Kansas. Of course, there is no money to take the trip.

Of course, there was no money for his wedding. Now this. We have to go.

Carol calls her father, who says he sees no reason for the three children to go there. Carol ends the call. She immediately starts calling her friends. Not going to Kansas to be with her uncle David is not an option for Carol or the boys. They insist we find a way. Carol calls Mary.

Only two hours after the sad news, Mary knocks at our door. "Carol is right. You all need to be there. I'm going to help you get there."

Mary knows I'm broke but about to start a good job. I want to reimburse her when I get on my feet. "Let's not discuss that now," she says. "Do you know when the memorial service is? Get the details so we can book your flight." She books the flight and secures a hotel room, paying in advance.

As we leave, she hands me three hundred dollars cash and says, "You need this." All four of us are overwhelmed by her generosity. We all hug her, and Carol hugs her tight.

My brother's home feels somber. The ultimate risk and the most unfair tragedy for any parent is the loss of a child. David and Kathleen ask me to do a reading at the memorial service. I feel honored, but between the incongruous image of their precious infant in an open casket and the depth of despair on the faces of everyone present, I'm barely able to read. I'm so fortunate not to know this kind of pain.

It's a short visit since I have a court date and a new job starting. I feel sad that I have let my family down leaving so soon. I have no wisdom or experience this level of grief to help David survive this. He and Kathleen choose to mourn privately.

*****

Today is my DUI hearing. I meet my attorney at the courthouse at eight thirty. We take our seats among well-dressed criminals who nod as attorneys whisper last-minute details. I've never been to court before. The atmosphere is abuzz with tension. My attorney coaches me, "You don't need to speak unless the judge asks you a direct question. I will handle this."

My arresting officer's presence makes my legs bounce up and down. I feel ashamed. There is not a single window in this courtroom where I can look at the sky and get my head together. My face and neck are hot, which means I may break out into large red blotches that will turn into hives unless I get control over my anxiety. If my breathing gets difficult, I may launch into a full-blown anxiety attack, for which I either need to run or lie down.

"Debra Ruth Mak." My case is called after about ninety minutes.

We walk forward to the judge's bench. I stand on one side of my lawyer, and the arresting officer stands on the other. The judge says a few words to them and then looks straight at me. "Are you Debra Ruth Mak?"

"Yes, sir."

He suddenly looks agitated. "You may call me Your Honor," he admonishes.

"I'm sorry, Your Honor. I've never been to court before."

The judge reviews the incident report and addresses my lawyer, "I'm sure you're aware Debra was driving legally drunk?" He allows no time for a response before asking the arresting officer, "How was Debra's behavior from the time you stopped her until releasing her from your custody?"

"She was emotional. She was also respectful and cooperative, Your Honor."

"Your Honor, today I'm asking you to reduce the charge to reckless driving so my client may continue to work in her job at Virginia Corrections. She needs the job and deserves a second chance."

He shakes his head like I'm the only bonehead, yo-yo mother on the planet with a DUI charge. I am two minutes away from telling him my life story. "You understand that if you make this mistake again, it's not a mistake. It's a conscious decision to break the law."

"You will not see me in your courtroom again. I promise you that."

The judge gives me a look that shows he has heard it all before then signs papers and looks at both the officer and my lawyer. "This will be reduced to a reckless driving conviction based on Debra's record. She is assigned 180 hours of community service work. Submit the paperwork within ten days. I'm waiving all fees."

He looks straight at me and continues, "If you appear before this court again, the outcome will be very different. You are dismissed."

My lawyer and I thank the judge in unison. What felt like an hour was less than ten minutes. Outside the courtroom, I sprint like hell to the water fountain, drink large amounts of water, and splash my face with it. My lawyer shows me the options for community service work. I select working at the local library, and the relevant papers are filed.

I seriously need a drink. Alcohol is the only thing that calms me down. My mind starts moving so fast with repetitive thoughts that escalate into a full rage. Sometimes, I have to tell the person in my head, "Shut up!"

I blast the music and drive as my breathing becomes shallower. I'm losing control of my breathing and stop the car near a tree. I stand up against it and lean over to catch a breath. Counting backward from twenty to one helps as I try to breathe.

I lucked out today. This is a huge break. You can bet I'm going to stop for a drink. I had a strong urge for alcohol the minute I walked into court. The power alcohol has over me is uncontrollable. Telling myself not to drink is like telling someone with diarrhea not to shit.

Sunday's Waterfront restaurant is within walking distance of home. I never drink there, but I can leave my car and have a few drinks. I'm not going to get drunk. The bar is small, and I'm the only woman sitting among businessmen having a liquid lunch. The bartender brings me one Michelob then another and another. After three beers, I feel better. My breathing is normal, and I feel okay. The guys are drinking Guinness, cocktails, and shots. Why the hell would anyone order oysters and zucchini chips while they drink? I drink to drink. My brain needs the buzz.

The conversations among these business robots sound boring. They know nothing about sexual violence, roaches in the bathtub, chakras, self-hatred, intuitive medical healers. They would hear my story and probably say they would pray for me, but they never really would. Stable humans don't understand me, which is why I go to dive bars where the broken hearts show up. Dive bars are full of people like me, and it's where I'm comfortable.

In a few weeks, my training at the academy begins, and I will probably fail the same way I failed my high school swimming class. I failed because I could not tread water without feeling like I was drowning. My mind spirals off as I think of failing.

A man wearing a Brandermill Country Club golf shirt orders me a cocktail. I've never had a cocktail. When I drink, it's beer or wine. I ask, "What's this?"

He says, "A cosmopolitan. Cheers!"

Sweet baby Jesus! Now I have to talk to him and pretend to drink like a lady? I hate sipping with the pinkie finger straight up. I can't do it. I turn away and stare out the window at the lake. The cocktail goes down in one gulp. I'm not fucking sipping.

What am I doing here after a DUI court appearance? Today was a wake-up call, yet I'm still asleep, drinking in the neighborhood bar. All these men, because I'm well-groomed, are probably thinking that I'm one of them. After one more drink, I know I had better leave before I vomit my emotions all over the friendly bartender and anyone else who will listen.

During the walk home on the winding trails of Brandermill, I encounter too many women in tennis outfits, fast walking and smiling, others with babies in strollers. I want to communicate with the birds, trees, and squirrels. Everyone is so cheerful on these trails. I break into a jog to get home faster.

At home, there's a message from Carol that she has a toothache at work. She works at Blockbuster and says she needs to work a few extra hours. Dammit, I can't drive over to give her some Tylenol. My eagle daughter is fiercely independent. She is the captain of the soccer team, editor in chief of the school newspaper, straight A student, and works three or four shifts per week to buy her own clothes. After Stephen's funeral, I gave her my bedroom to give her privacy. She studies every night until after midnight. Her application has been submitted to the University of Virginia. I have no doubt she will be accepted because she is a serious top student.

My boys are doing well too. Ryan has a natural intelligence and does not have to work hard for his high grades. Carol and Brock study daily. They all work so freakin' hard at school and in life.

I look at our house, and I long for a home that provides comfort rather than this place of brokenness. More than anything, I want to find a home in the same community that has working appliances, rooms that are not half painted, and art. Mason agrees to sell, which makes my day.

There's a cozy rental in Nuttree Woods, only one neighborhood away that is move in ready and has a backyard full of trees. We all love it. It has three bedrooms and a basement. It's freshly painted, and there are no holes in the ceilings. Even the ceiling fans work. The kids have their own bedrooms. I choose to sleep on the couch and keep my personal things in the basement. It's more important to me that all three children have their own spaces. I'll be satisfied with doors that lock and appliances that work. My monthly housing cost drops six hundred dollars. I won't need a second job. Perfect because the boys need closer supervision.

The house we are leaving is a major fixer-upper to be sold as is. It doesn't take long before a contractor gives us a lowball offer, and we accept.

*****

It's moving day. There is not enough money to rent a truck or pay movers. At least ten people show up with cars, vans, and pickup trucks. Moving etiquette includes providing coffee and doughnuts in the morning and pizza and beer in the afternoon for people kind enough to volunteer their free time. Loud rock and roll music kept everyone moving.

There are not enough boxes, so we use extralarge garbage bags. We are not even totally packed. At Ryan's suggestion, Brock starts dropping garbage bags full of clothes at least thirty feet from the upstairs bedroom to the ground. When the bags hit the ground, Cary and I schlepp two bags at a time from the yard to vehicles. Neighbors watch in disbelief, though no one offers to help.

Our new television won't fit in the packed vehicles, so Ryan and Brock agree to carry it from the house, down the street, through the golf course to the new house. Ryan is mortified from the experience. "I'm never doing that again, Mom. It was embarrassing." He walks away when I try to hug him.

Every neighborhood has one laughingstock, and *I am it* on Stoney Ridge Trail. We don't fit the upper-middle-class image. When the fireplace shifts, it stays detached. When the leaves fall, no one rakes them. There is absolutely no time or money to even paint the interior rooms. There's a mentally challenged boy who wants to paint, and I get him a gallon of green paint and reward him with a McDonald's shake. My kids think I'm crazy, but it makes him happy. He shows up daily with a driving lawn mower, saying, "I want to paint you house."

As I unpack in the new kitchen, I hear my three sprouts joyfully talking and laughing together in our new house. They can invite friends in now and not feel embarrassed. The undercurrent of inadequacy is gone. We are euphoric. My children are proud of my job and our new house. The Mak family finally has a comfortable place we can call home.

On my day off a few weeks later, the phone rings. It's my real estate agent calling to tell me the sale of our house won't be possible. It failed inspection due to the shift of the entire foundation underneath the house. Until someone can jack up the house and fix the foundation, no bank will finance a buyer. Our buyer's financing has fallen through. We have no choice but to move back there.

My kids won't be laughing at the news. They will feel foolish when they tell their friends. I hate so much that I cannot give my children the life they deserve, although millions of people live in poverty more extreme than this. It's a sunny afternoon when the four of us sit down to discuss the move. Carol, Ryan, and Brock make it easy on me. They blame me for nothing and are showing up today as masters of adversity.

Each day brings a multitude of moments when I see beautiful qualities in each one of them. They have walked through the gates of hell with me. Today, their individual lights reflect on me. What a wonderful thing to witness my three teenagers growing up with such inner strength. Our family is different, but we are good enough—good enough wherever we live.

Chapter 14

HOLY BALLS

My career in corrections has begun. This is job number sixteen. Before they spend money on our training at the academy, the new hires are observed for a couple of months to see if we have the right chemistry to perform well in this intense environment. The goal of the academy is to train officers to be professional, calm in crisis, motivated, and disciplined.

We travel by van at seven each morning to the Rappahannock Criminal Justice Academy ninety minutes north of Richmond. That commute makes for long days.

We can be terminated at any time for any reason during our one-year probationary period. Nights and weekends are spent studying for written tests. This is pass-or-fail time. There is no gray in corrections. You either make it or find another job.

The industry is dominated by males. So is the inmate population. There's only one other female in the academy and five working inside the facility. I'll be tested to my maximum level of fitness. I've made a few male friends, and we agree to study as a group as often as we can.

There are endless state requirements: legal terms, inmate classifications, intake processing, handcuffing, fingerprinting, strip searches, defensive physical tactics, contraband control, transporting of inmates, first aid, behavioral restraints, lockdowns, daily reports, and more. I'm shockingly calm and excited about having a real career before I hit menopause. My inner beast seems to be hibernating with this new focus. I'm challenged daily both mentally and physically, and I love it. I'm passing tests and feeling well received.

When the defensive physical tactics class begins, they partner me with someone who weighs at least one hundred pounds more than I do. I'm five feet four up against a male officer who's six feet five. I employ what I've learned about pressure points and score big when I can pull him down to the floor by his earlobes. The rape victim in me is wild and ready for this part of the academy training. Each day brings bruises, back pain, and a high five from the instructor.

Twenty-three years ago, I had the fight of my life. This is easy compared to sexual violence. I relish the reawakening of my physical power and breeze right through the challenge. No man will ever push me to the dust of a floor again.

It's a scorching hot August day, day one on the shooting range. Shit is about to get real. The morning wind is still. There are several orange five-gallon Igloo water coolers that keep us hydrated for eight hours. We are surrounded by woods in a large open space with no shade.

The instructors are setting up the movable targets. They look at least one hundred yards away. By law, we are required to hold, load, shoot, unload, and clean both a Glock nine and a shotgun. I've never even held a gun or been with anyone who owned a gun. I have witnessed the harm guns can do. I've held the anxiety of this part down deep. There's enough adrenaline pumping in me right now that I could escape. My main concern is that I will accidently kill someone out here.

A part of me thinks I can lose my job this week. Another part of me understands fears are not facts, and not all fears cause failures. In life, we try. If you win, you win. If you lose, you win. There's no loss in trying something different that tests you to the limit. This is a win-win for me because I'm giving my best effort. I've worked around many roadblocks in the past two decades. I'm holding on to hope that the firearms requirements do not sabotage my success, but if I fail, it'll still be a win because I did not give up trying. Anxiety is a part of me, and I'm learning to use it to push me forward. It's not going away. *I'm still that stupid cunt.*

Everyone is loading guns, and I study them. The other female officer hunts with her father, so she is comfortable with firearms. My best bet is to hang out with all the military officers. They are willing to assist, but there's not much downtime.

Holy Moses. We are being trained to "shoot to kill, straight to the heart." I feel the hot sun in my bones and keep drinking cold water. All officers have guns loaded, except me. What the hell am I doing here? This is not a spiritual calling. I need to run, run, run away.

The instructor blows a whistle and divides the group into teams of eight. The first team is called to the field. They shoot. There are no errors. The second team is called. They shoot. There are no errors. I'm on team three in the center. The whistle blows, and all guns are fired, except mine. Everyone moves up ten yards, except me.

An instructor walks over to me to see if I'm having trouble with the audio gear. He thinks I can't hear the whistle. "Are you okay, Officer Mak?"

(Definitely not.) I nod.

He moves me up with the team and says, "Make sure you shoot the gun this time right at your target."

(Oh, hell yeah.) Sweat is running down my face and back. My hair is wet. The whistle blows again. All shots are fired, except mine.

"Officer Mak, please step off the field."

(Oh crap. I'm fired.)

The instructor kindly reminds me, "You are aware that it's necessary for you to score a minimum of seventy-five percent to complete the mandatory requirements. Go over to the picnic tables and try to talk yourself down from the anxiety."

How does he know I'm anxious? Obviously, I am a major distraction on day one. It's not a positive sign. Thoughts are zinging. An officer tells me, "You really need to go to an indoor shooting range and practice tonight."

I have a better idea. "What if I could talk them into not sending me on transports so I don't need to qualify for shooting a gun?"

He laughs. "This is the law. You have to qualify, or you're fired."

Once everyone else completes round one, I'm told, "Don't go back on the field today. What we decided you need to do is hang back here with officers and learn how to properly load a gun."

(*Phew!* I'm not fired.) This might be the longest day of my life. All I want to do is go home, see my kids, take a hot shower, and lie in bed. I'm not going to an indoor range tonight at eight o'clock.

It's day two. We have the same lineup. Everyone is instructed to kneel and shoot, except me. I'm told to stand and shoot. Today I load the gun, but nothing comes out. The whistle blows. "Officer Mak, please come off the field."

(Dammit.) Yep, I'm failing. No one sounds angry.

I'm the only one who cannot shoot a gun on day two. All the instructors are now on the sidelines, putting their heads together about my inability to look at a gun, take arm, exhale, and pull the trigger. The entire team is at ease, waiting. I'm sitting on top of a picnic table, wondering if I should tell them the truth and even ask for extra help. It's either time to speak or quit.

I speak privately with two instructors. "Please understand I want this job. It's not anxiety. It's fear. I'm a rape victim, and I have a real sense of fight, flight, freeze going on here."

My rapist did not have a gun. He had a knife. However, I'm on a field with armed males. The gunfire and aggressive comments are interfering with my ability to focus. When I'm told how to do something, I can't remember it two minutes later. There is also a physical reaction. My body jolts, my heart rate speeds up, my blood pressure rises, and there's pressure in the back of my head. I think jumping out of an airplane would be easier.

The sergeant explains, "We have a problem that needs to be corrected. Tomorrow is day three, and you haven't fired a gun yet. We are doing obstacle course firearms, which require you to be on the ground and shoot. The academy wants you to be successful. You've done an excellent job at everything else, which tells us you can do this job. How can we help you?"

With a grateful heart, I ask the instructors, "Is there any way you would consider letting someone stand behind me who could slowly walk me through each step while I do these tests?"

They confer privately again and agree. "Yes, you got it. We can do that."

On day four, I ask to use a shotgun to avoid failing with the Glock again. Sergeant stands behind me, and my shot *barely* makes it. The kickback almost knocks me down to the ground and bruises my right shoulder black. I don't mind because the shot made it.

On day five, every other officer has qualified by noon, but since I have not, they are required to stay while I keep trying. Some are annoyed, others are laughing, and many are concerned because they want me to make it. Today, I'm holding the gun, loading it, and firing it, but I miss the target, and who knows where the shot went? The trees? Did I kill a squirrel? What the hell am I doing with a gun?

The lead instructor says, "Stand at ten yards and shoot, then move back another ten."

At ten minutes after five, I finally squeak past the required seventy-five percent to qualify at seventy-six percent. Classmates high-five me, throw water over my head, congratulate me, and try to carry me to the van. You'd think the Cleveland Browns had won the Super Bowl. There is a lot of mockery and laughter until I yell, "Shut up, you guys. All of you were killing squirrels at four years old. Let's see how we all role-play on Monday." My head rests victorious tonight.

Family members and friends fill the room at our graduation ceremony. Everyone has guests attending, except me. Sadly, I'm not surprised. There's a professional photographer, administrators from our facility, and the colonel. All the instructors are present and all the officers, dressed in uniform, sit together on the right.

The colonel takes the podium and asks everyone to be seated. "Thanks to all of you for coming today. This is my favorite part of the academy, when every officer is recognized for successfully completing the training."

One by one, we are called forward to receive the official badge, a certificate, and a handshake. The colonel continues, "There are three important awards we give to officers who show extraordinary efforts while at the academy. Once the awards are presented, I ask that the three recipients follow the photographer for pictures that are published in the newspaper and also added to the wall display at the academy. The first award goes to the officer who achieved the highest test scores."

A young man, with a huge smile, steps forward and remains standing to the left of the podium.

"The second award goes to the officer who excelled with firearms."

An older ex-military man stands and walks forward. His girlfriend takes pictures and acts like he won the Nobel Prize. He also remains standing.

"Our third and final award is the most important. It's the Charles E. Murray Jr. award. It commemorates a man who led by example every day of his career and lost his life while on duty. It is awarded to the officer who not only gives one hundred percent but also brings out one hundred percent in fellow officers. The academy calls it the leadership award. This year's recipient of the Charles E. Murray Jr. award goes to Officer Debra Ruth Mak."

Officer James taps my shoulder. "Mak, get up there. You won it."

Holy balls! This is an unfamiliar feeling. I try to collect my thoughts, but I never expected to be chosen, and I don't know what to say. My voice shakes, "Thank you for this day. With so much talent in this room, I'm shocked and humbled. Everyone who was at the range with me knows that I'm really a poet and a hippie at heart." I begin reciting poetry, and it's totally inappropriate.

"We come to work for more than a paycheck. Real leadership is about walking out the door after work a better person than when you walked in and bringing others along with you. Thank you again for today."

My eyes are wet, so I stop talking. Every single person in the room stands and applauds. This is the first day since I was raped that I feel the stinging sort of beauty that comes with a real feeling of self-respect. It's something I want to get good at. We earn it by respecting ourselves enough to give our absolute best. Giving respect to others is when the *magic* happens, when leaders selflessly bring out the best in people toward a higher purpose.

On my drive home, still in uniform, I decide to go to my spiritual place, the James River. The river has a spirit too. The deeper it goes, the quieter it is, and it brings out stillness. The river is like church, except it's better than church because nature does not judge. The flow of a river is the flow of life. Whenever I come here, my emotions surface. There's a cleansing that I can't feel anywhere else. The sun breaks through dove-gray clouds and shines cylinders of light through the water. I watch with both feet in the water. There is a new energy today I've never felt. It must be what *inner peace* feels like. It comes when a person can get control of their thoughts and feelings. I close my eyes and breathe. I feel a light mist of rain on my face.

Today's achievement calls for a celebration. I drive straight to Carytown to Bev's Homemade Ice Cream shop. I splurge and get an ice cream cone instead of stopping for a beer. After I pull into the driveway, I pause for a few minutes to inhale self-respect, hold, then exhale peace.

When I shower, there's a layer of inner filth gone. When I brush my teeth, floss, and brush my hair, I look in the mirror for the first time in a long time and give a half smile. It's not normal for me to look in the mirror. Tonight, I feel like the reflection looks different. Instead of any of the men in the academy with prior military and firearms experience, I was chosen as top leader. "Welcome to this beautiful feeling, Officer Mak," I tell myself. I'm grateful I survived long enough for this day, and I snap a sharp salute.

Chapter 15

THE CIRCLE OF LIFE

I'VE HAD EIGHTEEN YEARS TO prepare for this day. Double that would still not be enough. Carol and I are on our way to the University of Virginia this morning. She will not come back. My daughter will make her own stage and support herself well. It was my intention and hope the day she was born that I could raise her to take care of herself. Everything I did not achieve in life, I want her to have. We did well. She was raised by age twelve, and now she's raising me. She can expressively speak her mind. I have never been more changed of anything in my life than this *girl* of mine. She listened to everything I said when she was young and followed through. Now she's arrived in a higher place than I ever will. My dream came true.

As we head west on I-64, her eyes are on the lookout for exit 118-B. She is bursting with optimism that lights up the front seat while she sips ice tea and listens to Billy Joel. Her enthusiasm reminds me of the day I dropped her off for her first day of kindergarten—her sweet five-year-old face; her long wavy hair with that butterfly bow; her red dress, white tights; those shiny black shoes; and her Strawberry Shortcake backpack.

When she jumped out of the car that first day of school and I grabbed her arm and said, "I love you, Peaches," she didn't say anything. She ran up to the entrance of the school and never looked back. It bothers me that she probably won't look back today either. My emotions range from celebratory to the hollow realization that Carol will not be there when I wake up tomorrow…or the next day…or the next week.

We arrive on campus and carry boxes up two flights of stairs. All the other girls have decorated their rooms with cute, nonessential Target items. Carol has necessities only. She has no computer, car, bike, or allowance. Her father is paying the tuition, which is fortunate; she can graduate with no student loans.

We are busy unpacking when a cute girl stops by Carol's room, all smiles with a spark in her eyes, and says, "Hi, I'm Laura Beth." She's from South Boston. "Do you want to come with me to get our IDs?" They run off together laughing, as if they've known each other for years.

It's a sunny day with a gentle breeze in Charlottesville. There's a bench by Carol's dorm where I sit to wait. How proud I am that she is coming to Virginia's number one school. Today marks a milestone when the best part of me stays with my daughter and the worst part of me, she will leave behind. I'm not a perfect mother, but my imperfections did not make me a horrible mother. I love her perfectly, and she knows it. I gave her all I had every day of her life.

Carol has grown up strong within herself. Those are seeds I planted. I sacrificed all I could and more for her. Whether she understands that is not important to me. I raised her to become an independent woman with self-respect and self-confidence. I see it coming to fruition. That's all the reward I need. One tear falls as I overthink all of this.

Her first ambition is to earn a degree in English. Her goal is to become a magazine editor, along with rescuing two dogs, adopting a child, and living in the city…and *never* marry.

She has returned to the dorm. "Hey, Mom, would you like to go to The Corner and walk through the shops, have lunch?"

The Corner is five blocks of colorful eateries, bookstores, unique shops, bars, and markets. It's already Carol's favorite artsy spot. We order chicken and veggie quesadillas and talk about Laura Beth. "She's so much fun. I really like her."

Carol has not yet met her roommate from New York. I want to meet her and her parents too, but my daughter says, "You really don't need to stay all day. We've done most of the unpacking. Feel free to leave after we finish lunch. I really appreciate everything you've done for me today."

I reach across the table and touch her hand. We finish, and I pay the tab. I'm upset because the dreaded moment has arrived, and I'm not ready to leave, but when your daughter tells you to leave, you need to leave. I'm not going to cling to my *shooting star* daughter when she needs to start living a new life on her own.

We walk toward the car. I slip five twenty-dollar bills into her hand and put on my sunglasses. After eighteen years of loving and raising this beautiful young woman, she doesn't really need me anymore. I cry as I wrap my arms around her and squeeze her so tight. "I'm so damn proud of you, Carol. Call me. Let me know how you're doing. Call collect, okay?"

We arrange talk time on Sundays or anytime she needs me. It's hard for me to contact her because there are no phones in the dorm rooms. She'll call from a pay phone. We exchange our I love yous and goodbyes, and off she runs. How did my five-year old grow up and go off to college so fast? My eyes are glued to her until she rounds the corner of a building and disappears. She never looks back. My daughter is now a part of another tribe *so far away from my fire.*

I'm heartsick. I need a beer and a cigarette. I stop to get a twenty-four-ounce Budweiser and a pack of Marlboro lights. Then I remember my day in court. The beer is no longer an option, so I chain-smoke even though I'm not really a smoker.

Elton John's "The Circle of Life" comes on the radio. Whoa, what a powerful song for the day! It gives me the sense that some spirit guide is present. This song is forever paired in my memory with the day my daughter began her solo flight into the universe. A few tears fall as I try to assure myself that I'm not losing Carol.

Ryan, my anchor, is sitting on the front porch, waiting for me. I yell, "Hey, whatcha' doin'? Where's Brock?"

He answers my questions with questions. "How did it go today, Mom?" He doesn't wait for an answer. "Did Carol like her roommate? Did you cry? Did Carol cry? Why do you smell like smoke?"

The first thing I do is grab his big head and give him a playful Dutch rub, the kind his father always gave him when he was here. "Yes, of course I cried. No, of course Carol did not."

Not only do Ryan and I love each other, we really like each other. Some say not to be friends with your kid, but Ryan and I have our own set of rules. We really enjoy each other's company. My ADHD angel son knows how to provoke a strong emotional reaction from me that makes us both laugh hard out loud. Ryan is intrigued by my dark side. Carol is not. Brock simply accepts me and focuses on himself.

Brock is spending the night at Charlie's. Ryan invites me to Applebee's, a restaurant where the staff is familiar with him. Ryan drives like a '50s movie star playing the same song over and over and over.

We order food. Ryan can't sit still for more than six minutes. No matter what restaurant we go to, he is up and down, walking around, talking to strangers until the food comes. I'm used to it. Since he was a toddler, Ryan has loved meeting new people. He takes a bite of a chicken sandwich and declares, "Now that Carol is gone, it's my turn to take over the master bedroom."

Asian salad sprays right out of my mouth. "Carol used it for studying, not partying,"

"Why do you assume I want to party in that room?"

I'm laughing now. "Maybe because when Carol and I visited her college, we came home to a karaoke machine and Milwaukee's Best beer cans with cigarette butts in them, not to mention eight male bodies sleeping on the floor.

He says, "Carol is a nerd. She doesn't live in the real world. All she does is work. She hangs out with all the smart kids. I'm not like my sister. Don't you know that all the Brandermill kids are drinking, except Carol and her friends? Everyone has parties, Mom. When their parents go away, they drink. Don't compare me to Carol. This is not like when you and Dad were in high school and drank champagne the night you graduated and had sex on the ground by the Berea pool."

I'm pissed now. "How do you know that? Did your father tell you that?"

He answers, "I read it in your journal."

All I want to do right now is leave, but we keep talking. "Maybe I need to talk to all of your friends' mothers to find out if they know everyone is drinking." This conversation only makes me more inclined to say no to him having the big bedroom.

He orders another Dr Pepper. "Do you want a beer?" He walks to the bar before I have the chance to answer.

When he returns, I continue, "I did not want a beer, and this conversation is disturbing. If you're drinking, you are going to immediately find a job working Friday and Saturday nights. When I'm working an overnight shift, there's no need to be worrying about you. You also have a fourteen-year-old brother who is watching all of this. Seriously, Ryan, I hope ninety-five percent of what you're telling me is bullshit."

My beer arrives, and it's a tall boy. The waiter says, "Ryan said you're having a tough day. Congratulations on your daughter getting into UVA. The beer is on the house, Ms. Mak."

Ryan roams back to the kitchen. While he's gone, I drink the beer fast and order another. Later, I will have to find a way to get to Lucky's for more beer. The beast in me is in control again. I need to drink, and I need another one right now.

It's time to pay the bill. Ryan leaves a generous tip, and we walk out with his strong, protective arm around me. My son has been a challenge since my first contraction in the bathtub in Toledo. He reminds me that he's leaving in a year, and I have a meltdown. We keep talking, and by the time we are home, I surrender. "Take the big bedroom with the understanding that I will contact the mothers of anyone who spends the night if I detect any drinking."

At this point, if this is really going on with his friends, I'd rather Ryan be at home. There's no bar in my house. When I call Mary, she tells me, "They've all been drinking for a year. Stephen tells me when they stay at other houses, they get into the liquor. Ryan is telling you the truth. Keeping them under our watch is safer because they find a way to party. I'm more concerned about them driving home after drinking, so I stay home and supervise. They're all doing it, Deb."

Immediately, I put in for a shift change to days. Ryan works at the Brandermill Inn until 2:00 a.m. on weekends. This stops some of the partying.

My job is going well. They assigned me to central control, which is fast-paced and high-pressure. Mostly, I stand alone all night and watch several large screens that control the entire facility. Central control officers manage all the unit doors and supervise each unit by carefully watching each officer and the inmates for acts of violence or gang activity. Officers call me on the radio, "Central control, please send back up to K-Unit."

It's a multitasking position, and I do it well. They keep me here for a few months. Since it's a new facility, they are testing female officers in male units. Officer Pugh and I are the only two females given permission to work in the all-male units. It's not long before I'm tested in the male maximum security unit.

Our criminal justice system is full of caged humans who need to be in rehab instead of jail. It's very sad to realize criminal behavior is often a consequence of poverty or addiction because those conditions often pass from one generation to the next. Some of the inmates were born while their mothers were in custody. Throughout their childhoods, many of their fathers were in and out of prison. States are spending large amounts of money recycling criminals who are mentally ill. It's a revolving door. Society does nothing to help these people when they are released. They come back with another charge worse than the last one. They tell me it's harder in the real world after being released than it was inside the system. I bring empathy to work.

It's a cultural issue in need of drastic change. For the most part, I stand alone with my opinions. My beliefs are different, and I treat every inmate like a human being. My presence is respected. I'm not struggling to keep my unit under control. It's the opposite. Some cheer when I'm on duty. They even made up a song about me. "Officer Mak is back, back, back. When she is not working, she dresses in black, black, black."

Most of them share their life stories, and we connect because I identify with their problems. Their stories don't scare me. Nothing about any inmate scares me. I connect with all of them. Other officers need to stop acting like judges. Inmates have their day in court. I refuse to be a bully because I am aware of the fine line between officers and inmates.

So much of my past helps me do well here. If I ever have the chance to make real money, I would love to open a transition home where prisoners convicted of nonviolent crimes could be taught life skills they did not learn in childhood. Mental health should begin to be taught in the first grade.

I wish violent crime offenders who need to be institutionalized could be in a facility that would rehabilitate them over the course of years. What I find is that both men and women in this population have severe mental health issues. Many come from abuse the likes of which the average person knows very little.

*****

Carol calls, and I'm ecstatic. Yes, she and Laura Beth are close friends and have met a few others who are planning to get an apartment together in year two. Laura Beth is smart. She is also an English major with wit similar to Carol's. The first phone call makes me feel like my daughter does care about me. She calls on a regular basis and talks long and fast. I listen.

*****

One day, unexpectedly, my sergeant approaches me. "Officer Mak, the captain needs to meet with you at four tomorrow afternoon before your shift starts."

"Did I do something wrong?" I ask.

"I don't know. He didn't share anything with me. Make sure you're on time," he cautions as he walks away.

In almost eighteen months, I've never had a one-on-one conversation with the captain. Yep, I'm being fired because I'm too kind to the inmates. *Fuck it.*

As I lie on the couch, looking out the window, I can't help but assume the worst is coming tomorrow. Here goes my crazy life again. I've proven to myself over and over that I am employable. I'm a badass waitress, and I can find two jobs until another real job comes through.

At least Brock and Ryan are both working at the Brandermill Inn now, the police haven't shown up at my house yet, and Mason is still paying child support. For that, I am grateful. At times like this, I regret that my children have no father or grandparents close by. I can't possibly fill all their shoes. It's a life where I have them, and they have me. I'm doing it all.

On the way to meet with the captain, a panic attack starts in the car. I hear the voice inside me saying, *Here you go again, loser.*

I'm two minutes away from driving to Kinko's to send in a letter of resignation. My breathing is labored to the point of needing to get out of the car. I rock back and forth until I can breathe again. In moments like this, I wish I had a husband, a best friend, a sister, a mother. I'm alone in life with my past front and center. It comes up no matter where I go, whom I meet, or how I work. The last book I bought was Eckhart Tolle's *The Power of Now*. He believes there's a way to honor the past without losing yourself in it. Sounds good, but I have yet to master that.

I decide I must take the responsible road and face the captain. The ballerina bun is taken out of my hair. I march straight into the administration office and am met with a friendly welcome from the receptionist. "Hello, Officer Mak, you're early. Have a seat."

The colonel's office is right next to me. He looks up from his desk but does not acknowledge my presence, which does not bode well. A few minutes later, captain approaches me, and I stand up and offer a smile and a firm handshake. "How are you today, Officer Mak?"

He doesn't respond when I say, "Fantastic. How are you?"

"Hold all calls until I'm done with Officer Mak, please," he tells the receptionist.

He leads me to his office, shuts the door, and comfortably leans back into his executive chair. I take the lead. "Let's get down to business. Why am I here? What's the problem?"

He smiles, "Do you like to play golf?"

What the hell? "No, I think golf is boring. It's a sport for the elderly."

He chuckles. "I know you don't hunt based on your firearms scores."

"I passed twice. Don't worry about me. I have worked transports, and nothing bad happened with my gun." Since he appears to like sarcasm, I throw one back, "Do you like dancing in dive bars?"

He almost spits out his coffee and quickly sits forward to regain control of the conversation. "I didn't know you had a sense of humor. First things first: I like what you bring to the facility. We like your style of managing inmates. You're different."

About face. I'm not getting fired. "I love my job and think what I bring is needed here."

He stands, stretches, opens the door. "Would you like a beverage? Coffee, soda, or water?"

"Yes, water. Thank you."

He's back soon and continues, "There are several things we need to discuss. First, I want to compliment you. In the over eighteen months you've worked here, there has not been one single incident report from an inmate complaining about how you conduct yourself. No inmate complaints are a huge positive for the colonel. What you're doing is different, and we like it."

I interrupt him, "My heart is in my work. No matter what the challenge, I deal with it respectfully."

"Hold on a minute. Let me finish, Officer Mak." He sits with his fingers interlocked behind his neck. I am taking gulps of water when he says, "I'm offering you a promotion. The colonel and I decided we want you to have an administrative position. You would be the personnel director of hiring and training. The position has a lot of responsibilities that include hiring all officers, full training of all officers. You would report to both Kim and myself. We want more Officer Maks on board." He opens the door and points straight ahead. "Your office would be right there in front of mine."

I interrupt him. "What about Sergeant Bates? She hired me. Isn't she doing that job?"

He comes closer. "Your professionalism is what we need and want. She is to be transferred back to managing shifts. We trust you can find the right people and train them properly, yielding higher scores during our annual review. You will assist with improving the retention rate. I want you for the job. Think it over if you need time. The job is Monday through Friday, eight to five, with a one-hour lunch break. My only other request is I want to take some pressure off Sarah. She and I discussed training you to do the payroll."

"Thank you for your faith in me. When do I start?"

"Next Monday," he replies, "but please keep it confidential until an announcement is made."

I stand up and shake his hand. Bada bing! My mind is sooooo blown.

Ryan and his girlfriend, Kelly, have been dating for a couple of years. She loves his energy and humor, and he loves everything about her, including the prettiest smile I've ever seen. It's a healthy relationship, and I hope they grow old together. Our family adores her. They love cooking together, and tonight, they are making the entire meal in honor of my promotion. There's no chance that I will drink the wine they are serving because I'd risk getting hammered and passing out like a drunken slob on their pool table. Kelly and her family do not see that side of me, not tonight, not ever.

Brock calls and needs a ride home. He is at a friend's house, borrowing a computer. I hate when my kids need to borrow anything. They have never had senior pictures or yearbooks, and they are probably the only ones in their circle of friends who don't own a computer, yet they don't complain.

*****

A professor at VCU hosts a poetry reading that I attend. When he and I talk, he suggests I find a few readers while working on the book. He tells me to be sure they are all avid readers. "Expect honest, constructive criticism, but withdraw from anyone who disrespects you. It's not easy reliving tragedies through writing. Stand up for yourself."

Within a month, I have seven readers who are sending my writing back to me with comments. It feels urgent to have the support of counseling while I work with my group of readers. Unfortunately, therapist number thirteen is not a good fit.

Margaret Atwood says, "Blank pages inspire me with terror." That quote, along with other inspirational quotes by authors, are taped to the walls around my desk. With the next two days off, I work on the book. I sip tea and read through my journals, reflecting on the life I was given. I, the survivor, am joined by the rape victim, the black sheep, the single mom, and the beast. Which one will step forward, demanding recognition tonight? Which one can prevail? What will appear on the page? Will it resonate with anyone besides me?

I glance at the clock. It's suddenly 4:00 a.m. Paradise exists when the world is quiet and I'm alone, being creative, writing below the belt. The silence in the process of writing is healing, Patience only grows when we are under pressure. Ice cream is calling me. *So is God.*

Chapter 16

ZOLOFT AND MY BUNNY

THE CLEVELAND INDIANS LOSE THE World Series to the Miami Marlins after a season of eighty-six wins. Brock and I are enjoying mother-son time. We have watched game after game all season from start to finish, sitting side by side. I'm not a fan of sports, but I am a huge fan of time alone with my son. I'm loving every minute of it. There is something intoxicating about observing Brock's reactions to his hometown team. Sam, our black lab, watches us and snaps at the Doritos Brock tosses to her. Snacks are a part of this gig. The intimacy I feel in this time with my youngest child feels priceless.

Brock is having bouts of head pain behind his blind eye. We have an upcoming appointment with the Virginia Eye Institute, but when the pressure increases, making it difficult for him to get out of bed, I call for an emergency appointment. "My son needs to be seen today. He can't wait another two weeks to see an ophthalmologist. We are on our way and can wait."

Three hours later, the doctor tells us, "The pressure in his eye is very high." She gives us five different prescriptions. Brock must stay home, resting for five days, then return for another appointment.

The copay for the medicine he needs is eighty dollars. I'm thirty-six dollars short, and my credit cards are maxed out. Never having enough money is a source of shame for me. I leave the pharmacy with four of the five medications and cry, scream at myself out loud, on the way home.

That evening, Carol calls and hears about Brock's condition. Without hesitation, she phones the pharmacy and pays for the fifth prescription with her own credit card. I'm struck by the compassion my twenty-year-old daughter has for her brother.

The medications offer only temporary relief. "My head feels like it's going to explode!" Brock yells.

During the next appointment we learn the pressure is even worse. He tries other medications that don't help. The doctor decides the eye must be surgically removed. She leaves the extraocular muscles intact. There will be a hollow socket that needs daily treatment. I can handle this. I can. I will, I can do this.

Brock is captain of his high school soccer team. He is told he needs to quit playing all sports his senior year. He's not taking the news well. Neither am I.

The surgery is scheduled. We see another doctor who measures Brock for a prosthetic eye. It's an identical match to Brock's other eye that is as blue as a perfect spring sky. On the drive home, Brock makes a tight fist and repeatedly hits the palm of his other hand. "Mom, I'm not comfortable wearing a black patch for three months. Everyone will ask stupid questions. I don't want to do this."

I reply, "At least you won't be in any pain, and you'll get your life back."

He does not respond. Back at home, he locks the door of the big bedroom, which has been his since Ryan left for Virginia Tech. All he wants is a bowl of bean soup and solitude with television. The day his eye is removed, Carol, Ryan, Kelly, and Mason are all there to give him support. The complications are minimal, and the pain is gone sooner than later. Thank you, God.

Carol is euphoric over a guy she met. Max is a law student. They met while working together on a volunteer project. Afterward, Carol was mud wrestling, and Max decided to ask her out. What won her heart was his ability to have hours-long intelligent discussions. I can't wait to meet the man who stole a piece of my daughter's heart.

Max invites me to his rental home off campus. They seem to be on the same moral ground with plenty of potential for a committed relationship. My first impression is how he smiles all the time…and how lily-white and shiny he keeps his home. His cookware is also better than mine.

My administrative position does not pay enough money to keep us afloat. Both Ryan and Carol are in college, and the child support check has been cut drastically. Soon, Brock joins Ryan in Blacksburg, Virginia. I need to help all three of my kids as much as I can, and we help each other. When our refrigerator breaks, Ryan brings his from his dorm room. He gives Brock the truck he bought from Kelly's father. Ryan comes home often, but Carol wants to stay at school for the second summer to paint houses and pick up another class. My daughter has been a straight A student since middle school and has pulled all-nighters for exams for years.

Before looking for a second job, I find a therapist because no matter how well I'm doing at work or my kids are doing at school, I always feel there is something wrong with me. I care too much about what people think, and I don't understand why my relationships are strained.

Carol notices that my stormy past has a hold on me. We don't talk about it until she says, "The way you react to things is not healthy."

I'm not sure if my boys see what Carol sees. My mind constantly races with negative thoughts that trigger negative feelings. The spiritual path I was on is at a dead end. Kay and I don't speak. My father criticizes me at some point during every conversation we have. I crave human contact and connection but feel increasingly alone and uncomfortable.

Sweet Ryan forces my brother and me to speak. He loves Uncle David and tells me, "You're both wrong, Mom. Not talking to each other is wrong. Someone needs to put you two back in touch. You only have one sibling. I could never cut off Brock or Carol."

He calls David from a pay phone at the Waffle House on a calling card, and his face lights up when my brother picks up the phone. They talk and laugh for several minutes before Ryan hands me the phone.

It feels good to restore communication with David especially since Ryan is the peacemaker. When we discuss why we haven't spoken, David says, "You were mad at me about my wedding. You wanted to be my best man. Our relationship broke down when you refused to understand why you could not be in that role." He laughs. I'm not laughing.

I try to understand why that happened. What if everyone is right and I really am *crazy*? What if the man who took my life for one night also took my ability to ever live a stable life? What if his *crazy* is now my *crazy*?

My latest therapist is Karen. She's pretty and perky, and her positive vibe energizes me. Please let her be the one that can help me. We start by identifying all the inner trauma that follows me everywhere. She's the first active listener to my agitation and wants me to start taking *Zoloft*.

I refuse to be medicated. The problems I have are seriously screwing up my life. I want one person to tell me why I drink so much that I get drunk, why I quit good jobs, why I suck at relationships, why I hate myself, why I can't finish my book, why I do or say things and a day later wonder why, and why raising three children is the only thing I've done right? How can I be a decent person to them but not to myself? It feels urgent to find the answers to all my questions. There must be more wrong with me than being a rape victim. The attack happened over twenty years ago. Why am I not healing?

No matter what happens, my sidekick Ryan is there for me. Christmas comes, and he walks through the front door with a real tree. He doesn't care if there are no presents. Ryan wants me to have a tree. *Compassion* is an action word, and Ryan gets it. When things get tough around here, Ryan gets tougher. He refuses to believe his mother is failing in life. Ryan believes in me and wants everything to get better. I love his heart so much. He respects my survival in a way that no other family member does. He gives my tiny moments of pure logical joy.

In therapy, Karen brings up family in my next few sessions. We discuss my childhood, my adult life, difficult relationships, and how I'm doing with each one of my children. She hands me a stuffed animal and asks me to hold it for comfort and to try a little play therapy. A furry bunny on my lap is going to give me a healthy identity? Stop all my drinking? *Is she serious?*

I stand up to leave, but she stops me. "Wait a minute. Don't run away. When traditional therapies are not working, studies show that patients get in touch with their inner child while holding on to a stuffed animal. Would you prefer to hold a dog or a cat? All the problems you are dealing with come from not learning coping skills as a child. Engage with the bunny. See what comes out."

A fucking bunny is going to solve my problems? I'm done with Karen and her creative problem-solving. I return home, call off work, and start drinking.

Music at the highest volume can silence the noise in my head and take me somewhere else. I drink and dance to the songs "Maniac" and "Flashdance…What a Feeling" over and over. Now I'm drunk… and crying because I'm drunk…and because the third of my three precious birds I have lived with for so long will soon fly away. Brock leaves in eight months. I'm scared.

*****

Slammalammadingdingdong—our hellhole house has a buyer. Thank you, sweet Jesus. It's real this time, and Brock and I need to get out of here fast. Mason and I are the only former couple I know who have owned a home for fifteen years that is now worth less than its purchase price. Mason has to actually pay money to complete the sale. My goal is to find a new place where the kids can come home and know that love still lives there.

With no money to put down for a deposit and bad credit, I search for an apartment. This feels like situational bomb number eighty-seven hitting me. Brock and I are days away from being homeless when his friend's mother calls, saying, "Debra, I heard about your situation. Clayton and I want you and Brock to stay with us. There's one empty room with twin beds. Come stay with us until you find a place."

What a beautiful thing to have a person I barely know open her home to Brock and me. Linda saves us. She is an earth angel like so many others who have come to my rescue. Today is a day to give thanks for strangers. It's also time to give up drinking. There's no way I can go into the Nell house and get drunk.

It's pitch-black outside with a choir of stars. I pace the dilapidated porch, smoking a cigarette and then sit on the top step thinking about how many times I walked up and down these steps, wishing I were somewhere else…someone else. How I wish my children had new furniture.

Not once did I bring a man into this house thinking he could save me. Life is so hard when you're alone. I don't know the feeling of buying a new car or going to a furniture store to pick out what I like. I've never taken a week off, packed a suitcase, and gone on a vacation. The only traveling I've ever done was to the funerals of people I've loved, to help Kay move, or to seek medical treatment. I'm alive, but this is not living. I'm playing the cards I've been dealt, standing in the dirt of my story, and writing under a sagging moon. Victor Hugo wrote naked. I'm trying that tonight to see if I can get closer to my own piece of raw reality.

Someday I might buy myself a red rose. More likely, I'll die of a stroke laughing at myself. But one day, I hope to wake up and not feel crazy, finish writing my story, and send it out on the wind with the hope that one brave soul catches it and turns it all into gold.

Part 4

THE AUGHTS

Chapter 17

GRACE STREET

UNIVERSE, PLEASE FORGIVE ME. LIVING in a twelve-by-twelve bedroom with my eighteen-year-old son, with two beds three feet apart in a house that is not mine, makes me feel like an underwater volcano about to erupt. Poor Brock. What senior in high school wants to share a small bedroom with his mother? Thank God we are both busy and rarely here. Clayton is one of Brock's best friends, so when they are both home, he and Brock stay in Clayton's room. It could be worse. We could be living in a car. I'm not having luck finding a rental property in Brandermill that accepts me. The only way out is for me to move to the city. Of course, then Brock would have to commute. This is our best option. I'm grateful we have shelter.

I'm loading a wastebasket full of Bud Lights on ice into the bedroom. No one is due home. My boom box is here, so I'm listening to tunes while drinking beer. Brock is working late and has my car because Ryan's truck is not running. I'm organizing my uniforms in clothes baskets in the hall, where my ironing board also sits. The rest of my clothes are stored in the trunk of my car. Brock has the closet and the chest.

Linda spends a lot of time talking with her father at the kitchen table. He's a wonderful man. They invite me to sit and chat with them, but I confine myself to this room to try not to invade Linda's space. My rules, not hers.

After I finish my fifth beer, I realize being stuck in this room triggers rape flashbacks. I crush each can with my foot and then throw it against the wall. There's no cable in here, so I order it, adding the charge to Linda's bill without asking her. There isn't even room to pace, so I sit in a corner on the floor by the music and continue drinking.

Damn that rape dick, rape room, rape knife, rape smells, rape sounds, rape force. I'm listening to Abba and Don Henley. Still, I can't get the rape off my mind. My head is hung low as I dig, dig, dig deep into my scalp and let it bleed. There's blood under my fingernails.

*****

It's Christmastime, and all three of my children spend it in Orlando with their father. I'm off work, but I can't stay in this room. I don't have a destination, but once I get out of Brandermill, I head toward Virginia Beach. The hotel rates are cheap in the winter months.

I remember how Ryan bought me a tree last year, and I wonder if Carol remembers her box of European gourmet cookies that I bought her every year. It's important that Brock spends time with his father with everything going on right now.

There's no alcohol on this trip if I hope to avoid the aftermath of getting drunk, which involves making midnight phone calls having nothing to do with Merry Christmas. Apparently, I call people late at night to remind them about something they did twenty or thirty years ago. I never remember what's said, but they do. It's not funny. It confirms I have no self-control, and I am crazy.

I love this beach with lacy-looking foam that surrounds my feet as I walk for an hour with no negative chatter in my head. The wind flings icy sharp gusts. In between, I hear my mother's soothing voice. At times, it feels like her death happened yesterday, but it's been almost thirty years without her, and I can't remember her laugh. This moment in nature feeling a connection with my mother feels godly, but I have forgotten how to pray. The waves lapping on the shore sound like hope. Nature is a place of refuge that has always embraced me.

It's getting dark, so I leave the beach to find a restaurant with a salad, seafood, warm bread, real butter, and lemon water. I insist on making this holiday into a healthy experience with no regrets. I have no problem dining alone. Afterward, I plan to go straight back to my room, take a bath, watch a movie, and call my kids.

As I walk toward the restaurant, there's an illuminated sign with letters spelling B-A-R. Without hesitation, I walk right in and take a seat at a horseshoe bar already full with an assortment of men. I'm the only woman at the bar. Frank Sinatra is crooning from the jukebox. Before I can take off my coat, an older man yells, "Give that lady a drink on me!"

"Thank you. Merry Christmas," I say. I select what my mother drank on Christmas Eve: a white Russian with at least eight hundred calories. I order the second one with a double shot of vodka. Still no buzz. It's Christmas Eve. I'm in an unfamiliar bar with unfamiliar men in an unfamiliar city. It's not just risky. It's stupid. But hey, it feels like where I belong. At least I'm not alone for the holidays, and I'm close to my hotel.

At the bottom of my purse, there's a pen, and I grab handfuls of napkins and start writing. There's a quote from Emily Dickinson in my purse that I forgot to put in a journal, and I write it again: "If thy nerve deny thee, go above thy nerve."

A man shouts, "Give our sweetheart two drinks on me!"

Here we are, strangers in a paradise of colored lights, fake wreaths, fake presents under a fake tree. Next thing I know, a man in a green suit with a Santa tie comes over and sits next to me. "Did you get the two drinks I bought for you?" He sounds British.

"Yes, thank you," I answer, staring at my beer. "I'm just here to relax a bit before dinner."

He slowly tells a dramatic story of his mother's cancer and how she passed away. I can relate. "Losing your mother is hard," I say as I continue to listen attentively.

Eventually, I learn that his mother died at age eighty-nine. He starts crying. The bartender calls him a cab. Apparently, he's been here for seven hours and has cried through the last four. He stumbles out the door, waving an umbrella that almost knocks over the Christmas tree. "There but for the grace of God go I!" He shouts as he makes his exit. That's one man down.

Dive bars are *conflict theaters*, and I love the role of therapist. Being lost in someone else's problems is another form of escape, and I seem to attract the talkative, sorrowful souls wherever I go.

Another nose-blowing drunk yells, "How many *publicans* do we have in the bar?"

Eight guys raise their drinks, and he calls the bartender, "Hey, Bobo. Give all the *publicans* a shot of tequila on me." He yells again, "Give the whole bar a shot on me!"

How perfect and beautiful. I've never had a shot of tequila. Two shots are set in front of me. The dark amber enticement scares the hell out of me. "Shoot it. C'mon, shoot it down. It's Christmas," a chorus of male voices cheer me on. My finger dips into the shot glass, and I rub it across my lips. Here I go. One shot down, then two, and here goes a third. My throat and lungs are on fire, and my buzz is on now. I feel good!

The bar has a menu, and I need food. When I do the math, my tab is low from all the free drinks, so I order wings to go and a six-pack of Michelob. My body sways walking across the street until somehow, I crash into the right room. I can't believe I arrived in the right place.

All lights are out as I sink into the bathtub and continue drinking. I'm so drunk, it's hard to get out of the bathtub. I wrap a blanket around my naked body. The main reason I came here was to relax on the balcony overlooking the ocean with its healing power.

While sitting outside, I remember Ryan's first glimpse of the ocean. "Mommy, look! Hello, ocean. Good morning, ocean." His little legs ran in and out of the water and jumped in place with both feet. Ryan is on my mind until I black out.

Christmas Day is spent in bed. There's no possible way I can go to work tomorrow. Vomit explodes from my throat. Washing my face ten times, even twenty times, does not help the headache. I swallow three Advil tablets and rest. When I walk into the bathroom and look at the woman in the mirror, I scream, "Stop this! Stop this nonsense! Stop drinking! Stop it! Stop it before you can't stop it! You're drinking more than anyone in the bar! *Stop!*" Then I lie back down in bed and remind myself I'm not an alcoholic. Alcoholics don't raise healthy children and work two jobs. I work and drink. That's my life. I'm not an alcoholic. For the next few months, I stay sober.

Charlie's mom, Kathleen, calls. "We'd like to invite Brock to spend the summer at our house. We love Brock. He'll have his own room, and Charlie wants him to stay here. We all do."

Everyone at her house has chores, and Brock will be expected to mow their grass, which he can learn how to do.

Kathleen is a single mother of four who works with autistic children. Her youngest daughter Annie has Down syndrome. Kathleen's life is work, children, and her hobby working with stained glass. I'm beginning to appreciate all the people who proactively offer kindness to me.

Maya Angelou reminds us that people rarely remember what you said. They remember how you made them feel. I've felt protective arms around me from selfless people who care about people like me. In a world in which I'm stigmatized as *crazy*, people like Kay, Rubi, Mary, Linda, and now Kathleen helped me realize I've never really been alone. Someone has always reached out to me to offer a hand.

Cary invites me to stay at her house while I look for a place in the city. She is a Southern girl with a Southern accent. She gives me a room with a bathroom. Cary is a teacher who watches golf on the weekends unless she's enjoying her lover boy who is twenty years younger. We have good conversations. Finally, after six months, I am approved for my apartment on Grace Street, and she offers to make my car payments for two months so I can afford the deposits.

My new apartment is in an old building with tall doors and windows that create a cathedral feeling. It's only one block from the Richmond Library, where I can work on a computer. I love my Grace Street apartment with its three thrift-store bookshelves piled with notebooks and books about writing, two comfortable dark-red chairs, a bamboo table, and a rocking chair. A bed is not in my budget, so I buy an eight-foot, three-inch-thick floor mat and a body pillow and sleep on the floor five months. Cary gives me the gray comforter I used at her house. There are no closets but that doesn't bother me. I have locks on the door, a huge bathtub, and a renovated kitchen with working appliances. Plants eventually fill my windowsills, and I decorate the whole place from consignment and thrift stores. My mind is going in a thousand different directions thinking about how it feels to be in my own home.

I need a better car. I also need to start paying off credit cards. A weekend job comes through taking care of a lady with Alzheimer's who lives alone. On the first day, she tells me, "You must be a horrible woman if you can't find a husband." She forces me to watch golf with her for hours and to fetch her grapes. She yells at me, "Don't touch my grapes! Bring your own." She is verbally abusive, which I find difficult.

This lady may trigger my entire being. If I didn't need the extra five hundred bucks a month, I would have quit the job on day two. We take drives in her Jaguar, and we walk to the lake. Her demeanor improves when out of the house.

Her daughter lives close and takes care of her during the week. Her son lives in Norfolk, so we take a day trip to visit him. But when she accuses me of stealing her grapes and her bathrobe on the same day, she throws a glass of ice tea in my face at Long John Silver's, I call her daughter, and I quit.

Months after my move to Grace Street, I discover a gay bar right across the street. The bar becomes my living room on my days off. It's enjoyable because I don't need to be wary of any ulterior sexual motive.

My corrections job is going well. I have picked up the required computer skills thanks to the help of many. Still, the fact remains my finances require a second job. One morning, I impulsively request an opportunity to work more directly with inmates again. Although everyone is surprised, I am relocated to the Intake department, the most stressful part of the facility. I'm back on night shift. I pick up a second job working as a server at Denny's on Broad Street. Between Denny's and corrections, I'm working eighty to ninety hours a week. The osteoarthritis in my right knee is on fire. My running days are over. Both jobs are physical. I quit my job in corrections with no thought. What have I done? It feels like another inexplicable mistake. There are times when I need to tell the thoughts in my head to sit down and shut up.

Ryan is not answering calls, which is not normal behavior. Something is wrong. When I speak to his roommate, he says, "I'm not sure what's wrong with Ryan. Kelly broke up with him, but it seems like there's something more than that because he's not going to class. I think it's a good idea for you to come here."

Boom! I take three days off from work and head to Virginia Tech. Ryan answers the door in his boxer shorts, hugs me, and gets dressed. I take him to his favorite Italian restaurant to find out what's going on, why he and Kelly broke up, and why his major changed from industrial psychology to forestry.

We talk about Kelly first. He's not that upset. They plan to stay in touch with each other. Nothing bad happened. She is at the University of Virginia, and a long-distance relationship is difficult. After five years together, Kelly is closer to settling down. She wants to be an oncology nurse. Ryan is nowhere near ready to settle down. He's a bartender living off bar food and 7-Eleven snacks. The longer we talk, the more I realize my son made a mistake choosing a school well known for partying.

Brock works in a food court and is allowed one free meal a day. I send him twenty-dollar checks and tell him when it's safe to cash them. Carol's hair is falling out apparently from malnutrition. I need to start helping my kids out with food. They can't be full-time students and work full-time jobs.

Then there's the dog. Sam came to school with Ryan. "Where's the dog?" I ask.

Ryan grabs another slice of pizza, "She runs all over campus," he explains.

"Sam is an indoor dog, Ryan. She's your dog. You wanted her, paid for her, and decided she needed to be here. Why are you letting her run free all day? How irresponsible is that?"

He laughs. "Everyone knows Sam. She goes to classes here, and 7-Eleven gives her free hot dogs. Stop worrying about everything. She's fine, Mom."

Something is different with my son. He's not himself. This is not the time to be his buddy. When I start asking hard questions, he blows me off. His grades are bad. He's not happy. For the first time in his life, it sounds like he's failing. My high-spirited son doesn't appear to be bound for academic glory. We walk and talk and walk and talk. "I'm dating a stripper," he tells me. "Her name is Annie, and I want to bring her to Richmond to meet you."

Now I know something is wrong. I call Carol to see if she can take the dog. Carol is angry about Ryan's negligence, but she agrees to take care of Sam if I can deliver the dog along with a purple collar, leash, and food to Charlottesville. It's hours out of my way, and it shortens my visit with Ryan, but at least the dog won't be neglected.

Ryan and I say our goodbyes. He tells me Annie will drive them to Richmond in a month so she can meet me. While driving from Blacksburg to Charlottesville, I tell myself Ryan is going through a phase. It's only a phase. His brain works faster than mine. He and I have survived so much. Mini me and I can get through this one too.

Working ten- and thirteen-hour shifts a week is killing me. I'm almost fifty. After three days off, I need to rest for another weekend, so I call off my Denny's shift. Employees are fired when they call off without a medical note. Wanda won't fire me because week after week, my sales are higher than any other server's. She posts the numbers daily.

Wanda reminds me we have a court date and are expected to be there. Some guy at the coffee bar started masturbating, and I'm the one who saw it first. Kicking him out of Denny's would've been my choice. The guy is homeless and harmless. I'm not supporting the idea of charging him with disorderly conduct. The police came and removed him. I think that was enough. I wish Wanda would drop the charge.

It's early Saturday morning. I walk at Byrd Park on my favorite trail where the sunlight is diffuse. I'm a city girl at heart and an observer of the human condition. City life is a beautiful dance of chaos, diversity, and energy. Grace Street is exactly where I belong.

The walk in the park has me thinking about Ryan and what it will take to get him back on track. Many kids his age are not ready for the experience of living away from home. There's no shame in not going to school until you're ready. I need to check in with him again.

After my walk, I drive to World Cup where a variety of unpublished writers hang out and often share their work. I come here to meet strangers and hear their stories. I can hear the coffee grinder whirring as I approach. This is a comfortable place where people sit and discuss anything. No topic is off-limits. I meet other artists who seem brilliant and are funny, with lifelong dreams that have not come true. I want people like this in my life.

It's afternoon when I get back to my apartment. I shower and dress in a black skirt, boots, hoop earrings, and a hippie shirt. My writing bag is a gift from Carol. Today it is full of notebooks, pens, three books on writing instruction, and an apple. The bag will stay with me for the rest of my life.

I'm back in my car. My first stop is the Bamboo Café, a small bar that is intimate and superfriendly. They are discussing the Clinton impeachment and our current president, George W. Bush. The chattering is so loud, I can't write.

I move two blocks down to the Cary St. Cafe. I'm comfortably seated in a booth instead of at the bar. I order a pint of beer and take out my writing. It's darker and quieter here. Every few minutes, a guy at the bar turns to look at me. His eyes follow me when I walk to the restroom. He smiles and nods when I walk back, but I ignore him. His mountain-man look is a distraction since I love that rugged, earthy type. Now he's looking too often, so I move to the other side of the booth. He can't see me now. If this dude makes a pass at me, I'm out of here. Ten minutes later, he approaches me and says, "Hello."

I say hello back and keep writing.

He smiles. "You look busy. I don't want to bother you, but can I buy you a beer and talk for a short time, or do you need to keep working?"

I hand him a ten-dollar bill, saying, "Here, take this and buy us both a beer. I can take a short break." He tosses the money back at me. "What do you drink?"

"A pint of Bud Light."

"Cool, we drink the same beer."

"You've been watching me since I walked in here. What do you need?"

He laughs. "I've never seen a writer in this bar. Are you an author?"

"Hell no. I will never be an author. I write and stop, then I write and stop again. Do you know what I mean?"

He takes a long drink, "Yeah, sort of. You're an artist like me. What do you write about?"

With total sarcasm, I answer, "I write about saving the soul of America, which is why I will never be published. I can't save my own damn soul. What's your name?"

"Patrick. What's yours?"

"Debra," I answer as we shake hands. We talk nonstop for an hour.

Patrick is a carpenter who has been divorced for sixteen years. He has a daughter. He refuses to own a car. He rides a bike. He draws and smokes weed. His dream was to be an architect. I'm suspicious. "Why don't you have a car for work? Is your license suspended?"

He laughs out loud. "No, I ride my bike to work and walk everywhere in the city. When you work in the city and live in the city, there's no reason to own a car. Besides, I pay child support."

We talk about his "on again, off again" relationship with a woman twenty years older. Needing him to know, I say, "Patrick, this is a bar. I came here to relax and work. If you're trying to pick me up, you have the wrong woman, got it?"

He answers, "Got it. Are you a lawyer? Do you work in law enforcement?"

Shit! Is he one of my released inmates? I ask him, "Why? Have you been to jail?"

"No. It's a hunch. You have an authoritative manner and voice. I like it. Hey, can you wait about forty-five minutes? I need to go help a buddy of mine move an air conditioner."

I answer, "Maybe, maybe not."

He gets me another beer and taps me on the head, "You're a beautiful hard-ass. Please wait. I will hurry."

When he leaves, I ask the bartender if he knows Patrick. "Oh, yeah. Patrick's been a regular for years. He usually stops after work for a couple of beers. He's quiet and doesn't talk to women much. This is not his usual behavior. Enjoy yourself. He's a good guy."

A half hour later, Patrick is back, showered, dressed up with a portfolio of his work. I'm impressed with his landscapes, mountains, cityscapes. We keep talking and discover we have similar tastes in music. Patrick is the only man I know who owns an Enya CD. We both love nature and beer.

"Are you hungry? I'm starved. There's a place about ten blocks from here called Shaka's. They have great salads and sandwiches."

"Are you asking me on a date?"

He stands up. "Hell no, I'm asking if you want something to eat. You don't date men in bars, remember? Let's go. Come on. The walk is good for us."

Screw it. We are just walking. I'm going. What horrible thing can happen in the middle of the day? My gut tells me I'm not dealing with a monster. He opens the door and steps aside like my grandfather did for my grandmother. When we reach a busy intersection, he takes my hand. "You don't know how to walk in a city yet. Hold my hand."

Shaka's is a basement café with Dido playing on the jukebox. When we walk in, Patrick plays a few more tunes. We order food, and he puts a piece of his sandwich to my lips. I push it away. "We met a few hours ago. I'm not sharing food with you."

A few minutes later, I feel his feet wrapped around mine. He touches my face, and a piece of me melts. I can't remember the last time I felt the gentle touch of a man. It's been at least fifteen years.

Everything about this man feels real. It feels soft. It feels urgent for me to feel.

My heart has suffered so much neglect to the point of feeling unworthy of the love of a man, yet at this moment, he's pulling me in with his eyes. There's a static charge between us. The chemistry I share with him feels like a drug. There's a place inside me that has not been touched this beautifully by any man: my heart.

Schwoop! A man touches a piece of my heart. This feeling is larger than any horror I have felt for the past twenty-five years.

Chapter 18

CRASH INTO ME

BEFORE I DIE, PLEASE LET me know what it feels like to have unconditional love from a man. I divorced Mason with the hope of finding a soulmate and partner because that was missing in our relationship. I understand relationships can only be as healthy as the individuals involved. My heart knows I am not healthy enough to attract a healthy man, but Patrick brought to life a part of me that was dead. The chemistry we share plus the fact that he feels safe keep him on my mind. I'm not sure our paths will cross again. We did not exchange phone numbers.

What I seem to do best is make impulsive decisions. I'm working full-time at Denny's. I can't explain why I quit my corrections job with generous benefits to serve "grand slams" and chili-cheese fries all night. The decision was made and acted upon within less than twenty minutes. A smart thing would have been to give that decision time. So much of my life I've made snap decisions that backfired, so many consequences that have no logical reason.

Wanda, my boss, is tougher than anyone I worked for in corrections. She gives me the third shift Wednesdays through Sundays. Start time is 10:30 p.m. I will have health insurance in thirty days. I limp out to my car after working all night on my feet. The osteoarthritis is crippling me, but my need to stay employed is stronger than the pain.

Irvin, the dishwasher, is a single dad, and I drive him home even though it's out of my way. He works seven days a week, harder than any man I know with no complaints. He offers me gas money that I refuse. So many people have reached out to me to make my life easier. If I can make his easier, it's the least I can do. Pay it forward, Debra. Pay it forward.

The car payment for the black jeep convertible I just bought cost me my two days off. I'm hired as a parking lot attendant for the Richmond Airport. From eleven at night to five in the morning, I'm in a lit valet booth. Hours go by that I don't see anyone but when the two security officers on duty come by to warn me not to leave the booth. It would be so easy for someone to rape and murder me here. I'm jumpy, and I kill time by looking for signs of trouble. I feel calmer outside than when I'm trapped inside, visible, a target in a cage. I'm fifty years old working seven days a week again. Surviving financially is getting harder with age. Without any time for renewal, I know I'm headed for burnout.

It's Sunday afternoon. The sinner in me rolls over and pulls the comforter over my head. My car is parked at the bar I went to this morning after work. I don't close bars now. I open them. It's wine and dinner before noon, sleep five hours, work, and repeat. I'm not getting enough sleep.

Writing is the only thing that keeps calling me back. I get lost in my writing for weeks then lose my focus and ignore it for months. I often ask myself, "Who the hell cares if I ever finish a book?" Then I answer myself, "I do."

I feel the ceiling fan circulating air. My feet shuffle to the shower, where steamy rivulets of water on my head calm me. Thirty years postrape I still require a hot shower in the morning and a hot bath at night to zap the lingering filth.

I'm calling off the airport job today. After picking up my car, I buy a hot cup of 7-Eleven coffee and the *New York Times* and go to Ellwood Thompson's, my favorite organic market. Even though milk thistle is expensive, I buy it because it's good for the liver.

I notice a woman reading the ingredients on a box of toothpaste. I can't stop watching her. She looks so healthy. It seems like I have the equivalent of an invisible electric fence around me that shocks every healthy person who tries to get close. Maybe it's because I'm scared to death, they see who I really am. She turns her head to look at me, and I quickly walk away before I'm accused of being a crazy stalker.

Autumn leaves burn bright in Richmond. While eating lunch at Fountain Lake Park, I watch the Canadian geese. I wonder if I could disappear to a cabin in the woods for two years like Thoreau, could I focus enough on writing to complete a book? Carol jokes that the only way I could ever stay focused enough to finish is if I go to jail for an extended time. Carol has been an eyewitness to my inability to hold anything together in life, not a job, a relationship, my finances, or any therapist long enough to fix what's wrong with me.

When I get back to my apartment, there's laundry to do, so I gather it and head toward the basement laundry room. On the way there, Patrick suddenly appears on his bike and yells, "Hey, girl, how are you? Where have you been?"

"Gone butterfly hunting," I respond.

Patrick smiles, follows me to the laundry room, and starts helping. He was in the army and does laundry according to perfect military regulations. When I bend down, he starts massaging my neck like I'm a kitten. We pause for a moment and stare at each other. His fingers are moving through strands of my long hair. It feels so damn good, like I'm wrapped in a warm blanket. "What do want from me, Patrick? Why did you come here? Do you want sex from me? What? What do you want?"

He puts both hands on my shoulders. "Dammit, Debra, can we just talk? Have you eaten today?"

"Yes, I ate, and today is a writing day," I say as I walk away.

He follows me. Writing is cancelled. Patrick and I hop into my jeep and take off to Byrd Park. We share a love of nature. He runs laps while I walk fast. We sit down on the grass and allow our chemistry to create a subtle dance. Hours later, we go to the room he rents to enjoy more time together.

Patrick smokes pot. Weed does not have a therapeutic effect on me. It sends me straight into a heart-racing paranoia and brings up my personal hell. I refuse to smoke it. We spend the entire day together without alcohol.

No one I know approves of our relationship, but I really don't care. I've read poetry about what real love feels like, and this relationship gets closer to that description than any other I've known. It's not a connection that can be easily explained, except to say being with him releases shame, negative body images, self-blame, and a deep-seated fear of men. Patrick gives me energy that was sucked out of me the night I was raped.

A few months later, we are living together in his small room with rats in the walls, kitchen, and bathroom. The room is right next to Cary St. Café, where Patrick and I met. Is this another mistake or a blessing? It's one way of cleaning up my credit card debt, which is over ten thousand dollars. Our love affair takes off fast. I like him. I love coming home to him. He's not a man I would ever marry. He's a man who is healing parts of me that cannot be touched in therapy. Who cares if there are rats in the house?

My boys are showing signs of financial stress. Virginia Tech, located in Blacksburg, is so isolated, it's hard for students to find work. The only jobs are on campus. Ryan's changing personality is *loud* while Brock's is *quiet.* The only real solution is to convince Mason they both need time with him and could work and live in Orlando. When I call Mason to discuss the idea, he supports it. We talk for an hour and make plans to move Ryan to Orlando first. Months later, Brock follows his brother. They both leave school and work sixty hours a week to support themselves. Within a few months, both boys are working in Mason's medical business with health benefits. Ryan starts out in sales, and Brock runs the warehouse.

Ryan is officially diagnosed with ADHD. He needs medication but refuses to take it after a few weeks. My boys seem happier. They discover a few of their best friends are going to school at Full Sail in Orlando. This was a good decision. My sons need time with their father. They need a new beginning. I made the right decision for them, for all of them.

After a year of living with rats, Patrick and I move to Belmont Avenue in the Fan District. We spend time on the rocks at the James River. Patrick goes to the library, mass, and bookstores with me. We often walk and talk at Byrd Park. We eat breakfast in restaurants.

Patrick is obsessed with personal hygiene, and it turns me on. After long showers, he smells like a walk in the forest. As we lie in bed one morning, his fingers move slowly around my face, neck, arms, and inner thigh. The scars from my mastectomies don't bother him. He massages my chest as though my breasts are there. Lying in bed, we are entangled in each other.

He is aware of what rape did to me and is patient with intercourse. When I need to stop, he stops. I am becoming unstuck. We spend time skin on skin with my head resting on his chest. I can hear his heartbeat. Our connection transcends the physical. We make love in the shower, in the car, in the woods, on the floor, in the middle of the night, and first thing in the morning. He kisses my eyelids and take strands of my hair across his face. There's not an inch of my body Patrick does not touch.

It takes the heart of a lion to restore what was *destroyed* in me. Patrick helps me love my body again. Weight is dropping off fast. I can't get enough of him. I crave him on top of me as I look into the blue eyes of a man, not the eyes of my rapist.

We take a drive to Powhatan, and Patrick brings his telescope to show me the night sky. In an open field, we make love on the hood of the car. What appears wrong to the outside world is right with me inside. I can't break away. I'm numbed by his touch that removes my inability to hate my body, to fear the intimacy of a man without the fear of violence. It's been over twenty years, and I'm not leaving him no matter how this looks to the world. I don't care what people think of him. He brings back oxygen to my soul.

*****

Carol has graduated from Virginia Commonwealth University with a master's degree in social work. Her first job offer is with Catholic Charities in Washington, DC. She's been renting a house with two close friends, and we have a huge celebration. My grandmother, who is in her nineties, sends Carol a congratulations card with five dollars inside. My daughter says it is the best gift ever coming from her great-grandmother with a third-grade education. Carol wants to save the five-dollar bill as a reminder of how little things in life can hold more value than big things.

Her five-year relationship with Max has ended. He has moved to Puerto Rico for his internship. Carol dates other guys, but she still loves Max. She often talks about him with me. Eventually, she meets Andrew, who wants to marry her. They are in a serious relationship when Max is hired to work in Washington, DC. Max e-mails Carol occasionally, and they meet once for coffee, but nothing changes. Carol is committed to Andrew.

On one of my trips to visit her, she brings up Patrick. "I'm seriously worried about you. There's something about Patrick that is not right for you. I see another train wreck coming at you fast and hard. Why are you with this man?"

I don't know how to answer her.

Carol continues, "Think about what you're doing. We have talked about the reasons you and Dad divorced. You've told me you want a healthy and mature relationship. Please, Mom, don't spend your life with a man that can't offer you anything other than sex."

I stand up and walk to the restroom to get my anger under control. My twenty-five-year-old daughter is telling me how I'm screwing up again. When I return to the booth, I tell her, "I can't talk about this with you. I'm sorry. This is deeply personal to me, and I can't make you understand any of it, okay, Carol?"

She shakes her head. "No, it's not okay, Mom."

I pay the tab, and we leave. Carol has no furniture yet. It's her first apartment without a roommate, so I tell her to come to my apartment and take whatever helps. It's all used furniture, but she can take it all if she wants. I know how to start over.

A week later, she gets a van and takes the rocking chair, dishes, a bamboo chair, two bookshelves, a coffee pot, and some plants. I've kept Sam until she could get settled, but Sam is now going back to stay with her.

She does not bring up Patrick. When I ask her to stay for lunch, she answers, "Not today, Mom." She thanks me, hugs me, and leaves in a rush to get back to DC.

On Mother's Day, my boys drive up from Orlando to spend time with me. We eat at Sidewalk Café, and we laugh hysterically at the various, sometimes awkward memories we share. With every memory that triggers me, I fire back a positive. "Ryan, do you remember when I picked you up from school on your birthday, and the two of us took a train to DC? And Brock, do you remember how many times I drove from work to watch you play soccer then had to drive back to work? Do you remember how I stayed on the cul-de-sac playing baseball with you until you wanted to quit when I don't even like sports? You guys can't make me feel inadequate as a mother. Look at you two! You're winning in life. You're driving better cars than your mother. I must have done something right."

Ryan hands me a CD by Enya. "I found a song on here for you, Mom. I think it would be a good title for your book. It's the thirteenth brightest star in the universe, sixty-five times larger than the sun, Aldebaran."

We play the song while Ryan drives. Next thing I know, they've stopped the car outside of a tattoo parlor. Ryan grabs my left arm. Brock grabs my right arm. They drag me toward the tattoo parlor with me yelling, "No way, guys. I'm not going in there. You know how I feel about tattoos. Stop it! Stop pulling me!"

My boys are both over six feet tall, and I'm suddenly standing in a tattoo parlor while Ryan searches for the star Aldebaran. Next, I'm in a chair being poked a hundred holes per minute while my boys stand by and watch. Ryan says, "Always remember that you're a writer, Mom. This is a reminder from your sons. Write the book." Aldebaran is permanently tattooed on my upper left arm.

Before leaving for Orlando, Ryan and Patrick throw a few football passes back and forth. My boys don't seem to have a problem with him and ask no questions. When Ryan finds out Patrick loves astronomy, he tells him, "Take my mom out with your telescope to see Aldebaran."

My boys have touched my spirit. As I watch them drive away, I get emotional about how they thought this would be a good way to keep the writer in me alive. What a Mother's Day gift. What a gift that they are not judging me. I love them.

Patrick acts annoyed with how much time I spent with my sons. His mood grows dark. We go out to a bar. He angrily explains that he doesn't celebrate Mother's Day or ever talk to his mother. He talks about the hatred he has for her and how hard it was living in nine different foster homes, having to learn how to fight. When I suggest therapy might help with childhood issues, he yells, "Stupid bitch! What could you possibly know about it?"

I don't engage in the hostility, but I don't like being his target. I leave the bar. He follows me, continuing a loud verbal onslaught. "What the hell could you know about any of this? You had a mother and a father. You weren't raised in foster homes. Shut up about Mother's Day."

His behavior scares me. I ask him to leave for the night, and he leaves for a week. When he comes back, his behavior is even more controlling. He is jealous when I call my kids. When we go to bars, he doesn't like me talking to anyone. I wish our relationship could be like it used to be. I'm so confused by the changes that I'm back in therapy again. We move into separate apartments on the same floor of a building.

At a coffee shop one morning, I see a blind homeless man come through the door. I feel so sorry for him that I buy him a huge breakfast and ask him, "Would you like to take a shower at my place? Spend the night on my couch while I'm at work?"

He smiles and takes me up on the offer.

Patrick comes to my door, sees the man, and explodes. He sweeps the desktop contents onto the floor. A neighbor hears the ruckus and wants to call the police. I stop her and send Patrick away again. A few weeks pass with no contact.

A UPS package from Ryan arrives for me. It's my first cell phone. In the note, he writes, "I bought this for you so we can talk more. You are added onto my plan so no worries about the money. Call me when you can. I have news. Love you, Mama."

Ryan is marrying Christen in six weeks. I met Christen last Christmas, and I like her. I purchase two thrift-store outfits and buy an airline ticket. The wedding is fun. Christen's mother, Dulce, is from Cuba. There's three hours of dancing at the reception. I never stop.

Ryan wants me to move to Orlando. He calls daily and leaves messages. Some days, he calls multiple times. "Mom, there's no reason for you to live in Richmond. Please come and live here near Brock and me." He calls with the same message for months.

Patrick visits my apartment, but he constantly pulls me into fights. I grew up with parents and grandparents who didn't raise their voices, curse, or throw things. The day he takes a swing at me that connects, I throw him out. For eleven days, I cannot get out of bed. I won't face the world with a black eye. Wanda sends Dee, a trusted coworker, to find out what's wrong. She is kind and supportive and wants to help me, but there is nothing anyone can do. This isn't simply about rape, a hard life, drinking, or even an abusive boyfriend. My brain is not working, and I have never felt so depressed. My body is stuck in bed. Something is wrong.

Every good feeling felt with Patrick is *dead.* After twelve days of total shutdown, I start packing. I leave behind Patrick, my job, and an apartment with decent furniture. I pack plants, photos, writing, books, and clothes. I don't ever want to see Patrick again, but I won't forget that he gave me back a part of me that was taken away in the rape room. With 180 dollars in my checking account, I leave Richmond and drive eight hundred miles to Orlando. Eagles soar alone. I'm like all the wildflowers that have no name. I need to start life over.

Ryan, Christen, and Brock share a house. They don't know I'm coming until I call them from South Carolina. Ryan opens the door with a huge grin, singing along with the Dave Matthews song "Crash into Me" playing in the background. He hugs me tight. Christen and Brock are smiling. It feels right to be here. My beautiful sons rescue me.

Chapter 19

CRAZY BRAVE

WHEN YOU MOVE EIGHT HUNDRED miles away with only 180 dollars in your bank account, there are consequences. I jump from one Denny's to another trying to find one where I can earn more than fifty bucks a night in tips. My jeep has been repossessed, so I take the bus now. I have no health insurance. I'm penniless. Moving here feels like a mistake, and if it weren't for my boys, I would drive straight back to Richmond.

Florida's heat is merciless. It rains a lot. Even the birds stand still in the humidity. The only way to pick up some fast cash is to sell all my hardcover books to a used books store. Once I have the sixty bucks, I head straight to Muldoon's. It's a horseshoe bar in a Cape Cod style house with live bands, laughter, and lively conversations.

After three months, I find a job paying eight bucks an hour. I take the night shift so Ryan can pick me up there at 11:00 p.m. The office is fifteen minutes from Ryan's place by car but takes ninety minutes by bus.

I'm making enough money to survive but not enough to save for a car or my own place. Four months later, I'm still living with Ryan. Brock has moved out. There's not enough room for the four of us. Brock and I move his life by using cars. I'm the only one helping him.

The move is necessary for his independence. We spend an entire day moving boxes into an efficiency apartment where he will embrace solitude. I'm proud of him. He's living on his own for the first time.

My Richmond depression follows me to Orlando. Most days, I lie in bed until it's time to work. Ryan knocks at the door. "Mom, why are you lying in there? Please get up and do something."

I don't respond. He gets mad and knocks louder. I'm so low on energy, I am physically unable to stand. Something is wrong. I need a therapist. I need lab work done, and I have no health insurance.

The gift of being in Orlando is that Ryan and Christen are expecting a baby boy. It's my first grandchild. It gives me a reason to stop drinking or at least to slow down.

I'm only drinking two days with five days off rather than drinking all seven days a week as I did in Richmond. While sitting in a bar, I find a pamphlet in my purse that Mary gave me when she wanted me to go with her to Alcoholics Anonymous meetings. I never read it until now. It has twelve questions that indicate whether you have a drinking problem. I answer yes to all twelve. Their recommendation? "Get Help Now."

I tear it up and toss it in the trash. Screw AA. Their questions don't apply to me. I'm not an alcoholic. I drink, but I can take breaks from drinking. I don't start drinking vodka at seven o'clock in the morning. I'm working.

Eventually, I'm promoted to night manager of a company, supervising a staff of about sixty. I'm able to buy a used Mazda truck, find a small apartment in Winter Park, and stop off at Clicks after my shift to drink until 2:00 a.m. every night. My only day off is Saturday. I'm making more money than I ever have in my life. One-hundred-dollar bills are tucked under my mattress. My boys get one often. I'm falling in love with the almighty dollar.

Therapy is back on my list, and I can afford to pay out of pocket to meet with therapist number thirty-one, and on and on I move through therapists. None of them are helpful until I meet what seems like therapist number thirty-four, who is different from the rest because she asks a lot of questions that no one else has asked before. "Has any therapist recommended a full psychiatric evaluation, Debra?"

I think for a minute. "No."

She's writing down every word. "What about people who were close to you? Your husband, brother, your friends—did any of the people who labeled you crazy or knew how much you've struggled ever suggest you might benefit from seeing a psychiatrist?

I think back. "No, no therapists or people who have known me personally ever suggested that. Once, I was told to go on lithium, and I refused. Another time, it was Zoloft, and I refused. Why are you asking?"

She keeps writing and then looks at me. "It's concerning to me that no one who saw these behaviors—addiction to alcohol, bouncing from job to job, bad credit, inability to sustain a healthy relationship—did not suggest a psychiatrist. Has anyone in your family experienced mental health issues or was anyone an alcoholic?"

I give it some thought. "My grandmother Anderson was strange. She seemed angry and moody, and I did not like her. My uncle Paul was an alcoholic who stayed sober for decades and then relapsed in his later years. Another uncle died of alcoholism."

She sighs with empathy. "I want you to see a psychiatrist immediately."

This comes as a shock. "Why? Do *you* think there's something wrong with me?"

"I am not qualified to give a diagnosis. That's why I'm referring you to a psychiatrist, but I would not be referring you if I did not see indicators going back decades."

She writes the referral, and I stuff it in my purse. I'm not going to a psychiatrist. I function just fine. I'm never going back to her again either.

It's a Friday night at Muldoon's. I need to drink. I'm fighting the beast in me. I'm obsessing over the fact that my last therapist wanted me to see a shrink. A guy dressed like a funeral director sits next to me. He drinks Guinness and chain-smokes Camel Lights. I've never seen a man in a dive bar wearing a suit and carrying a briefcase. I find out he's a math professor who graduated from Case Western Reserve in Cleveland. With Cleveland in common, he talks a little more. "Where did you recently move from?"

I answer, "Richmond, Virginia. What's your name?"

I notice a French accent when he answers, "I don't give out my name in bars. I'm not here to meet people. The only reason I come is to relax after work. Please don't take it personally."

What an asshole. My head turns the opposite direction, and I say, "Well, I'm not comfortable speaking to strangers who won't share their first name. Please don't take that personally, Monsieur Arc de Triomphe."

Two beers later, after complete silence, he whispers in my ear, "My name is Zachariah. Everyone calls me Zac."

A full conversation about both our lives begins. He's the first person I've met in Orlando who speaks freely about anything. Nothing is off-limits. We like each other.

*****

One coworker and I click immediately. She sits in her cubicle with her high heels off, painting her fingernails, and smiling all the time. We become friends even though I'm a manager and she's twenty-five years younger than I am because we are both weirdos and love the weird in each other. Renee Kumar is beautiful and has a heart bigger than the state of Florida.

One night, Ryan appears at my office. "Mom, come with me. Can you please get off work? Christen is in labor. I really want you with me."

Ryan and Christen allow me to be in the room to witness the birth. What an honor. Ninety minutes later, Forest makes his entrance. I'm the first family member after his parents to touch my grandson as his tiny fingers curl around my pinky.

*****

With little notice, the company I manage is going out of business. I get drunk for a week before I start job hunting. Every couple of days, I check to make sure the psychiatric referral is still in my purse even though I have no intention of making an appointment.

My kids freak out when I take a job with Mears Transportation as a taxi driver. My plan is to make a grand a week, and when it is slow, I can write in the taxi. There's no GPS, and I'm not that familiar with Orlando since I've only lived here a year. I do not know where I'm going. Experienced drivers suggest arriving at the Peabody Hotel by six in the morning for a jump start to the day. All the fares are to the airport and usually include big tips. My trip to the airport fails when I get lost and my passenger misses his plane. Holy mother of God! During week one after paying for gas and rental of the cab, I clear twenty-seven dollars working seven days.

I buy a map and ask the passengers to help me figure out where we're going. I'm working from six in the morning until my last pickup at SeaWorld at ten at night. I sleep five hours a night. The only upside is I can't drink. Week four, I hit another snag when driving to the Florida Mall just forty-five minutes from the hotel. Three hours later, I still can't find it. My passengers beg me, "Please, please, take us back to our hotel. No more driving, please."

I pick up a woman passenger with kidney stones, and I can't find the hospital. A family of five wants to go to the Magic Kingdom. I drop them off at EPCOT. They all scream at me in Spanish. A family of four is so stressed out the wife slaps her husband across the face. I pull over and lecture her. When I drop them off, the husband hands me a fifty-dollar bill, the largest tip of my career as a taxi driver.

It gets to the point that if potential passengers are not staying on International Drive, I tell them, "Sorry, I don't know where you're going," and I drive off. But the word spreads to avoid cab 801—my cab—so sometimes when I stop to pick up passengers, they wave me away.

Brock and Carol tell me to quit. They're worried I'll be murdered. Ryan jokes about patting down my passengers for guns. "You're not thinking smart, Mom," he says. "No one should work a hundred hours a week for eighty bucks take-home pay."

When hurricanes Charley, Frances, Jeanne, and Ivan all hit Florida, Disney temporarily becomes a less-desirable destination, forcing me to quit. I'm totally broke. Checks have bounced, and my account is closed. I manage to get through the hurricanes by drunk dialing. My next Orlando job is seven days a week pitching environmentally friendly bacteria-producing enzymes also known as septic helper over the phone to people in rural areas eating meat loaf while I try and sell them. If any job is going to take me to the brink, it's this one.

My next therapist tells me my drinking problem is the result of my parents flip-flopping from evangelical Baptists to atheists. I don't go back. None of my problems have to do with childhood. I found that out when I became a mother. There's no such thing as a perfect childhood or perfect parents. We live in an imperfect world as imperfect beings.

Zac is still in love with a woman in Cleveland. It doesn't matter that it never works out. He and I become friends and lovers. We spend most Friday nights together. He loves talking to me about my writing. We really enjoy our conversations. We are intellectually a match.

Ryan and Christen get a divorce, and Brock breaks up with his girlfriend of a few years. Carol has reunited with Max, and they have chosen the wedding date: November 26, 2005. They will marry in a chapel then hold the reception in the huge ballroom at the train station. I'm so happy for my daughter. She is marrying the man she really never stopped loving. She calls me, saying, "Mom, you are the only guest I'm worried about inviting. You're the one who could ruin my wedding day. Please don't drink, Mom."

I force back tears. "Scratch that worry off your list. There's a zero chance I will drink before, during, or after your wedding. I am not touching alcohol while I'm with you. Let me come to DC. I want to buy your dress. I'm going to do everything I can to make your wedding day stress-free. Let's never have this discussion again, Carol."

By July, I have medical concerns but no health insurance. I need a friggin' colonoscopy, that long and winding road. A friend, who goes by the name Flap, and I are sitting at a bar as I tell him about the wedding, how I need money, that I have health issues but can't afford a doctor, how bad my drinking is, and feeling like I'm going to die soon. Flap listens to my whole life story over the next several weeks. He's an active listener and reminds me of Grandfather Anderson.

One Saturday afternoon, Flap looks at me and says, "I don't have money. I screwed up my life trying to be a famous country rock singer. I've listened to you talk, and I know there's something wrong with you, and it scares me too. Don't take this wrong or lightly, but the one thing I can do for you is marry you. You'd have great health insurance in thirty days. We don't have to tell anyone, and we can live together to share expenses or not. You can still see Zac, and we'll end the marriage when your life becomes stable. I can't stand by and watch you destroy yourself any longer. You seem like a really smart and good person that needs help."

"It's really sweet of you to offer, but it feels immoral. I couldn't do it, but thank you, Flap."

His argument is pragmatic, a marriage of convenience, no romance, no sex, no I love you—just access to health insurance. It takes only a week to persuade me. We meet at the courthouse, get married, tell no one, and a month later, I have health insurance. This might be one of the weirdest things I've done in my life, but I'm convinced I have cancer. I'm also worried about my brain. Who gets married for health insurance? Only those who are desperate.

Seeing a medical doctor is my priority. I find out I don't have cancer. Talking with a psychiatrist is next. After twenty minutes of questions, the doctor hands me a prescription for Lamictal. "This may be bipolar I disorder. Take this medication daily and see me in a month. However, if you break out in a rash, stop taking the medication and come to my office immediately."

The next morning, I wake up with a severe full-body rash and drive straight to her office. She looks at the rash. "Stop taking Lamictal. As soon as the rash goes away, come back, and I will start you on a different medication."

I read that Lamictal can cause a potentially fatal reaction called Stevens-Johnson syndrome. Not only that, how can she diagnose someone in twenty minutes when my life has been wrecked for decades? She doesn't know me or my story. All I did was answer twenty minutes of questions, and she treats me like I have an ear infection. I hate her. Bipolar disorder? What does she mean? I don't know anyone with that condition, except some of the inmates I worked with in corrections. Her diagnosis is a mistake. No one will ever know about this bipolar thing, especially my kids.

Flap has made me an authorized user of his credit card for Carol's wedding. He tells me straight up, "I believe you're going to find your way. I want to help you. She deserves everything you can give her. I want you to use this card so you can pay for whatever is necessary to show up as the mother of the bride with respect. It has a huge limit, so don't worry about that. All I need you to do is make the payments and pay it off as you can."

Flap helps make Carol's wedding day perfect. When I tell her what he did, she says, "This is the kind of guy you need to marry."

I will *never* tell Carol I married Flap for health insurance. She does not understand that level of desperation. My kids will never know about this marriage-of-convenience thing.

*****

Arthur Batson looks like a professional model. He's sizzlin' hot. He's the owner of the investor relations company where I interview for a job potentially paying six figures. He sends me to his brother's office for the second interview. Art concludes by saying, "I've owned this business for twelve years. No women have lasted. I'm not trying to scare you. I want you to know the facts. You go on straight commission in ninety days. You are required to build a book of clients. If you can't find new clients, this is not the right job for you. My employees make money, or they go elsewhere. You need thick skin. The stock market is a risky business, and it takes time to build relationships with financial advisors."

Market language is foreign language to me. What flips my light on is they pay me two thousand dollars a month for the first ninety days of probation, the hours are sane with weekends and federal holidays off, and Art Batson is caring. He asks if I can start the following Monday. "I'm going to give you a shot because I like you."

I'm in love with this new boss because he actually has a soul. During the interview, he showed me his grandmother's picture and tears fell down his face. And he's seriously *hawt.* Like Los Angeles modeling *hawt.*

To keep this job is the reason I need to go to Alcoholics Anonymous. In the first month, I succeed at getting new buyers to listen to my cold calls. Art raises my pay to three grand a month, which allows me to start paying Flap back.

Art uses me as an example in meetings with all the guys. "Look at Debra's call time. She spends more time on the phone than any of you."

Jeffrey, a coworker, takes a personal interest in helping me succeed. Almost every night, he gives me a few minutes of coaching. We become friends. Our office manager Carla is smart and capable of handling all of us. Although I love her fire and want to be friends, I keep a safe distance because no one at this job can know about my totally screwed up personal life. I don't drink with coworkers *ever!*

I attend AA meetings at five thirty on weekdays and Saturday and Sunday afternoons. I go straight to the bar after the meetings. A sober person cannot feel good on demand the way a drunk can. Not only have I found a real friend in Flap and a real job making real money, I have also found a therapist who tells me to take sobriety seriously. He wants me to meet with the psychiatrist at his office for an evaluation. He tells me the changes I want to make are possible provided I do the work.

"Going to bars after AA meetings is not how anyone gets sober," Jeff explains. "We can't move forward until you change that behavior. If you're not taking sobriety seriously, I cannot take you seriously. Do you understand?"

He wants to guide me every step of the way. We make weekly Saturday morning appointments. I feel lighter. This therapist is finally someone I can trust. His faith keeps me going to AA meetings. It's also becoming important enough that I stop filling up big 7-Eleven Gulp cups with beer to take into a meeting. I stop going to bars after the meeting. AA is the room that reeked of miracles that creates a spiritual thirst.

"One day at a time" is not working for me. I'm sober for five weeks, drink for two, sober for three months, drink for a month. I go through eleven sponsors. I refuse to do the steps. I buy books about alcoholism but refuse to say, "My name is Debra, and I'm an alcoholic." Instead, I say, "I'll pass."

I break all the rules of AA but continue to go to meetings. I hear the stories of how lives were destroyed by alcoholism, how men and women lost jobs, lost contact with their children, lost marriages. The stories of the brave people in these plastic chairs are what I love about AA. I manage to stay sober for nine months, never missing a meeting, never missing a session with my therapist Jeff, and never calling off work with a hangover. AA becomes my sanctuary, therapy my battleground.

Then out of nowhere, after almost a year of sobriety, my urge to drink grows strong. I start driving past the old dive bars. The beast wins, and I call off work and drink all day on a Sunday.

Flap and I share a condo. One day, I slip on olive oil on the kitchen floor and take a hard fall. Brock comes over to help me get into bed. The next day, I'm ordered to stay in bed by an orthopedist. My depression becomes so bad again, I don't get out of bed for a month. My body feels like I need a cab to get from the bed to the bathroom. I cry on the phone to coworkers and anyone else who listens. It feels like any gains I made are lost.

Art allows me to work from home. I try to hide my depression because I can't lose my job. Carla sends my paycheck every two weeks, and I work as much as I can. Before long, by five o'clock every day, I'm at the bar again. Now I'm drinking vodka and diet coke.

One morning, I am collapsed on the bathroom floor. My car is missing, and my purse is gone. Flap is gone. I have no strength to stand, and I lie there thinking about Jesus and about dying. I crawl to the bedroom to get my bottle of water. Hours later, I locate my purse and car parked in another parking lot close to the condo. I'm living one minute at a time.

The next day, I drive to Macaroni Grill because they sell alcohol. I order a glass of Riesling and food, which makes me physically sick. This is the worst I have ever felt. I don't know who the fuck I am anymore and why the fuck I fuck up my life every fucking time. Back at home when I get out of the car, I collapse onto the trunk and call my therapist Jeff. I cannot live one more day like this! Jeff is with a client, so I tell the receptionist, "It's an emergency. Please tell him to call me right away."

I stay lying on the trunk until he calls. "Deb. What's going on?"

I scream, "Please help me, Jeff! Please help me!"

He answers, "Are you drinking?"

I stand and answer, "Yes, but I'm not drunk. I need help."

"Where are you?" When I tell him I'm at home, he says, "Listen to me, Deb. Call a cab. I want you admitted right now. We have to do this now."

I ask, "Admitted where?"

"Go straight to South Seminole Hospital and voluntarily admit yourself. You need to be admitted to a mental health facility for a full in-patient evaluation. Can you do this, or do I need to do it for you? Are you suicidal?"

I'm crying, "No. There's something wrong with my body. It won't move. I can't work. I can't think. Something is really wrong with my head, Jeff. I'm scared."

I drive myself to the hospital, and two hours later, in a not-so-private, curtained-off section of the ER, I'm admitted to the psychiatric unit of the hospital. The only call I make is to Flap to confirm I have health insurance for this. He assures me, "Yes. Thirty days. Stay there until they find out what's going on." I'm exhaling relief.

He promises not to tell anyone but then breaks his promise, telling Ryan the truth. Ryan calls Carla and lies. Ryan knows I can't lose my job.

My belongings are taken from me and secured. I'm given a gown. When I fall into bed, I feel the weight of years of suffering. The room feels safe. It's like the universe put the brakes on my exterior world and rallied up my interior life to look deeply at what I've neglected.

Thank God for strangers. If it were not for Flap, I would've never landed in this safe place.

On day two, the questions begin, questions that go all the way back to the beginning of time. I see other patients who appear to be struggling more than I am. I think about the stigma, the struggles, and the hijacked hopes and dreams of all of us who are someone other than normal. A woman throws pillows at the wall. She talks about how she wanted to set her body on fire after losing a daughter. Her pain hits me hard. How could any mother survive that?

By day three, I want detachment. Life has taken too damn much from me. After all I've survived over the years, this hospital room, my bed, my pillow and blanket—this feels like home, and I want to stay here, sequestered from the real world. This is a silent retreat. The first vacation of my adult life. I'm tired of wondering if everyone is whispering, "She's crazy," yet the people in plastic chairs at AA believed in me. No one in those rooms called me *crazy*. Flap saw the real me on a barstool and never called me *crazy*. Jeff had expectations that I would heal. He never called me *crazy*.

I'm on four medications. A nurse speaks privately to me, "I don't understand how you survived. All the traumas, loss of life, and self. You've been through too much. I hope you consider going on disability. Your mind needs rest."

In this moment I realize how my dreams have energized me through decades of problems.

Everyone is kind to me and encourages me to leave the room, but I only leave for consultations. I prefer lying in bed. Time has stopped, and I have no clue how I'm going to be able to walk back out into the world again. Some people who come here never do. I could be one of them. My children are raised, and I've never felt the peace of solitude in a bed. I'm praying I can stay for months, not days. I need to be here. Christmas is spent in a psychiatric unit, and I don't care. The beast in me is resting. The sun is rising and beer, Madonna's music, and kettle chips are not the highlight of my day. With unblinking eyes, I spend Christmas staring up at the ceiling. My prayers grow wild. I feel my spirit slowly awakening.

After consultations and test results have been analyzed, the day finally arrives for a diagnosis. Everyone agrees that I have been suffering from bipolar I disorder for decades. It is evident in my mood swings, periods of depression, ruminating thoughts, insomnia, alcoholism, impulsive decisions like cutting off therapists who could have helped but whose advice I distrusted and dismissed, quitting good jobs, compulsive spending, bad credit, poor judgment, and failed relationships. They explain exactly what it means and which medications I need to stay on for life.

They praise the strength of my character, explaining how the combination of undiagnosed bipolar I disorder and trauma were especially challenging. According to the doctors, I handled it well. Mistakes I made were due to my brain chemistry. The alcoholism was self-medication. Bipolar disorder is not a weakness. It's a mental illness. Few undiagnosed people raise healthy children; few undiagnosed survive it in later years. I'm one of the survivors. All I needed for the past thirty years was more sodium for my brain and weeks of nothingness with mental health professionals. I needed more space.

One person finally understood that, one single person finally directed me to the appropriate care. I don't hate anyone for not doing something for me who repeatedly thought of me as *crazy*. My sanity will forever be due to a stranger in a bar, who saw something, did something, and cared enough to help. Flap, who gave me health insurance, this man is my North Star.

I walk in circles around the room and burst into tears. It has a *name*, bipolar I disorder, and it can be treated. On this day, a full-blown miracle happens as my mind and body are slowly releasing decades of negative energy.

The initial treatment is lithium, Cymbalta, Abilify, Xanax, and Ambien. The medications are monitored often and adjusted accordingly. The anger, shame, and hopelessness are gone. When I walk out of the hospital, *I never* pick up a drink again. The urge to drink is gone a few weeks after I begin treatment with appropriate medications.

As if I were promoted, I send announcement e-mails to everyone. "I'm bipolar, and there's treatment." I want the entire world to celebrate with me.

E. E. Cummings said, "It takes courage to grow up and find out who you really are." I get goose bumps thinking about the future and how everything is going to be bright, and I can grow old with my three children and do things that make them proud. All three of them are relieved that I have a real diagnosis. None of them are embarrassed, not even Carol. The best gift in all this is that my children see who their mother *really* is as I continue to heal.

I'm strangely in love with what the disciplines of this diagnosis means. I'm exercising daily, my diet is organic, I read—more reading. My body is back to a healthy weight. When I read a book now, I can remember what I read. Colors are more vivid. I notice the quality of the air and how coffee smells. I start to look at everything, including my moral code with more clarity. I smile at strangers and become a kinder person. I love who I am becoming.

The only sadness I feel is how long my diagnosis took. I'm fifty-five years old. I lost a huge part of my adult life to people, both personally and professionally, who were not paying attention to me. It was easier for them to call me *crazy*, treat me as an inferior, and write me off as someone with no hope. The signs were all there. Everyone who knew me saw them. I'm not feeling pity for myself. All I want to do is become a better person. Eventually, I'm able to let all of that go and not blame anyone for anything. None of this is anyone's fault. It's my responsibility to heal.

Even if it takes the rest of my life, I will write about this. My story needs to be heard, not because I'm special but for the sake of anyone with a mental disability who has endured harsh criticism and anxiety due to unkind and inaccurate labels. My story needs to go out into the world so others like me can refute the harsh criticism by our culture around mental illness.

When I return to work, I'm promoted a few months later to Art's first general sales manager. My credit score rises, and I'm no longer afraid of who I am. I feel strong and believe all my days of suffering are over. None of us really know we have hit rock bottom until we are on the way back up. Nothing will take me down to the bathroom floor again.

Part 5

THE TEENS

Chapter 20

THE BLACK AND WHITE OF LIFE AND DEATH

One of the many gifts of my diagnosis besides a sane inner life is economic stability. I'm paid well, and I hope to work with Art for a long time. My bonus is in the five figures this quarter. Money is not everything, but it's important. I'm finally free to buy what makes me comfortable, save a little, and enjoy spending money on others. I'm loving life right now.

What I want to do is throw Ryan a surprise thirtieth birthday party. I enlist Renee to help organize it. I've been sober three years and have enough money to rent a Hummer limo that's packed full of Ryan's favorite people, balloons, and snacks from Whole Foods. Ryan is not an easy one to surprise, so this takes some planning. The money I spend is well worth it when I see a few tears fall down Ryan's cheek as the limo pulls up and he realizes what I did. With his arm wrapped around me, he says, "Thanks, Mom. You shocked me. Thank you." Ryan hasn't cried since he was a toddler. He will remember this birthday long after I'm gone.

I would have been willing to sell my soul in exchange for a bipolar diagnosis earlier in life. Talk therapy is a part of my diet—to understand, forgive, and accept the decades of mistakes before the diagnosis—but it is challenging. I try to second-guess how I would have acted had I witnessed someone I cared about going through the hell I did. I would have had to do something to act on what I saw happening. Is it true that no one really cared enough about me to assist me with getting help?

So much from the past comes up. No doubt my children would've been spared a lot of chaos had they been raised by a mother who was properly diagnosed and medicated. Mental clarity gives me new insight into my true self as I attempt to measure and accept what was lost. I'm not stuck in the past but intend, making a future out of it somehow, someday.

There remains a stigma in our culture around mental illness, and it's wrong. *I am not my illness.* Many people in our country who are disabled cope with stress from how they are treated as well as from the actual disability. There's a nudge from my doctors and the universe to step out on the stage and speak about my experience. Every psychiatrist I have worked with believes more personal stories from those who have experienced mental illness need to be shared. I lost a large portion of my adult life to an undiagnosed disorder. It would be selfish to stand on the sidelines as my life gets better and not extend a hand to others. When I recognize certain familiar behaviors in other women, I realize *I was her.*

*****

Brock cries tears of joy after helping deliver his first child, *Noah.* I hear the baby's first cry from outside the birthing room. Noah and I bond when he is four minutes old. One month later, Ryan's wife Andrea gives birth to *Rose.* I am invited to be present. Andrea is like a lion and pushes Rose out with no anesthesia. I hold her hand the entire time and keep cold compresses on her face. I am honored to cut the cord. Carol is ecstatic to meet her first niece. Another of the many gifts of sobriety is that my grandchildren will never see me pick up a drink, nor will any of them see me drunk.

I attend the Unitarian Universalist Church. I enjoy both the teachings and the people. It is a community that celebrates justice, equity, and compassion. Rarely do I miss a Sunday service. It shines a bright light on my healing and writing each week.

I'm on my way home from work when Ryan calls, "What are you doing?"

"I'm throwing up lithium right now in a parking lot."

"Mom, you need to get off that drug."

I explain how it does not make me sick. It just makes me throw up twice a day.

He says, "Can you meet me at Publix on Aloma?"

It's on my way home. "I'm close by. Why?"

He hangs up. Ten minutes later, Ryan shows up in his new Lexus. With his promotion to sales manager, he is earning a six-digit salary. Ryan is making a lot of money for his father's company, and he is helping to grow the business. Not many are more comfortable speaking with people than Ryan. He sees something worthwhile in everyone he meets. I'm proud of his success. He wants me to drive his car, so I do. We take a half-hour spin, and I think about his five-hundred-dollar truck that would drive maybe five miles and then break down. Because of the way all three of my children grew up, they appreciate everything they have.

Ryan gets excited when he buys new appliances. Brock is happy with new clothes. Carol is living her dream and traveling. All three of my children own homes they bought themselves. They are thriving and loving life. Nothing is taken for granted because nothing was handed to them. They worked for everything from a young age. Maybe the guilt I have of raising them without everything needs to be put to rest.

Carol calls with heart-stopping news. She and Max are pregnant with twins. They move to a home in Arlington, Virginia, where the public schools are among the best in the state. Carol is now working for the Special Olympics International and travels internationally to many events. She has a staff, is being promoted to acting vice president, and will begin working directly with Timothy Shriver. She is also pursuing her doctorate in social policies at Catholic University.

How she will simultaneously travel for work, raise twin babies, and work on a doctorate, only my daughter knows.

When adult children begin having children of their own, there is an opportunity to appreciate or at least better understand their own mother's efforts. My daughter and my relationship is something that holds value now. Because the past includes some bad drinking memories for Carol, she respects my present sobriety. She also corrects her brothers who order alcohol for themselves when they take me out to dinner. She may not trust my determination to remain sober, but she is really trying hard to wrap her head around the diagnosis. It's another gift of my diagnosis that includes sobriety that I can tell my daughter is gaining respect for me.

One day, a call comes from Carol with a huge request. "I'm so nervous about leaving the babies in day care. If there were a day care at work, that would be okay, but there isn't. I'm trying to find a way to keep them out of day care until they are two."

I stop her. "Are you asking me for help?"

"Yes, I'm wondering if there's any possible way you could take care of them for two years. I know it means leaving your job and the boys—"

I interrupt her, "Honey, stop right there. I would love to come and help you." *Dear God, my daughter trusts her mother again.* What a moment. "I'm going to run this by Max and call you back, okay?" Five minutes later she tells me, "Max is more excited about this than I am."

We make plans over the next few days. Carol is put on bed rest at thirty weeks. She works from her bed at home. My move is scheduled for January 25, shortly before the babies' due date. She's covering all expenses, including my coming into Arlington to get an apartment. The move cost me zero dollars.

After Jade Olsen and Grant Miller are born six weeks early, I drop everything and take a plane to Arlington. The preemies are discharged from the NICU breathing on their own. My daughter and I take shifts during the night. When one baby cries, the other cries. Carol wants everything documented. We both make do with only three or four hours of sleep for two weeks. I'm back in Orlando for only one week when Carol calls, "Can you come back? We are losing our minds over here." The move is still scheduled for January 25, but I agree to come immediately and stay until a week before the official move.

It's January 19. Carol wants to take her warm heart out into the crystalline joy of winter for a walk with her boys. They are wrapped in layers, shielding them from the cold. The snow crunches under our boots as we walk out the driveway. Two pairs of eyes open and close above pink cheeks as we walk the tree-lined streets under the low gray sky. For the first time since my diagnosis, Carol brings up a stored memory, "When I was at the University of Virginia, I was so worried about how you were acting that I went to a therapist."

My first reaction is shock. "Really? What was the outcome?"

She stops a minute to check on the boys. "My therapist told me *then* you were probably bipolar. I didn't want to tell anyone. I was only twenty." By the look on her face, I know she feels bad about not sharing this with me when she first learned it.

I put my arm around her. "Well, she was right, and it's all okay now as long as you understand that anything you saw that was disturbing was not just me but the side effects of an undiagnosed mental impairment. Do you understand the difference now?"

"Yes, of course, I do."

She changes the subject to her babies. We walk another hour while having one of our best talks since she became an adult. I remind her of the many good things I did for her, and she remembers. It feels so good to have a real conversation about hard things.

I get a real boost of integrity from our long walk and talk in addition to the respect and trust my daughter demonstrated by asking me to stay with her children. This is the first time since she was in high school that I feel like she needs me. There's not a chance I would decline this time with her. Our relationship is starting to heal.

While walking home, it occurs to me my phone is back at the house. "I wonder if Ryan has answered any of my texts by now. You know your brother and texting. He always responds. I sent him a couple of e-mails earlier too, but nothing came back."

When we get home, there are multiple messages on her phone and mine, saying, "Call immediately."

As I listen to messages, Carol calls her dad. Her face looks pained. I grab the phone from her. "Listen to me, Deb. This is really bad news. Please sit down."

I don't sit. "What's wrong with Ryan?" I'm instantly numb with a racing mind.

Mason says, "He's in a coma on life support. Brock and I are in the emergency room, and they are transferring him to the ICU. How soon can you get here?"

I freeze, and Carol grabs me while I feel a blow to my body. We are crying, holding on to one another, feeling the same fear of a threat. She calls Max, asking him to come straight home. There are no flights to Orlando out of any airport until tomorrow morning. For the next few hours, I call everyone I can think of to find out what happened to my son. All they can say is he never showed up to get Rose at day care. He was found in his work chair unconscious. They rushed him to the emergency room, where he was put on life support. Right now, scans are being done to see what happened to his brain. No one knows anything more.

Renee wants to pick me up at the airport, so I collapse into bed and proceed to watch the clock all night, anxious to be in Orlando, anxious to hear that my son is doing better. While waiting to board, I call Carla. "Oh, dear God. Oh my god. This is not good. I wish you were not alone right now. Please call me when you get there and when you know anything."

She stays on the phone with me until it's time to board. Carla and Renee are my two best friends in life, my most sacred vessels.

For the entire two-hour flight, I lean my head into the seat in front of me. It never moves. I can only tell myself we will get answers about what happened, and Ryan will get better. He'll need help with recovery. He can move with me to Arlington. I can handle him and still help Carol. Ryan is going to be okay. He's going to be okay. I say this over and over until my Jet Blue flight lands in Orlando.

Renee and I stay at the hospital all night. She holds my hand. We sit by him, stand up, walk, sit back down. Neither one of us eats or sleeps. My son lies motionless from an intracerebral hemorrhage. Without warning, it took his vision. When he wakes up, he will be blind, another massive blow to my heart. The nurse tells me he needs to learn how to walk and talk all over again. Dear God, hear my prayer.

When I hear the report, I don't believe it. "Don't you dare die, Ryan. Do you hear me? This is your mother talking to you. Wake up. You can't leave me. I love you. I love you. I love you."

Another night nurse says if he survives, my son will be in a vegetative state. I can't hear it. "Bullshit! It's all bullshit! He almost died once, and he made it. Ryan has the spirit to live to one hundred. He is not going to die!"

He's my shining extrovert son who loves his mama. It's a gift to be best friends with your son. He is not dying on me. I know Ryan. *He will not die.* Life stops for our family as we wait together, hour by hour, for a miracle.

Carol and Max drive from Arlington to Orlando with their newborn babies. When Carol takes her first step into Ryan's room, she throws her coat against the wall. "What the hell happened to my brother?"

People are coming and going, but no one except immediate family is now permitted in Ryan's room. The relaxed attitude of Ryan's neurologist makes me angry. He shines a light into Ryan's dull, unblinking eyes. It seems like my questions are a waste of his time. I want Ryan transferred to another hospital.

Hope is not dead until the heart stops beating. Ryan's heart is beating strong. My eyes are locked on his breathing. All I know to say is, "I love you. I love you. I love you." That's all I want him to hear if he can hear anything. *I love you, I love you, I love you.*

It's Friday afternoon. I've spent twenty-nine hours in this room without food or sleep. Ryan's doctor calls Mason and me out into the hall and says, "Ryan has no neurological function of the brain. The brain stem has separated, which means there's no coming back from this."

I don't believe it. "Show me. I need proof of what you're telling us."

He looks down. "The proof is in the scan."

Mason and I look at each other. "Show us the scan."

The three of us walk down flights of stairs into a basement. The doctor explains everything. We listen. He shows us where the stem is separated, which means Ryan is brain dead. There is no recovery when a person is brain dead. *My son is going to die.*

The news spreads fast, and more people come and wait. Nurses talk to Mason and me about when we want to take him off life support. They explain how long after removing the support it takes for his heart to stop. I tell the nurse, "If he's going to die, then I don't want to watch him like this." Knowing my precious, spirited son will never open his eyes, laugh, talk, or be here to raise Rose and Forest is emotionally unbearable. Mason and I decide to take him off life support at nine o'clock that night.

At exactly nine o'clock, the nurse removes my son from life support. Andrea and Christen, the mothers of Ryan's children, are there. Max and Carol, Mason and his wife, Brock and Stacy, and Flap, a total of nine of us surround his body. Each one of us holds on to a part of it. I'm at the top of the bed, resting into his shoulders, holding his hand and sobbing. We are all sobbing. My hands move across his face and head. We all say, "I love you, Ryan." Mason picks up his son's foot and kisses it. A hundred times we say, "I love you."

At nine-thirty-seven, my son is pronounced *dead.* He is thirty-three years old. He dies as I lay my head on his head, his shoulder. He dies two days after being admitted to the hospital. We had him for only two days after admission. Two days, and he's gone.

He woke up on a Tuesday morning and took a shower before going to work. A few hours later, he slipped into a coma. He had called me the night before to talk about seeing a movie at the Enzion when I got back. Nothing was physically wrong with him, except a few friends told me he complained of high blood pressure. Ryan shared so many things with me, including things I did not want to hear. He never told me he had high blood pressure. He did not tell the one person who would have insisted he see a doctor and get treatment.

Renee drives me back to his house. When I walk through the door, I feel the deepest regret about not spending more time with him. Renee stays with me awhile, and I try to plan practical next steps, such as buying Rose a dress for the memorial service, anything to avoid talking about my dead son. When she leaves, I sit in the chair I bought for him. The two teacups we drank from are still on the coffee table. I can still remember the steam rising up from our last cup of tea together. We sat and talked about my move to Arlington. We talked about his graduation ceremony and how we would both attend. His cap and gown are on the kitchen counter. I hold them up to picture him in them, and I sob.

I cannot sleep. The Ambien is not working because *I'm petrified.* I have no idea how any of us survive this. Carol always said, "No one makes me laugh harder than Ryan." Brock lost his best friend. How will Forest and Rose grow up without their father?

Ryan was the family conductor. He orchestrated every holiday, every occasion that brought us together. He knew what was going on with everyone in the family. He was the glue that held us all together. He was head chef, and I was his assistant. He loved cooking for people and sending leftovers home with them. He was a gentle giant who loved to make us laugh.

I sit on the side of his bed, look into his dresser mirror, and say out loud, "You will not start drinking. You will not spend one day in bed over this. You will not relapse." I make myself a promise not to destroy what took fifty-five years to create. I'm going to keep that promise. Ryan wanted me to write a book. He titled it. I promised him I would. I'm keeping that promise too.

I sit on the couch and pick up the teacups. After a few minutes, I throw them in the outside garbage can. None of this makes sense. How can my son be gone in two days?

I walk into his room, get several of his shirts, and collapse onto the couch where we last sat together. His scent is still on a couple of the shirts. I breathe it in. I can smell my son. There's wild rain beating against the window panes. I hear it and remember Lance's arm around me when we ran from his car to the house in pouring rain. He told me, "You and I could live together the rest of your life,

Mom, if nothing else ever works out for us. You and I could always survive."

The crying begins again. I can't stop crying. It's a suffocating feeling. My heart fell to my feet. I love my son *so much.*

Chapter 21

MY PRAYER FOR PEACE

IN MY MIND, THERE'S A relentless replay of the moments between learning Ryan was on life support until his last breath—the ICU nurses coming in and going out, his dead brown eyes, the monitors the moment his heart stopped. I can smell the room where he died. For at least one hour each day, I collapse on the living room couch because the mental images of my dying son force me there. If I didn't stop and let the images move through me, it feels like they would take up permanent residence in my head, causing unforgiving pain, preventing me from remembering Ryan alive.

Witnessing the death of my child divided life into two parts. One half of me feels dead. The other half is merely pretending I can live life without my son. Grace as a grieving mother in the first few days is God's power that shows us what we need to do to survive.

A few of us are meeting at Brock's to tell Forest his father died. Ryan's time with Forest was short but packed full of family activities, sports, and laughter. I doubt that any seven-year-old can understand the purpose of a memorial service or grasp how permanent death is, but he picks up on the sadness in the room and sits quietly next to his mom, unable to express his feelings or ask questions. We all process loss differently. Rose, who is two, is much too young to understand.

Flap is moving to Arlington with me. This is not the time to be making life-changing decisions. He was close to Ryan and is grieving too. All three of my children love him.

Carol calls. "Your apartment has everything in it. Max's father has offered to move both of you and your car via Amtrak to make the move easier on you. Any idea how much stuff you'll be bringing?"

After a pause, I answer, "I had intended to give almost everything to Ryan. The things I'm bringing can be loaded into the Volvo. Tell Max's father thank you."

The ride on Amtrak takes twenty hours. I'm practically in the fetal position the entire time, staring out the window in shock. I don't speak to anyone.

The apartment on Monroe Street in Arlington is a little over five hundred square feet. Carol has forgotten nothing. There is art on the walls, brand-new furniture, and a fridge full of food. She even bought me a "grief chair." Her card reads, "Every mother needs her own chair to sit quietly, comfortably to deal with this kind of loss."

The apartment is three blocks from the metro and five minutes from Carol's house. Arlington has an energy I've not seen anywhere else I've lived. I hear foreign languages spoken everywhere I go. Many people walk, run, and ride bikes. There are lively restaurants. Everyone seems kind, smart, and healthy.

Brock and Stacy are in Arlington when we arrive. He and Ryan were scheduled to meet their two nephews and watch the Super Bowl game together. For most of the visit, we gather around Carol and Max's kitchen table, talking about Ryan, eating good food, and drinking adult beverages. I'm not touching alcohol. I'll stay sober in the aftermath of my son's death. The best part of my son's visit with his wife is we played Scrabble at my apartment. We actually enjoyed the company. It was pathway for grief to settle for an hour.

I grieve for Ryan, but I also feel my children's loss of their brother, especially the severe loss Brock feels. He was close to his brother his entire life. It's as if a part of his own identity has disappeared. For the first year, I plan to fly into Orlando every six weeks to spend a weekend with him. I cook food, stay up late and talk to Brock, and stock their fridge with food. My grief will not spill onto

Brock's grief. When I go there, I try and help him. His grief sounds as bad as mine.

For the first month, my day begins with the alarm clock going off at 4:00 a.m. We arrive at Carol's by five to give her and Max one extra hour of sleep if the babies are awake. Carol and Max wake up each morning to a fresh pot of coffee and come home to a dinner I've prepared. Being with Carol feels like a heal-your-heart boot camp. She talks with me in the first few months for as long as I need to talk.

When I get home, the first thing I do is log on to Facebook. Ryan created my account, but I rarely used it. Now I'm becoming addicted to it since hundreds of people are reaching out to me from across the country. I start another page titled "Shine On, Ryan," where mothers show up with their own personal stories of losing a child. For me, Facebook is therapeutic. It serves as a channel for my grief. It's the only place where I can speak freely, and people reach out to me. I'm not alone when I'm on Facebook.

Carol makes an appointment for me at the William Wendt Center in Washington, DC. I attend Saturday sessions with a grief counselor. After giving birth to and raising a child who grew up to become one of my favorite adults, it is such an indescribable emotional blow to now live without him. As the shock wears off, the anger, guilt, fear, and overwhelming sadness are all I feel. The guilt I feel is lethal.

The psychiatrist who assists with my medications for bipolar wants me to stop taking lithium. Depakote is added to my list of medications. All other meds stay the same.

Jade and Grant are positive distractions who keep me busy all day long. It's double the diapers, double the feedings, double the baths, double the love. Max and Carol suffer from sleep deprivation until Max decides to train the boys to sleep longer. Carol can't do it. She high-fives her husband when, within a few days, both boys are sleeping five hours at a time. Carol and Max leave home by seven to catch the metro and arrive back home by six.

When Carol travels I spend the night. My days are busy taking care of the boys, running errands, doing laundry, encouraging their attempts to walk and talk, and playing continuously. I'm up and down two flights of stairs all day long. My osteoarthritis is not responding to over-the-counter anti-inflammatory medication. My knees swell to twice their normal size. My right leg is hard to bend enough to get in the car when I leave each day. Flap has to rub it to reduce the pain.

While sitting on the front porch with the babies one afternoon, my phone rings. It's a friend from long ago calling out of the blue. Shayla and I were high school majorettes together. I haven't spoken to her in decades. She suddenly lost her fifteen-year-old daughter Jolie to meningitis. She is the first mother I speak with who lost a child. She encourages me to believe Ryan's death is survivable; she gives me hope. I feel so much relief knowing she understands how the grief of losing a child is different. This grief does not have stages or closure. It's a constant for a long time. It takes raw guts for her to reopen emotional wounds and share her pain. Everything she tells me makes sense. Shayla is a godsend. I can't thank her enough. We stay in touch and plan to get together one day.

If Carol had not hired me to take care of my precious grandsons, I may well have spent each day in the grief chair, gazing out the window. The first Christmas without Ryan I spend alone at a Waffle House restaurant, playing with the hash browns on my plate while trying to read a book. The words fly across my brain. I can barely finish a sentence. All I wanted was to be left alone.

The grief is harder in year two than in year one. I miss my jolly, extroverted, big-hearted son and all the beautiful little things that used to annoy me. Triggers are everywhere. I break down at the most inconvenient places. A bottle of hot sauce forces me to leave the store. The Food Network channel makes me cry. I can't look at photos of Ryan, but I cling to his blue sweater. I try to attend a Compassionate Friends meeting but walk out in the middle of it. I can't listen to mothers who have experienced the holy terror of losing a child of any age from one month to fifty years old from cancer, suicide, overdose, texting and driving.

Age or cause of death do not mitigate the grief process. Grief is not something we let go of; it's something we learn to carry. I haven't learned how to carry it yet. It's too heavy. My grief comes with anger and guilt. It comes with insomnia. I light candles for Ryan at night, speaking into the silence, hoping he's somewhere hearing me, and looking for a sign from him. My grief counseling continues. I realize I don't want to give more power to death than to life.

During the spring of 2012, the twins reach fifteen months old. The physical stress of a job that requires me to be on my feet all day long has become crippling. I see an orthopedic surgeon who tells me, "You really don't have a choice at this stage. Cortisone shots will not help. You need a double knee replacement, or you may end up in a wheelchair."

When I research double knee replacement, I choose to do one at a time, starting with the right knee. The scheduled surgery forces Carol to quickly find another caregiver for the boys. She's not happy, which makes me feel horrible for her. After my total knee replacement, I'm so grateful to have Flap with me in Arlington. He assists with ice and groceries, and we take daily walks together. He comes with me to rehab three times a week. Being stuck in a chair all day long is giving me too much time to think about Ryan. The seventy pounds I lost is back on my body. I don't care.

I'm barely functioning and not talking to anyone but Carol, Brock, and Flap. My psychiatrist makes a change in my medications. It helps a little. Flap and I continue to take my walker to the metro and beyond to grief counseling. Two years after Ryan dies, I'm still sober. If losing a child does not throw me into a full relapse, nothing will. Holy mother of God, I have not picked up a drink. Sobriety is not for the weak.

It's year three. Flap and I move to Richmond, where things are familiar and affordable. I'm ready to attend Compassionate Friends where I meet hundreds of mothers who have lost a child. With the acceptance and support of my army of wounded healers, I begin to face the realities of losing Ryan and mark my own progress toward healing. The facilitator asks me to take over the Richmond chapter, and I put my grief to work. Every mother who walks through the door at St. Andrew's Church for the first time is paralyzed with grief.

The grief community is similar to Alcoholics Anonymous. Through listening and sharing with other grieving mothers, we each carve our own path to discover a way through. We are powerless over death. Every mother knows if there were anything we could've done to save the life of our child, we would have done it.

I'm now living in a basement apartment with no kitchen. My cooking is done on a hot plate. I decide to go on social security to write my book. Authors encourage writers to work with a team. Over fifty people volunteer their time. Some are not avid readers. Others are just curious about my story. Eventually, the reader group reduces down to fifteen. I'm writing seven days a week.

Nine months later, Max and Carol also move to Richmond. They buy their dream home. It's a 1905 eight-bedroom home on one acre in historic Ginter Park. Carol renovates it while working on her dissertation. Carol is offered a professorship at Randolph-Macon College. She is filling in for Tim Kaine, who is Hillary Clinton's vice president choice. Baby Landon becomes the fifth member of the family. I take care of him while Carol is at work.

For three months, I've had a lingering cough that my primary care physician dismisses as allergies. When blood appears with the cough, I demand an ultrasound, which indicates nodules and a goiter. My next step is to see an ear, nose, and throat doctor who removes my thyroid. The goiter turns out to be a tumor. The pathology report comes back benign, and the cough disappears. I know there are gifts of recovery. However, since my recovery began, I have lost a child and undergone two surgeries and feel like I'm unemployable.

I need to pray for peace. During a half-hour prayer, I ask God to please protect my two children and me. Please give guidance to my readers. Please don't let anything happen that will stop me from finishing my book. Please grant sanity in my life until I can finish writing. And I make a promise to God that the rewards will be spiritual, that I understand I have no control over how the universe receives my story. It's the first time I've prayed in years. I'm on my knees with tears in my eyes. It's a prayer for peace. *Four months later, Carol is diagnosed with breast cancer.*

It's the first year in which I have felt some sense of normalcy after the loss of Ryan. But now another nuclear bomb has dropped in my lap with Carol's cancer. I try to convince myself that first, breast cancer is survivable; Carol will survive it. Second, how many mothers lose two children? Less than two percent who live to be ninety. There's no reason to panic. Carol will get her noncancer life back. My focus is to fight for her and with her every single day. Whatever the need, I'm one text away.

Alcoholism was like a parasite under my skin. I'm proud every single day of my sobriety. How would I be here for my daughter if I were drinking. God…bless…me and all the humans who sat in the basements and churches with Alcoholics Anonymous. The recovery stories helped me recover. It's another miracle.

The toughest challenge for me is that Carol is no longer my little girl. At thirty-nine, she makes her own decisions. Every decision she's made in life has been smart and right. I'm supporting her the way a mother should. She's never given me a reason not to since age twelve.

Meanwhile, I continue writing. Chapters are sent to the readers while I attend to my daughter's needs, including helping with her three boys under the age of four. Therapy is needed again, and I'm fortunate to find a woman who meets me where I am. We talk twice a month, and she supports me with my grief, my writing, and Carol's cancer.

Thanksgiving arrives, and Brock and Jenn spend it at Carol's home. We enjoy dinner gathered around the dining room table, and everyone gives thanks. Carol is off chemo this week, and it's the first time in months she can enjoy a little wine. When dinner is over Max, Carol, Brock, and Jenn go to the historic Jefferson Hotel. Brock proposes to Jenn at the top of the elegant red-carpeted staircase. Jenn accepts, and our family has something to celebrate.

Hysteria breaks out in the living room by the fire when Brock complains to Carol about his foot and the boot he needs to wear. She compares cancer to an ankle sprain with words that only the Mak offspring could understand. She compares his Tylenol to her chemotherapy as the bantering between Carol and Brock continues for two hours. Carol lets it all out. I'm in tears laughing. It's the first time since Ryan died that our family is having the kind of dark humor we had for thirty years. It's laughter only my children and I could appreciate. My daughter took the stage. What amazing grace she has while fighting for her life.

Carol is in Brock's beachfront wedding in Clearwater, Florida. When I see her dancing, my heart dances with her. There's no language for the feeling a mother has when her child is cancer-free. Her wavy hair is growing back; eyebrows, eyelashes, toenails are back. The cancer that was in her body is gone in November 2016. *Gone.*

Christmas 2016 is a happy time with family, food, and wine, with fireplaces lit. Forest, Christen, and Rose spend a week with us. Christen brings her parents. There's a sound of laughter in every room. The holiday season is perfect.

Carol is taking a spin class and returns to work with the Special Olympics. She wakes up early to walk her one-hundred-pound dog Lola and takes care of her three sons. Grant and Jade are in kindergarten, and Landon is almost three. Her energy returns, and she's happy and humbled to be a cancer survivor. The only complaint she has is a little back pain and substantial vision loss. When I ask her about both, she answers, "I've seen the doctor, Mom. It's a side effect of the tamoxifen. Everything is fine."

I know she's fine because she's texting me about politics five times a day.

In January, she and I are invited to attend a roundtable political discussion with fifteen women. When Carol starts talking politics, she's unstoppable. She does her research and is a formidable debater. She is bold, influential, cause driven, and wants social and political change. She has chosen social policies for her doctorate. It suits her. For me, the best part of the night is listening to her.

We are encouraged to attend the Women's March, a worldwide protest the day after the inauguration. It's on the anniversary of Ryan's death, so I decline. That is one day I spend in spirit with my son. Carol also declines. That surprises me.

The Special Olympics needs Carol in Vancouver at the end of January. I agree to stay with the boys for five days, but I worry as Carol leaves because it's obvious her back pain is worse. Grant tells me, "Mommy throws up sometimes when she eats." She reminds me again that it's the tamoxifen and that some cancer patients must take another drug for the side effects. She sounds confident.

Once she's back home, the texts about politics stop. She meets me at the door and does not want me to come into the house. There's something wrong. When Valentine's Day comes, Max is out of town for work, so I pick up the boys from school. I take them to dinner. We buy Carol flowers and a teacup, and they each write a note on the card. When I call her, she says, "Keep them as long as you want. I'm resting." My daughter does not rest unless she is sick.

She's refusing my help with baths and wants me out of the house. "It's okay, Mom. They are going to bed right after baths, and so am I." Carol never goes to bed at 7:00 p.m.

The next time I speak to her, she's in bed at 5:00 p.m. For three weeks, she is not texting me or wanting me around for more than five minutes. I don't hear the voice of my daughter. *I hear cancer talking to me.* Signs are everywhere by the end of February that this is more than the side effects from tamoxifen. There's a difference between imagining what could be wrong and knowing what's wrong. I need to know. *I brace myself.*

Chapter 22

DEAR DAUGHTER

February 25, 2017, Saturday

My daughter outshone herself with today's event. It's Landon's third birthday party, and Carol has rented a guesthouse at Maymont Park with a trolley to carry guests to the petting zoo, the nature center, and the gardens. She has arranged for fruit, cheese and veggie trays, Chic-fil-A nuggets, raspberry lemonade, coffee, and birthday cake. At least thirty chubby-cheeked toddlers and their parents are here to help Landon celebrate. Watching them makes me smile. The first beam of morning sun to penetrate the clouds flashes across the sky, briefly turning it light orange. I pull in a deep breath that tastes like mint.

Carol vomits four times in the first hour. She looks weary and walks like she's in pain. "Don't forget I bought gluten-free cupcakes for the kids with allergies," she reminds me. She told me this five times yesterday. My daughter normally does not repeat herself.

"I can tell you are not feeling well enough to be here," I speak to her privately. "Please consider going home. I can handle the party, and Landon will never remember when he's older that his mother didn't feel well on his third birthday. Please don't be stubborn. Just leave and get some rest. I can take care of everything here."

I rub her back, but she pushes my hand away and says, "Don't do that. My back hurts today. No worries, Mom. I'm okay to stay. Just feeling sluggish. My joints have been stiff. It's not a big deal."

She spends most of the two hours sitting, trying not to draw attention to how she feels, but others notice. A few ask me what's wrong. I eventually take charge and end the party early, fearful that this is more than stiff joints. Carol asks me to come back to her house to help Landon open gifts. On the way, I blast music on my car radio to drown out my anxiety that made me fat again.

Carol collapses on the couch like a wounded soldier. She occasionally shoots a worried glance at me. Otherwise, her eyes stare up at the ceiling, detached from Landon's excitement about his presents. I ask her, "Can I make you a cup of green tea with ginger? That should help your nausea."

She answers, "Sure, thanks."

While making tea, I ask Max, "What's going on with Carol?"

"You need to ask her," he replies.

Carol takes a few small sips of tea and throws up two or three times.

"Honey, please tell me what's wrong with you."

There is a vacant look on her face. "Mom, it's nothing. Most likely I'm getting smacked hard with side effects from tamoxifen. The drug often needs another drug for its extreme side effects. With some patients, it's not tolerable at all. Let's not panic about this, okay? Everything is fine, Mom."

"When do you see the oncologist?" I ask.

"Monday or Wednesday, I don't remember. I need to check the date and time."

She doesn't remember her next oncology appointment? "How long have you been throwing up like this, honey?"

"Mommy throws up every day," Grant interrupts. "When she ate a Girl Scout cookie, she threw up, Grandma. It was her favorite one, the thin mint cookie."

Max directs the boys to play outside.

My daughter, who is supposedly cancer-free for the third month after fifteen months of grueling treatment, is protecting me. When I lost Ryan, her mission toward me became *protect my mother*. I'm the last one to get medical updates.

When Max mentions the twins are doing a sleepover with the neighbor boys, I ask, "Why don't I take Landon for the night? With all three boys gone, you'll relax better. Good idea?"

Carol agrees. "Yes. Thanks, Mom. Max, can you pack a bag with everything Landon needs for an overnight?"

Carol has not left the couch all afternoon except to vomit and to follow me to the front door. She gives Landon a kiss. "I love you. Happy birthday."

I yell back from my car, "Please watch a movie and rest. Have good sex with your husband." As soon as I blurt this lame attempt at humor from my unfiltered brain, I realize how inappropriate it is. Carol is sick, and no one is laughing.

"Screw all that. I'm going straight to bed," she responds and closes the front door. It's four something in the afternoon. Carol does not ever go to bed at four in the afternoon.

I escalate into my massive anxiety disorder, swallow two clonazepams, and drink a large Diet Coke. I make a quick call to my friend who has Pollyannaish optimism and tells me I'm overreacting. His phone call, the antianxiety meds, and my grandmotherly love help me ensure that Landon enjoys the rest of his special day. He throws all his toys on the floor and wants me on the floor with him reading books and making food out of Play-Doh. He squeezes an entire tube of bubble bath into the tub and uses all my Tupperware to pretend he is making soup. We laugh a lot. Then Landon and I snuggle in the rocking chair, and even though I have rocked my three children and six grandchildren, this moment with my youngest grandchild asleep in my arms on his third birthday is a precious moment I will never forget.

Day two: February 26, Sunday

Sunday morning brings blueberry doughnut holes, apple slices, milk, and my version of Twitter—birdsongs. Landon loves the

Children's Museum, so we head there before taking him back home. As I drive north on I-95, my cell phone rings. Carol screams, "My cancer is back, Mom! My cancer came back!"

I press down so hard on the brakes of my Toyota that it starts to slide and scares Landon. With static in my head, I say out loud, "Get off this highway. Find a parking lot."

Carol is sobbing and screaming while I drive. "My cancer is all over my body! It's in my lungs, my liver, my bones, Mom!" She repeats the same horrifying words over and over as I exit the freeway onto streets with traffic starts, stops, red light, green light until finally, a CVS parking lot. I stop the car.

"How did you find this out, Carol? What do you mean it's all over your body? Honey, there must be a mistake. This is not possible. Please, please, Carol, calm down for one minute, okay? I'm only a few minutes from your house. On my way, I'm going to call your doctor. Stay calm, honey."

She continues a crying fit that I've never heard from my daughter in her forty-one years of life. "The doctor just called. The cancer is in my lungs, bones, liver. It's all over me, Mom."

The walls, all of the walls I so carefully erected starting on day one of her breast cancer diagnosis, are collapsing. This is not happening. This cannot be happening.

Carol hangs up, and I hit my head several times against the headrest. How stupid of me to tell my daughter to calm down. I am so angry with myself and with that doctor. Why didn't the doctor call Carol into her office with this news? Why call a patient at nine fucking thirty on a Sunday morning with a cancer recurrence like this? Is Max with her, or is my daughter alone right now getting this news? With trembling hands, I grip the steering wheel so tightly that my fingernails dig into my palms. I forget that Landon is in the back seat until I hear the crack of his sweet-pea three-year-old voice, "Grandma, is my mommy sick again?"

I turn around and rub his little leg, answering, "Yes, Mommy is sick, but we are going home to take care of her, okay?"

Landon stares out the window. I keep talking to him, but he does not respond. Landon sucks his thumb. I shut off the radio. Silence.

Fear is a hallucinatory trip, a kind of madness. For nearly five decades, fear had its way with me, but at age sixty-five, I've learned to take fear by the hand, feed it faith, let it wake me up, and ignite me to do things in life that need to be done. I own it and even trust it. Fear is part of being human, being bipolar, being a mother of a daughter who could be on her deathbed.

I am afraid to meet Carol face-to-face after that phone call. I am terrified of losing another child. But right now, I must take hold of my fear and walk through Carol's front door. I need a couple of minutes for my insides to thaw from what feels like buckets of freezing-cold ice water dumped all over me. My best skills—caregiver, warrior, protector, even comedian—all available to those I love and to myself in times of suffering suddenly seem nonexistent.

As I walk in, Carol grabs me. We hold on to each other fiercely, cry softly, and feel the spiritual force that binds us together. My heart screams, "Do *not* give up hope." I feel her calm down. I focus on her spirit, not her cancer. I kiss her face twice.

I know what it feels like to have no hope. Hope is not some illusion. It's a promise I am making to my daughter. Hope may be all we have, but it strengthens your heart with courage you never knew you had and keeps your spirit alive. I will not give up hope. I couldn't possibly. This is my daughter. Carol knows that I believe she can walk with the other ten million cancer survivors on this earth and that we are going to beat this one day at a time, one scan at a time, one new diagnosis at a time. There are miracles in life, and she's earned one. Deep inside me, I believe she will be okay. Somehow, she's going to come back from this.

An hour later, Carol's brain is buzzing like an electrical circuit struck by lightning. She is on her laptop with the Cleveland Clinic, on her phone calling family and friends, on her iPad searching survival rates, treatment for breast cancer metastasis to bones, liver, lungs. She shows me the data, indicating that 23 percent of breast cancer patients get a recurrence in the first two years. She is doing all of this with her one-hundred-pound dog Lola half on her lap. She doesn't complain about the pain this animal is probably causing her as she continues to vomit every five or six minutes.

It's not surprising that Carol has a one-hour breakdown but then gets to work on solutions. She's never spent a day in her life depressed. Carol does not easily get sucked into anything negative, not outwardly anyway. The girl does not reveal emotional pain to others. She never made one Facebook post about this cancer during sixteen months of treatment, and she told me to keep her medical challenges off my timeline. Carol does not depend on Facebook likes or comments for inspiration like her mother does. I love Facebook. She hates it. We are so different in all the right ways, which makes this relationship challenging and fun. At least we agree on politics. That should have been my first clue that she was sick: when I stopped getting texts about Donald Trump.

She frets about how she might not get to her next work event with the Special Olympics that requires her to travel abroad. At the same time, she is being kind to Joseph and Michael, the neighbor kids who just walked into the house asking for a treat. I give them each a fig bar and then remind the boys that friends need to remain outside today and that we're not serving snacks. Max tells me that Carol let all five of these boys, under the age of six, lie down with her in her king-size bed two days ago when she needed to rest. Even while waiting on cancer scan results, my daughter remains kind. I'm so proud…and so scared.

Laura arrives. *Shit is about to get done.* This girl is a doer. Carol and Laura met in college and were roommates for two years. She is one of Carol's five best friends and has a PhD in nursing. She works at VCU hospital, where she just got Carol admitted. Laura calls the oncologist and reminds Carol to stay hydrated.

VCU Hospital is the Cleveland Clinic of Richmond. It's where all of Carol's hospitalizations have been. Karri arrives next. She packs an overnight bag. Carol decides to take a bath. Next, in walks Jennie, who has been a best friend from sixth grade through college. They rented a house for three years together when Carol did her master's. They got married two weeks apart, were pregnant at the same time, and both have cancer. Jennie was diagnosed with multiple myeloma one month after Carol's diagnosis. She packs lunches, makes a grocery list, answers calls, and cries when Carol is out of the room. No tears flow in Carol's presence. Everyone knows my daughter does not want all that emotional hoopla.

Carol says goodbye to each one of the boys and then asks to speak to me privately. "I know how badly you want to come to the hospital. Would you please stay here tonight with the boys? Max wants to spend the night with me. Laura is going to come with us to help with getting me admitted. She can move things along fast. Besides all that, I don't want the boys with anyone but you or Max. Are you cool with all this, Mom?"

I hug her. She knows that asking me was not necessary. Truth be told, I'm not at all cool with being away from her for one minute, but I'll deal with it. Carol is not five years old. I watch as she gets in the car. My eyes stay on her car until she's out of sight. She does not look back.

On the front porch, I breathe in and out deeply and slowly. This hospital will be her fifth in eighteen months. I tell myself when she's hydrated, gets the vomiting under control, and the doctor begins a treatment plan, she will return home.

Deborah calls. She is one of the original cofounders of the Make-A-Wish Foundation. She knows people in high places. She and Carol met at Catholic University, where they did their doctorates together. Deborah is one of Carol's best friends. "I want you to know I'm already working on getting her into Dana-Farber in Boston within two to three weeks. Once we have her vomiting under control, we can get her to an oncologist there who can do an eval and let treatment begin in Richmond."

She is also recommending a consultation with MD Anderson in Houston with the top breast cancer oncologist in the country. "This is all positive news, Debra. I personally know a woman with the same diagnosis as Carol's who is still in treatment but alive. It's been almost ten years, and Carol sees that same oncologist. I'm extremely optimistic about all of this. I know you are too."

Her hopefulness makes me feel two hundred percent better.

The boys are fed and bathed. Each one picks out a book for me to read. While brushing his teeth, Jade says, "My friend in school was right. He told me Mommy could die from cancer. Is she going to die, Grandma?"

"I don't want you to worry about that. Some people die of cancer, but plenty of people with cancer don't die. Your mother is getting another doctor, and *we* are all going to do everything we can to make sure she'll be okay. But I want you to talk to me anytime you are worried, okay?"

He nods and jumps on the top bunk of his bed.

Grant yells, "Stop talking about Mommy's cancer!" He is kicking the wall and screaming, "Shut up! I don't want to talk about this! You are going to have bad dreams again!"

Now Grant is crying, and Jade is fine. Landon starts screaming, "I want my mommy! *I want my mommy*!"

Grant covers his head to shut out the noise. It takes at least an hour for all three boys to relax enough to fall asleep.

A neighbor calls to tell me they want to start a meal train. I tell her I need to check with Max. I'm overwhelmed by the love and support that pours in immediately.

Max texts, "They did a CT scan of her brain to see if that's why Carol is vomiting. It came back clear. No brain cancer. Carol actually cried with the news. We are moving her soon. I will text you with info. Thanks, Debra."

Brain cancer? They suspect liver, lungs, bones, *and* brain cancer? Why brain cancer? She's not complaining of headaches. This day can bring an atheist to her knees. Life gives you wild cards, and then all you can do is pray. One tear falls down my cheek, realizing I never taught Carol to turn to prayer. I thank God that my daughter does not have brain cancer.

When Ryan died, a Cleveland mother, Lynette Macias, sent me the book *God Never Blinks* by Regina Brett. Lynette has no idea how much that book helped free me from my guilt. I need to read it again. The author writes, "If we meet the face of God in the afterlife there will only be one question. Did you love? As long as you loved—you lived. That's all that matters."

I loved Ryan, I love Carol, and I love Brock. I taught my children about unconditional love by example. But when it comes to prayer, I've been so inconsistent, and I worry that Carol might need to pray right now. She nearly has her PhD in social policies, but I forgot to teach her how to get on her knees when there is nothing else to do but hope that something more powerful than us is out there. I fucking forgot to teach Carol how to pray.

I feel like getting stoned and drunk and disappearing. I take a sleeping pill instead and go to bed early, but my mind is dark with horrible thoughts and scary words. Am I the reason Carol has cancer? If she dies, will it be my fault? I text a nurse and a friend from high school. She calls me back, and my sanity returns.

It's 2:00 a.m. The sleep meds are not working. I curl up on the couch downstairs with questions that have no answers and problems that have no solutions.

Day three: February 27, Monday

Morning comes. I drive the three boys to their private school through darts of cold rain. Grant asks, "Can we see Mommy at the hospital after school?"

"Let me check with your dad. I know you'll be going, but I don't know when."

He kicks the back of my seat several times. I ignore it. He is in kindergarten and needs a release. These young boys are going to have questions and react to the answers, especially Grant. I speak to their teachers and learn that Max has already e-mailed them, explaining the situation.

Time to drive straight home, take a shower, feed the cat, send my readers an e-mail, change clothes, and grab snacks. There's no possible chance of my leaving my daughter's room.

The halls of VCU Hospital are something out of *Star Trek*. Whatever can shine is shining. I'm getting more calls and texts than I have time for, but that's because Carol is loved by an army of angels. My girl has cords hanging all over her: two IVs, morphine drip, catheter, oxygen, and monitors. The nurses are constantly in and out.

They have started antinausea meds and steroids. She wants ice chips but barfs them up. I ask her main nurse what meds they are using for nausea. The doctor has ordered another one, and they're waiting for the pharmacy to deliver it. Zofran is not working. Holy crap, my girl has never been this sick.

Carol's oncologist enters the room and announces she will be in Florida for five days. She tells us the name of the temporary replacement who take care of *things* in her absence. An MRI of the brain has been ordered, the lung biopsy is tomorrow, then more scans and more meds. The doctor tells my daughter that by the time she gets back from Florida, Carol will be back home. She should call now to make an appointment to begin a treatment plan, which cannot be determined until all tests are complete. Carol tells her, "They already did a scan of my brain, and it was clear."

The doctor replies, "We have to take every possible step to find out why we cannot get this vomiting under control with medications."

Carol says nothing, but I follow this doctor out the door to ask her why an MRI of the brain is necessary. She answers, "Liver cancer would not cause this much vomiting."

"What the hell would?"

"Brain cancer. That's why I ordered the MRI."

"When was the last time you scanned my daughter?"

"Carol has shown no symptoms that indicated the need."

I follow her as she walks away. "Hold on, you're trying to tell me that a BRCA1-HER2-positive-DNA breast cancer patient with five positive lymph nodes after months of chemotherapy does not warrant another scan?"

I'm positive this oncologist will never speak to me again. Carol had positive lymph nodes upon her initial diagnosis. I wanted the surgery first. Carol's oncologist felt confident the chemotherapy first could help prevent a future recurrence. Meanwhile, my opinion is the cancer was spreading all over Carol while she was in chemotherapy and the drugs were not reaching it. The result is an entire body full of cancer.

Carol wants a bagel when I get back to her room. She is starving. She also tells me, "I stopped at the ATM and got you sixty dollars for your parking and expenses. Take it all, Mom."

How can she be thinking about my financial situation while worrying about her own survival? Kindness again. My daughter is kind when she has every reason to be pissed.

I break the bagel up into child-size bites. "Take one bite at a time and chew it slowly. I bet it will stay down."

She is so excited about this damn bagel. She takes four small bites, pukes at least five times, then tosses the bagel into the trash.

Max is leaving to go home. We decide that someone needs to stay with Carol 24-7. Max and I make a schedule. Away from Carol's room, Max cries like a little kid. "I want you to know, if I could change places with Carol, I would right now, Debra—right this minute. I want my boys to have their mother." He's emotional, steps into the elevator, and waves goodbye.

I return to Carol's room and kiss her forehead. There are too many people coming and going. Carol is too sick for constant visitation, so I ask the nurse if we can put a sign on the door. "Yes. Let's do it now."

The signs says, "NO ONE IS TO ENTER THIS ROOM WITHOUT CHECKING WITH A NURSE"

It's been five surgeries, months of chemo, months of radiation, three months of life back, and now this: a liver full of cancer; at least three tumors on her lungs; bone cancer on her spine, lower back, and shoulders; and possibly brain cancer? This is her reward for treatment? We might need a miracle. I believe they can happen. I've experienced them in my own life. There's a prayer circle going all across the country. My friends and family are scattered and everyone prays. There are churches of strangers praying for my daughter this week.

Her friends would like some time with her, so I take the opportunity to run to Carol's house to pick up a blanket, yoga pants, tank tops, and her own pillow. There is encrusted bird shit all over my car window. It has probably been there since Landon's birthday party, but I just now noticed it. Driving is incompatible with my current stress level. I'm preoccupied, making hasty lane changes, too many sudden stops, and jumping red lights in a vehicle with expired tags. My budget does not allow me to pay for luxuries like current tags. I'm grateful I can afford gas. I dodge cops and dare one of them to stop me. I decide to enforce new driving rules so I don't kill someone: soothing music only, no more talking on the phone while driving, no highways, and my hand out the window at all times to direct the wind toward my face.

The most gorgeous magnolia tree I've ever seen in my life stands in front of Carol and Max's home. It covers the entire front yard. Carol hung a tire swing on the tree. It hurts to look at this house. I'm filled with dread as I drive into their circular driveway. I can picture her running out that red front door, but I wonder if she will ever meet me at that door again.

I glance over my right shoulder and see Max starting a run with his neighbor buddy. He is wiping away tears. I have only seen Max cry once before at Ryan's memorial service when he read the letter Forest wrote to his dad. He sees me drive up and comes over. I hear the anguish of the man who is in love with my daughter. "I don't know what to do, Debra. I am scared that Carol is not coming home. I have never felt this scared in my life."

"I know, Max. I know you're scared, and I understand. I'm scared too. I came here to pick up a few things that Carol wants. While we're alone, though, I need to tell you that I cannot be anywhere right now except at that hospital. Please do not sign me up to watch the boys. I need to be with my daughter. My plan is to sleep for a while and then spend the rest of the day with her. There is so much support coming in for the boys. Please take those people up on their offers."

Max's tone is sympathetic. "Carol and I talked about this already. She knows you want to be with her. She also thinks it's important that I spend time with the boys every day while she's in the hospital because they're anxious and confused. We're all thinking alike."

As we wave goodbye, I reflect on the difference between Max's worries and mine. He is feeling the impending death of his wife. I'm anticipating some flight I will take with Carol to Houston, Boston, Cleveland—wherever we need to go to get treatment to extend her life. I am determined that my daughter won't be dying anytime soon. I have moments when I fear death, but more often, I am sure she'll live. Cancer is tricky and unpredictable. I know people who were on their deathbeds with this disease who are alive today. Her cancer will take a positive turn, and my daughter will be here to raise her three sons.

When I walk into Carol and Max's house, each room presents a different flashback. In her office, I see her on conference calls, waving people out. In the bedroom, I see her throwing five different outfits on the bed, trying to decide which one to wear. She's looking for a book in the library, chilling with Max and wine by the fire, running up and down flights of stairs in seconds, throwing tennis balls for the dogs, tossing a football to Grant, and blasting the kitchen radio while dancing with her boys. I look out the kitchen window and see her jumping on the trampoline with them. I remember her excitement the day she texted me to come over and check out her new dining room table. I was there in twenty minutes to admire it. The memory of Christmas dinner just two months ago sends tears streaming down my face. We feasted together and laughed and talked four hours with family.

I collect the things she asked for, but I'm starting to breathe weirdly. I need to get the hell out of her house. I'm juggling too many emotions at once and can't stop crying as I drive. I already miss seeing Carol in her house. She's everywhere in that beautiful home she created.

Back in Carol's hospital room, I meet a doctor who is taking charge of her nausea medications. There is also a pain specialist. I tell him straight up, "This is too much pain. Carol has a high tolerance for pain, but she can't take this any longer. We need more medication."

They both ask her questions, and an order is written for ten milligrams of morphine every four hours around the clock plus a rescue dose as needed every hour. He explains that every patient is different. She may experience more insomnia or feel agitated, but she will feel immediate relief from bone pain.

Carol looks happy with this plan and tells them, "Thanks so much. I appreciate your getting right on this. I'll let the nurse know if I need less or if there are any unmanageable side effects. I'm smart about this, but I'm looking forward to less pain. Thanks again and have a good day." Kindness.

I laugh when they leave. She gives me a sober look and says, "What's funny?"

"Carol, honey, I have watched you teach all three of your kids great manners. Your first word was *please*. Your second was *cookie*. Your third was *thank you*. Considering how shitty you feel right now, I wouldn't be offended if you didn't use good manners."

She finds no humor in this. "Why should I be an asshole? It's not the medical staff's fault that I have cancer. Can you help me roll over onto my side?"

She can no longer move, sit up, or lie back down without assistance. When we change her position, she cries out and rings the nurse call bell. Nurses promptly respond. "Can you please remove this catheter? It's an aggravation. Someone is here 24-7 to assist me with the bathroom."

The nurse checks the computer. "I'm sorry, Carol. The order says that you are not to leave your bed right now. Can I get you anything else? Your meds are being changed now. They will be here soon."

"Great. Thank you. Please close my door."

When the nurse leaves, Carol looks at me. "Get this goddamn catheter out of me. Come on, Mom. You can convince these nurses. Do something, please."

Soon after the catheter is removed. Mothers will make things happen faster than anyone on the planet. We stay in the arena, stay in the fight when it's our kid.

Morphine is having a different effect on Carol than anticipated. It knocks her out for twenty minutes. Then she wakes up foggy, and within ten minutes, she's back out again. Even under the influence of maximum doses of morphine and other medications, she maintains her dignity. I stare at her while she sleeps and think about how she has not smiled, laughed, brushed her hair, cared about her phone, tablet, or lip gloss for three days.

I hope I can continue to greet each new day with the energy of a climber greeting a mountain. I wish Ryan were here to help me with Carol. I'm thinking too much about Ryan. Early morning texts from my best friend remind me, "Good morning. I'm praying. Stay in touch. Love you." Between this friend and at least fifty other people who love me, call me, text all day long, I remain hopeful that despite this sudden godforsaken unraveling of events and despite increasingly negative reports, my daughter will be given more time in her precious life.

Brock and his wife are flying in from Orlando in two days. Brock is afraid he may be losing another sibling. He has been getting the latest updates and, like Max, is less optimistic. I'm comforted to know he is coming. We need each other's support.

A doctor arrives with two nurses and Laura and Max. Carol wakes up when the doctor sits on the side of her bed. The six of us surround her bed as he starts, "Hi, Carol, your blood tests came back today, and I have updates. First things first: we were able to determine that the recurring cancer is the exact same as the primary cancer—your breast cancer. This helps the oncologist with decisions about the right chemotherapy drugs to use to target this cancer.

"The second finding is not good news. The oncologist ordered a test that measures the rate at which this cancer is moving. An aggressive spread rate of twenty percent is considered high." He pauses. "Your cancer is moving at a rate of sixty-seven percent, meaning it's more like a wildfire in your body."

There is dead silence in the room. No one speaks. No one moves. Carol doesn't want to discuss it, not at all. "Thank you," she says. "Please close the door when you leave."

Everyone walks out, except me. She does not ask me to leave, but I respect her need for silence. She keeps her eyes shut. The doctor's description is too graphic, invoking an image of deadly embers carried on a lethal wind through a once-vibrant young body, landing on healthy tissue, sparking more fire and more embers, and raging out of control. Did she already have stage 4 cancer at her initial diagnosis? We don't have two or three weeks to get another oncologist. She needs to go to Boston, Houston—wherever there is availability now, right fucking *now!*

Max walks back in, and I leave. I call Kelly, Ryan's former girlfriend, who is now an oncology nurse and a friend who talks to me any time of the day or night. "Damn, Debra, the problem is that these oncologists need her physically there. You would need to do a medical transport. Is Carol strong enough for that now? My advice is this: when her friend gets in from DC, find out if this report can be e-mailed to her oncologist connections in both Boston and Houston and see if they can collaborate with Carol's doctors in Richmond to start a treatment plan there immediately."

I text Carol's friend Deborah. She is on her way to the hospital about a half hour away. This is great news. We need her optimism.

Carol's cognitive functions appear weaker with these new meds. She is losing decision-making control. It's so out of character, but Max and I agree that some rest and relief from her pain are more important. She wakes up, needs to go to bathroom, throws up twice on the way, and again on the way back. I have never seen someone vomit this much.

Deborah arrives with her life-affirming, wildly philanthropic heart; snatches away Carol's ticking time bomb; and replaces it with plans and action steps to get treatment. She has appointments already scheduled and is so optimistic that for a moment, I believe Carol will be cured of this cancer.

I'm a realist, though, not an optimist. My life has fallen into so many puddles and ditches with hellish outcomes that I can't inwardly be positive. But outwardly, I know how to act and speak.

Max's dad shows up next and breaks down in front of Carol. He is seventy-nine years old and loves Carol is if she were his own daughter. This man brings flowers to her every almost every time he comes to the house. My daughter has fallen in love with green and blue hydrangeas. She places one in mason jars around the kitchen. No other man in her life bought her more flowers than her father-in-law. We are limiting visitors to two at a time. Carol has become extremely antisocial due to her increased meds and the recent news.

Carol's father, Mason, arrives at 10:30 p.m., and Max asks him to stay at the house instead of a hotel to help with the boys. But first, he needs Mason to spend tonight at the hospital with Carol because Max hasn't slept in two days. I update him on the day, kiss Carol, and tell her, "I love you. I will be back early."

She is shaking. She asks, "What's going on?"

Mason talks to her, and with stifled tears, I walk out. Tomorrow is lung biopsy day. In the parking garage, I rely on the exit signs because I've forgotten where to go. Today's rations of grace and courage are used up. I hate the thought of waking up to a lung biopsy. I feel alone and terrified of what may lie ahead.

Black is an interesting color. It's formed by the absorption of all other colors and represents grief, class, evil, strength, rebellion, mystery, and authority. Seventy percent of the clothes I've purchased since my experience with sexual violence four decades ago are black. It's the color of midnight, which is precisely the current time as I drive home. I'm drowsy. The radio is off. I have no interest in gazing at the moon or stars.

My favorite therapist, who walked me through sobriety, had the balls to ask, "My question is personal, Debra, but why do you always wear dresses and skirts and black? Do you own a pair of jeans? Do you ever wear pink, yellow, or orange?"

I could use about a four-hour session with Jeff Woods about now. He's in Orlando, but I'd consider driving the several hours to see him. He helped me get myself back after being lost my entire adult life. He guided me through the recreation of my identity, and I love the woman I am now. I didn't know the answer to his question, so I answered it with another question, "Why do you think I don't wear jeans and wear black?"

"You refuse to wear jeans because of your anxiety disorder, and you wear black because of your intense energy. You need to move to New York City. It's a city of artists, and they all dress like you. People who wear black all the time are on a mission."

I miss him and need him right now. I absolutely love this man. He was there for me when Ryan died. What therapist gives you his cell number, e-mail address, and permission to contact him 24-7?

What therapist stays in touch with you when you move eight hundred miles away? I need to talk to him about Carol.

I make it home without hitting a curb, blowing out a tire, or being pulled over by the Virginia State Police. Mercy, my cat, greets me with her gleaming mint-green eyes. I fall into my rocker like a building collapsing. Despite the image of a cancer wildfire destroying Carol's life, I cannot do grief, sitting in this chair with two dead children. That's how I know Carol will survive. No mother loses two children.

I'm nervous about tomorrow, not because I believe her lung cancer is serious. It's not. She is not coughing, spitting up blood, or showing any signs of terminal lung cancer. They can remove part of her lung, taking out the three tumors visible on her scan. She'll be fine. I'm nervous because this is day three of watching Carol lose her mental and physical strength. The oncologist said she would be going home in five days, but she is worse now than when she was admitted. Carol got a raw deal today. She deserves none of this. God is not fair.

Day 4: February 28, Tuesday

Max texts me early. "I'm with Carol. Mason said she was restless and uncomfortable all night. He did not sleep. They are coming to get her for MRI first then biopsy. See you soon."

My phone has nineteen voice mail messages that I don't have the energy to answer. I need to get to the hospital. It's almost 9:00 a.m. I'm expecting a lot of visitors today. We are within hours of knowing the full lung cancer report. Finally, my daughter will get some good news.

There is a ridiculously long line of cars waiting to get into the hospital parking lot. As I wait, my Richmond therapist calls. "Good morning. Can you talk for a couple of minutes?"

"Yes. Thanks for calling," I reply.

"I am worried about you and wanted to offer a session whenever you can find time to meet. Let's talk, Debra."

"Honestly," I tell her, "there is nothing to talk about. We still don't know how serious this all is. Tests are being done today and tomorrow. I don't have a clear picture of what Carol is dealing with. Our family is getting support from everywhere, and I'm hanging in there."

"My concern is your mental health. You are aware that new trauma can trigger past trauma. I want to be sure you are safe."

"I'm surrounded by a lot of love. I'm also holding on to hope that cancer patients can beat cancer at any stage. I'm not thinking of Carol dying. I'm focused on her treatment."

"What about your medications? Do you need an increased dose?"

"No, I'm not taking more meds. I need to run. I'm at the hospital. I appreciate your call, and I promise I will call you if I need to."

We say our goodbyes. For the love of God, do I need therapy right now? No, I need a relief for my daughter of this unshakable mind and body pain.

When I arrive on Carol's floor, six people are in the family waiting room with no Carol updates. I'm greeted with a hug from Amy, Carol's friend from Chapel Hill. Today, all five of Carol's closest, most cherished lifelong friends are at her bedside. These girls teach me a lesson about friendship. Real friends may not call every day, but if you are in crisis, they're in it with you. They tell their husbands to watch the kids; they fly, drive, take trains and buses and time off work. They don't worry about what it costs; they stop their life because yours has stopped. They're here because they love Carol. She has real friends because that's who she is, a real friend. And real friends attract real friends and stay with you through everything.

Carol returns four hours later. She looks pale. She moans. Her catheter is back in. Her oxygen is increased. Nurses are in and out, and the doctor steps in. Carol is crying, "Please. Please! Please!"

I feel a huge wave of crushing pain, and I suck it up fast. Moving her from gurney to bed causes unbearable pain. She has thirteen visitors waiting to see her, but she wants only Max. When he eventually walks out, I walk in. "Where are my boys?" she asks me. "Are they coming tonight?"

They give her morphine, and she's out.

Hell is this moment. Hell is my kid with four cancers. Hell is this room where my daughter cannot breathe, eat, drink, sit in a chair, sleep for more than twenty minutes, or get relief from a disease that is on fire in her bloodstream. Hell is standing at one child's bedside, watching him die. Hell is the apparent assumption of any god that I can survive the loss of another child.

I need air. Amy and Deborah are with Carol, so I leave, grab a Diet Coke, throw down two more clonazepams, and take a brisk forty-five-minute walk to rid myself of this hell and to convince myself that I will not lose my daughter.

Hours pass, and Carol wants the room quiet and dark with only one person at a time. She doesn't feel like talking. I notice the biopsy results on a computer screen outside her room. It's been left open by mistake, but I can't ignore it. I text Max, and Max texts Mason. Carol's nurse appears. "Debra, you shouldn't be looking at this, but I'm going to walk away right now because if it were my daughter in that room, I would want to read it too. I know you need facts. Don't tell anyone I saw you reading her report. Got it?" She walks away.

I feel light-headed and lean against the wall. The report says there are many malignant tumors on Carol's lungs. Max arrives, starts to read, and walks away. Mason reads everything. The size of each tumor is listed: seven millimeters, one centimeter, two centimeters, five millimeters. Laura arrives, reads it all, walks away, and shouts, "Fuck!"

Carol's boys will not be visiting tonight. I will not be going home tonight. There is no chance in hell I am leaving my daughter after reading this scan.

Day five: March 1, Wednesday

It's 1:00 a.m. In the quiet moments as Carol sleeps, I contemplate her three lives—her life before cancer, during cancer treatment, and now trapped in this private hospital room with a stage 4 recurrence. The hardest part of this is sitting helplessly, filled with urgency, as I watch the thief, cancer, steal this beautiful child of mine from us all.

I need to cry, but I don't. I pretend to be okay all day long, but I'm not. I feel powerless and pissed. The fear I feel is unlike any other fear I have felt before. It is terrifying to watch my own child, my girl, my amazing daughter get kicked out of life by an illness. I cannot be weak because she is drawing strength from me. I must assist her every waking moment and hope for a positive turn without letting her see how this is chilling my bones.

Cancer doesn't discriminate. It doesn't matter if you're young or old, rich or destitute. You can be intelligent, educated, and resilient, but none of that can save your life. Our Book of Life opens the day we are born and closes when we die. All we can hope for is to survive long enough to love someone, raise our children, and raise ourselves well enough that we find peace in both the mess and the beauty that comes with being human.

I refuse to leave Carol's side since she only sleeps twenty to thirty minutes and wakes up needing immediate assistance. My skirt has been inside out all day, and seventeen hours later, I notice. I don't care, but I could really use a toothbrush, toothpaste, and caffeine.

Deborah confirms that an oncologist at Dana-Farber has agreed to work Carol in any day of the week. We also have a March 20 appointment at MD Anderson, Houston, with a top oncologist who works with breast cancer recurrences. This is all positive news. Carol tells me, "I have a work commitment at the end of the month where I need to travel. Mom, I need to be well enough to get there."

I ignore her work ethic and offer more ice chips. She's out again.

Carol's moans are louder and more frequent today. My poor girl cannot even adjust her pillow without pain. I match my breaths to the beeping machines while she sleeps to silence the screaming thoughts in my brain. It's a fitful night. Her vitals are now taken hourly. The rescue dose is given hourly. Her oxygen is turned up to over ninety percent.

I don't understand why her respiration has become more seesaw since her lung biopsy. She reports a stabbing pain under her armpit all the way down her right side. God knows her breathing is awful.

She keeps repeating, "Where are my boys? When are they coming? I need to see my boys."

"Later today," I assure her.

The nurses at VCU hospital are stellar. We've had not one bad experience in four days as they deal with nonstop gloom and doom. A mother draws strength from the caregivers of her child. It's heartwarming when a nurse takes an extra five minutes to talk to me and offer genuine empathy. Nurses are the glue who hold a hospital together. They are so skilled, so compassionate. They help families cope, keep communication straight with doctors, give quality care to their patients, prioritize demands moment by moment while documenting every move they make.

Carol's night nurse walks over to me and gently rubs my back. "Your daughter is a star in her world, Debra. I can see how many people love this girl. You didn't raise an ordinary girl, did you?"

"Thank you," I reply. "She gets the credit. Carol was raised making her own decisions and designed her own life. She knew who she was by age thirteen."

"You must have invested a huge piece of yourself, moved heaven and earth for her in those first thirteen years because I've been in this profession for twelve years, and Carol is one of the kindest, coolest, bravest patients I've had. She keeps herself under control. We are all impressed with her."

She continues, "I complain about sleeplessness, working nights, all the responsibilities that come with being a woman. Nothing compares to what you're going through. Can I get you anything—a blanket, pillow, beverage?"

"I would love coffee and a toothbrush and toothpaste. Thanks for asking," I answer.

She is back in five minutes with all of it. Carol is awake. She needs more oxygen. I quickly hide the coffee. It sickens me that she has not been able to drink or eat for days. I won't eat or drink anything in front of her.

Carol throws up for five minutes. Her memory seems foggy. The nurse sanitizes her hands, puts on new gloves, and works with her for a few minutes. She is also concerned about Carol's breathing and calls the house doctor. Carol is scheduled for a chest X-ray in the morning. She is extremely anxious, wants her blankets and yoga pants off, and lies there in her underwear.

They come and draw more blood, and my fragile creature says, "Mom, seriously? It's 3:00 a.m. Is my world coming to an end so fast they need to wake me up every thirty minutes now? Can you talk to them and see if they can bring my meds and check my vitals at the same time?"

She throws up again. "This shit is really getting old. My life is about throwing up, lying here with morphine that suddenly is not working, and my breathing is worse. This white-and-yellow crap coming out of me is because the cancer is not just in my lungs, liver, and bones. It's also in my head. Brain cancer will be my next good news."

I place my hands on her hands lightly due to the IVs. "Let's not lose hope. Let's look at this brain cancer logically. You have no headaches, visual problems, dizziness, problems with speech, and your CT scan came back clear. I'm not worried about brain cancer. They need to get this vomiting stopped so you can eat, and we can get to Boston. This is serious stuff, but every doctor says it's treatable. All you need to worry about is getting rest. Everything else is being taken care of."

"When are my boys coming?" she asks.

"Today, I promise."

"How can I go home like this tomorrow without a hospital bed or a nurse?"

I respond, "I will be your nurse. I can handle everything. I will move—"

Carol passes out halfway through my sentence, perhaps to avoid discussing things. She might be talking to Max or her friends. I don't know, but she is emotionally absent with me. Carol has not asked me about the lung biopsy results, and I won't bring them up. I was really hoping tonight would be a chance for a heart-to-heart talk but only if she needs it. She seems too sick, shut down, and wants to isolate to escape this reality. She stays out for more than twenty minutes, which brings me to my feet.

It's 4:00 a.m., the hour when people cry alone. I check messages while looking out the window at tops of buildings, streetlights, an arriving ambulance. I see a 10:50-p.m. text from a friend: "Thinking of you a lot. Hope we talk in the morning. Love you."

Carol has now been peacefully asleep forty minutes. This is a first in five days. I sit up closer to her, watching every twitch, breath, and moan in total disbelief. One month ago, she was doing a spin class three times a week, working full-time with the Special Olympics, flying to Vancouver for an event, walking Lola for forty minutes every morning before her boys woke up, and taking care of three boys. She had her life back. How did she go from that energy to not being able to dress herself, roll over, check her phone, or even take a sip of water without throwing up?

I feel a righteous fire within me that will see me through this. I cannot give up. I am lit.

Morning comes. Her MRI has been cancelled, and Carol has just been transported for an X-ray. There are several people here already. Kate texts next,

> You have not left her room for two days. I'm not taking, "NO" for an answer. You need real food. Will let you know when I get to hospital.

Amy also tells me to take some time away, hands me a bag of granola, and promises Carol will not be alone for a minute. Max is hopeful my daughter will see her three boys soon.

I take some time away. When I return to the hospital, Carol is still declining, but her boys arrive soon. She insists on being out of bed, sitting in the chair with her oxygen off and asks, "Mom, could you please get the boys each a cookie? If they have M&M cookies, get those. Otherwise, chocolate chip. Can you hurry? They are going to be here soon."

The nurse allows only a few of us to be in the room. Carol holds the cookies, but sitting in the chair is not a good idea. She is uncomfortable, and she cannot sit up. She also cannot be without oxygen.

I tell everyone, “Let’s all wait outside. Give Max and Carol private time with their boys.”

Out in the hall, I hear, “Grandma!”

It’s Landon with his brothers. I hug them and tell Max the rest of us will be in the waiting room, but he asks me to stay. The boys hesitate when they see Carol. Jade walks up first, gets his cookie, and then runs out of her room. Max calls him back, but he stands away from Carol. She needs oxygen.

Grant gets his cookie and runs toward the door. He says, “Thank you, Mommy. Grandma, can you come out of the room with us?”

I open the door but remain in the room. Landon is the only one showing no anxiety. He hugs Carol twice. At this point, she can’t sit up in the chair any longer, and Max calls for a nurse. This visit is challenging; neither she nor the boys can handle it. Max and I each fight back tears.

Grant and Jade are afraid to be with Carol, but Landon is last to leave. Max tells me he is taking them home. With tears in his eyes, he tells them, “You need to walk in there, hug Mommy, and tell her you love her.”

One by one, each son hugs their mother goodbye.

Carol asks to be alone. Outside her closed door, I wonder if this is the last time she touches the faces of her boys. I hope that was not the last goodbye. Jesus Christ, will they ever see her again?

I can’t stay here any longer. I know my eyes are working because I can feel them blink, but my ability to think, feel, stand, or finish a sentence is gone. Everyone tells me to leave. Max is spending the night with his wife.

At home, I collapse into bed. I’m consumed by the love I feel for my daughter. For forty-one years, she’s been a source of pride and laughter. She has shown me what real integrity means. She’s been a near-perfect daughter, and our relationship has grown since she became a mother. In the last six years, we have only had one conflict. It was over a Facebook post.

Love is not an emotion. It is our essence. It is life. It’s the reason people are brought together, the reason the world lights up. My relationship with Carol has taken me to the highest dimension of myself. She can't die. She can't die. She can't die.

Days six through nine: March 2, Thursday, to March 5, Sunday

Waiting is excruciating. I arrived at Carol's room this morning to see a team of seven doctors and nurses working frantically around her as she screamed, "I *can't* breathe! *Please* help me! I *cannot* get a *breath!*" Then she lost consciousness, and my sweet girl was rushed off to emergency surgery. If her lung collapses, she will go straight from surgery to ICU.

Two of Carol's close friends, Deb and Amy, and I are sitting in plush chairs in the surgical waiting room at VCU hospital. I keep studying the screen that tracks each surgical patient's progress by color. One color indicates the patient is still in surgery, another color indicates they've moved to recovery, and so on. To pass the time, I also speculate about which lighter-hearted people are waiting for less complicated surgeries—the gallbladder or appendix removals, the knee replacements, the bone fracture repairs—and which ones must be here for the far more serious last-ditch-effort surgeries, those whispering to God like me.

I have learned to use these waiting periods to direct myself to be here now. May I be brave for Carol. She needs all good energy. May I release my fear from this truth of life. My daughter has stage 4 cancer, but no one can know for sure how long she has.

We are all using our phones to update others. We're high on caffeine. People around us are working feverishly on laptops or discussing compelling topics such as the location of the vending machines, the weak Wi-Fi signal, or what can be spotted in the parking lot from the window. I need a milligram of clonazepam.

My knees bounce compulsively from nervous energy. By my side is the expensive black leather writer's bag, a gift from Carol that will last a lifetime. The impulse to write might strike at any moment, and writing is my therapy, except that writing won't be happening today, not here, not now—maybe later, maybe never. My daughter was not a huge supporter of writing my book. She is private and knows the story requires me to tell the truth. Much of the truth is not something Carol wants me to share with the universe. All I know is the book is not for my family. If I lose them, it's going to be sad. I'm writing it for human beings who will relate to my suffering and recovery. If anyone in my family is ashamed of that, shame on them!

After three hours, the waiting room phone rings, and the hospital volunteer summons, "Debra Mak?" All three of us go to the phone. The thoracic surgeon is on the other end. She tells me he drained at least one liter of blood from Carol's lungs.

"Oh, for Christ's sake! How did this happen? Is she okay?"

"She did extremely well. The bleeding most likely resulted from the lung biopsy. I placed a drainage tube in the pleural space that allows excess fluid and air to be removed. This needs to stay in for two days, and she will need to stay on her back the entire time. We're probably looking at the tube coming out Saturday, MRI on Sunday."

"When can I see her?"

"We are keeping her for a while longer than usual for observation. You can wait in her room. I don't anticipate she needs to go to ICU. But while I have you, I feel you need to know that I was able to see a lot of malignancy in her lungs. They are covered with cancer."

"We are aware, doctor. I read her CT scan report. I have no further questions, but I would like for you to contact her husband by phone. Do you have his cell number? He may have questions."

"Yes, I have it, and I'll call him now."

"Thank you. Please call me if anything changes with Carol's condition while she's in recovery."

"Will do."

We go back up to Carol's floor. Brock and his wife are flying in today. I text Brock to stand by at Carol and Max's house until we see how she is doing.

I'm fiercely possessive of the forty-five minutes I get alone with her when she gets back. She's comfortable and asleep. I stare at her nose, cheeks, wavy hair, eyes, lips, fingers. I watch her breathe, make sure she is covered and warm, watch her vital signs. I stand like a mountain watching over her.

My daughter is gorgeous, but her physical beauty is the least impressive thing about her. She gifts the world with kindness and contributes something positive in her work and her personal life. I feel so guilty about not telling her enough times how proud I am to be her mom. I have not observed one unkind word. She thanks medical personnel who come into her room. Being kind to everyone in her life is a chosen lifestyle.

I'm not as kind as my daughter. I have anxiety and grief vertigo. I get angry. I'm angry at the oncologist and every single day she suffered only to get this horrific outcome, but I need to stop this kind of thinking. There are a hundred different would've-could've scenarios that lead to nowhere. She's not dying, she's not dying, she's not dying. I say it over and over and over.

About an hour after Max arrives, Carol says she doesn't want anyone in the room, including Max or me. She wants silence and solitude, and everyone understands. Some people leave; others wait in the family waiting room. Max and Laura leave to get a bite to eat, and I grab a folding chair and sit right outside Carol's room. I will sit here for twenty-four hours if that's what it takes. I'm ten feet away if she needs me.

I run down to the lobby to buy more water, and I break down unexpectedly in the elevator in front of six strangers. It's the stifled tears of the last year and a half. A man puts his hand on my shoulder. Others avoid looking at me. Another man says, "Hard day. Hope things get better for you."

The elevator doors open. I step out, blinking heavy tears. A frail elderly lady with a voice that sounds half her age rubs my back like I'm a cat and says, "Honey, what is making you cry? Walk with me for a little bit. Let's go to the chapel together. I want to hear what's wrong and pray for you."

I wipe my face on my sleeve and reply, "That's so nice of you. Really, you are a dear lady, but no thank you. I'm not going to the chapel."

She's still rubbing my back. "Why not?"

"There is no God in there."

I cry a little harder, wishing that I could believe prayer would help. I have prayed hundreds of times in my life, but none of those prayers were answered. Why would that change now?

I hug her and walk away, feeling the effort of each step. I feel fatigued from too little sleep for too many days. This is hard—incredibly hard—and there are other people hurting right along with me. I'm doing a terrible job of supporting them.

I purchase water and snacks and head to the restroom for privacy and lean my head against the stall wall and discover my favorite long hippie sweater is floating in the toilet. Good thing I have a blouse on underneath. I rinse the sweater in the bathroom sink and head back upstairs.

I'm back in my chair, where I will remain until Carol calls one of us back into the room. A family member must stay close by. Every hospital patient needs an advocate.

Carol and I would drink coffee, vent, laugh, debate. We could hardly stop talking. She would tell me funny stories about her boys every day. These days, she says so little about anything. Everything around her is in slow motion. I'm in with her fighting the fight of her life. This is a blizzard of pain.

I'm waiting for the next bomb to drop. My inner psycho speaks to God, "God, what are you doing now? What is this lesson? Goddamn you. My son is dead, and now you want my daughter? Taking Ryan out of my life wasn't enough? I come from Christian people, learned how to pray when I was very young, was saved, baptized, read the entire Bible once. I sat in church pews for decades, brought my children to church, and gave money I couldn't afford to give. I have taken care of homeless people. I care about our world. You make all things possible, make miracles happen. You let Charles Manson see his eighty-third birthday, but you won't let my daughter, who has made good choices her entire life, stay on this earth and raise her three sons? Fuck you, God! Fuck you and your omnipotence that kills mothers and children! You do not exist, not in my world."

My anger is out of control, and I need air. I walk as fast as I can to the nearest outside exit door because otherwise, I will pick up my folding chair and slam it into the wall. I'm not angry with the oncologist or God. The truth is I'm more terrified than angry. I'm utterly terrified that this wretched disease is going to kill my only daughter.

I take two milligrams of clonazepam, buy another Diet Coke, and go to the chapel where I sit in silence for a half hour, not to pray or meditate but to tell myself that I'm allowed to feel this way and that feelings are not facts. My emotions are erupting because I'm traumatized.

I feel my body relax. Dwelling on the unfairness of all this gets me nowhere. I stop thinking those thoughts and bring myself back to a space where I care enough about myself to keep going. I must remain Carol's badass mother and be what she needs right now.

After another ten minutes of silence, I walk back and sit back down on the chair and keep my head and my spirit in high order. I observe patients going by on gurneys, accompanied by strained family members. I hear moans. Doctors walk like soldiers. The nurses are overworked. I sneak a quick peak at Carol. She's in a heavy slumber. I hope she is dreaming a good dream. My head is resting in my hands for an hour, thinking about how bloody short life can be for some of us.

It's 4:15 p.m. when the Doctor arrives. He spends three or four minutes in Carol's room. His face looks like a brick when he walks out. He stands next to me while making notes that take even longer than he spent with Carol. Then he taps my right shoulder. "How are you doing, Mother? Are you hanging in there?"

"I'm hanging. Thanks for asking," I answer.

He pats me another couple of times and shakes his head back and forth. "We will have a treatment plan soon. All we need is the brain MRI, and it will start. Your daughter is a perfect patient."

He walks away. I guzzle a bottle of water and cling to the chair like it's a life raft. I feel like I'm snapping again. Another day, another child, another illness, another hospital. If Carol dies, just lay me down within these same four walls and let me die with her because how does a mother survive this twice?

Life can lead you into dark holes that trap you. It's happened to me too many times. We can only crawl out when we remember the honor of being human, that each day is a gift, and we must show up for our own humanity. I've pushed past the edge of a rapist's knife, cared for my dying mother, cared fully for family in the aftermath of a madman's gruesome murders, faced urgent and radical surgery, authorized my son's removal from life support. I must not forget the honor of being human.

I need to flip the switch in my mind from fear to love. That's what brings me back to survival. That's what being human means, the humble acceptance that whatever life brings, love is the only force that allows your humanity to evolve.

I receive a text from Carol. "Mom, are you still here?"

"Yes, honey, of course. Can I come to see you now?"

"Yes. What time is it?"

"It's eight minutes till five. I will be right there."

I slow jog to get back to her room. The nurse is replacing her morphine drip with hydromorphone. It's ten times more potent. New doctor's orders: around the clock, two milligrams, every three hours. She is in crippling pain, a constant ten on a scale of one to ten. Her vomiting has increased. She tells me, "I'm so sick of this, Mom. Take me home, please. I want to go home."

She passes out before I can speak. I take her hand that does not have an IV. I hold it, squeeze it, kiss it, and do not let it go. The nurse tells me they are going to start a blood transfusion, another new order. All visiting is cancelled, except for Max and me.

Saturday comes and goes. Brock and his wife visit Carol for only five minutes. She's too sick for them to stay in the room. She thanks them for coming. They both walk out with tears. Brock's sister was to weak, too sick to have more than a five-minute conversation with her brother, who flew in from Florida. This is some serious shit going on.

Sunday is MRI day. Max goes with Carol to the procedure, which begins around noon. They look at her head, neck, and spine cross section by lovely cross section one quarter of an inch at a time. It takes two hours. Results are rushed and ready early tomorrow morning.

I am not worried. I'm more concerned about the cancer that's been confirmed and wonder how we are going to transport Carol to Boston or Houston in her condition. By late Sunday night, the hydromorphone is doing its job. Carol is in and out, mostly out. She wakes up to throw up then falls back to sleep. She says it hurts too much to change positions.

Before I go home, I tell Max, "I have an important doctor's appointment that I have already cancelled twice. How would you feel if I came in tomorrow morning after that? I know the oncologist will be here with MRI news."

"Of course," Max says. "Take care of that. Laura and others will be here. Don't cancel your appointment again."

"I hope she sleeps well tonight," I say. "I'm expecting good news tomorrow. Text me with it, okay?"

Max answers, "Sure, no problem. Drive safe."

I kiss Carol and tell her I love her, although she hears nothing. Then I drive home with the radio blasting to drown my thoughts.

Mercy, my cat, meets me at the door. We both sit in my grief chair. I have sat on this chair every single night for six years, ending my day talking with Ryan. I want no computer, no Facebook, no calls, no texts, no TV, no lights on—nothing but Mercy and I sitting in this chair.

I'm afraid to admit that Carol may be past the point of no return, given the relentless parade of crap happening every day bringing more bad news. If I'm afraid, what must my daughter be feeling?

I cannot yield to this wretched disease. Never because that would mean giving up on my girl, my crazy brave girl.

Day ten: March 6, Monday

My eyes are clouded as I drive to my doctor's appointment for labs and a scheduled ultrasound. I check my phone for texts every three minutes. It's 9:00 a.m.—nothing yet.

I jab at the radio then silence it. Everything hinges on today's report. She needs to keep both appointments: Boston and Houston. We need to start treatment. I take my first clonazepam of the day, run a brush through my hair, add some blush, and walk into the doctor's office. It's 9:10—still no text from Max. I text him. No response.

I'm not a woman who cries often or breaks down hysterically. My eyes dried out from four years of daily crying after losing Ryan. But now, my eyes are filled with tears because I'm away at my own doctor's appointment when I should be with Carol. It's 9:25—still no text. Too long now. No news is usually not good news.

Dr. Rogers tries to comfort me. "You know how your brain works, Debra. You go to the worst possible place and stay there until you find out the facts. Please don't do that to yourself. There may not be a report yet."

My blood pressure is high. She checks it again. I wait for meds. Staff come in and out, giving me hugs. Everyone knows me in this practice. Hypochondriacs get attention. It's 10:10—still no text.

Friends are calling. Family, other texts—not the one I want. Everyone is saying the same thing. "Try not to worry. Everything will be fine. Thoughts and prayers."

I'm done with that expression. I know people mean well, but I want real talk. Tell me how hard this must be and that you want to be a part of it. Tell me you will call me later. Tell me how horrible this must feel. Offer to send a meal over for Max's boys. Ask what you can do. Tell me you are sorry that Carol is going through this. Ask questions about what is going on with her health. Listen to me for five minutes. Say anything, except what the entire universe says when they don't know what else to say. *Thoughts and prayers.*

I stop at Dunkin' for an extralarge brew because I slept for two hours last night and need caffeine. Coffee is sloshing all over me as I speed down 95-N. It's a frustratingly long wait for valet parking. I'm twelfth in line, sipping coffee, listening to classical music. I spill more coffee and stop at the hospital coffee bar. There's an eternity of a wait for the elevator.

In the family waiting room, Mason and his wife are sitting alone, heads down, not talking. I melt into a chair next to them. "We got some very, very bad news this morning," he says. I descend into a quicksand of dread. "Carol has cancer of the brain, brain stem, and spine."

I want to walk to the window and jump out but there's not enough strength in me to stand. This is not a cancer we can escape.

Lungs, bones, liver, and brain? The three of us sit side by side, processing the news like ghosts, not crying, not cussing, not talking, not moving. I feel like I'm in a different world. "Where is Carol right now, with Max?"

Mason nods. "She wants private time with him."

Several minutes pass, and Max walks in, pushing Carol in a wheelchair. "I assume you know," he says.

I nod. Carol looks grim and cannot lift her head to look at me. She has shut down. This is the hardest moment of my life with my daughter. This is too much suffering. It's fucking *hell.* But I must support her in any way I can to give her what she needs. It's Carol's human right to deal with this in her way, and her way has always been the high road. She processes pain logically, privately. I'm the opposite. I need to let pain out, but Carol needs me on her road with her. "Do you feel like moving?" I ask her.

She picks up her head and answers, "Yes, let's move."

The others stay in the waiting room.

"Tell me what we used to do in your childhood when you didn't feel good?" I refuse to talk about brain cancer unless she brings it up. I do everything I can to distract her from this misery, even if it's only for a second.

She doesn't answer so I keep talking, "Okay, how about I go to *Barnes & Noble* and get some magazines?" Whenever Carol was sick, I would buy her tea, crackers, soup, peppermint patties, and magazines.

"Magazines would be good," she manages to respond. "Let's stop and get my phone, so I can text you the ones I want. There are too many to remember."

She texts, "*Life and Style*, *The New Yorker*, *People*, *Women's Health*, *Us Weekly*, *Elle*, and *Time*."

As she finishes, her nurse walks in. "Just letting you know, Carol, we received doctor's orders to move you to palliative care. This will happen within a half hour, so perhaps your family and friends can help collect your belongings." She touches Carol on the back and walks out.

Carol's head drops again. The rest of the family and Laura arrive and start packing. Laura quickly puts a positive spin on the move. "You are going to be one hundred percent more comfortable. They will manage your medications more closely. Patients go there for pain management while they are in treatment. There is a huge, comfortable family waiting room. The nurses are assigned to only two patients. I promise you, Carol, this is a saner environment, and you will feel better. I'm glad they have a room for you."

Everyone loads Carol's belongings onto a huge cart. I assure her that I will check her room twice to make sure all her belongings are moved. I pick up her I pad and place it on her lap. Max says, "Debra, I forgot to tell you. Carol asked me if you could spend the night with her tonight."

"Of course. Carol and I are going to stay up all night and read magazines."

Carol is in the hall with Laura, thanking all the nurses. She calls them rock stars and gives them her flowers. Even after a brain cancer diagnosis, kindness matters to *my girl.*

In nine days, we have gone from Landon's birthday party to palliative care? A month ago, Carol was in Vancouver in charge of an event for the Special Olympics International. She was working eighteen-hour days for a week. How did we get from there to here?

Max takes her to be measured for a mask that must be bolted to the table during ten whole-brain radiation treatments scheduled to start tomorrow at noon. They give Carol a 50 percent chance of extending her life for a mere but still precious three months.

Her brain cancer has a name: leptomeningeal. Cancer cells have spread to the membrane surrounding her spinal cord and brain, and cancer cells may be floating in her cerebrospinal fluid.

It's a death certificate. She will not survive this. My own mother found out she had breast cancer four decades ago but with treatment, went into full remission for two years. Then a lung cancer recurrence took her life but not for months. Carol was diagnosed seven years younger than my mother at diagnosis, but her outcome is much worse.

The family waiting room in palliative care is lovely, with a window, sofas, a full kitchen, social workers, and our own chaplain. But all I feel is gloom. Rohit Nanavati, Max's father, is here. Our eyes lock with shared understanding. He is crying nonstop, shaking his head in disbelief. His pain is making mine worse. Max's mother and aunt are here, a few neighbors, Carol's friends, and Kate is on the way.

Carol's friends all took time off work today, and the room is packed. More people are coming from Ohio, New Jersey, New York, Florida, California. I tell them not to come right now please. Carol can't handle it. Rohit is not allowed in Carol's room because he can't control his emotions. I look at him and feel sad for him. He loves my daughter.

A woman walks in, asking for me by name, and I stand and shake hands. She's a therapist. "I just wanted you to know that if you need to speak with anyone, we have 24-7 support for palliative care families. I'm sorry about what you are going through. It helps to talk about it."

"I have a therapist," I say, "and I prefer to process this with someone who knows me already."

She continues, "I understand, but she may not be available at times when you might need her. If so, you could talk to me about your grief, what you are feeling, what this is doing to you."

I ask her, "Did you ever lose a child?"

"Thank the good Lord, no, I have not," she answers.

"Have you ever talked to a mother who has lost two children?"

"I need to think about that one for a minute. I'm not sure." She is taking pamphlets about grief out of her bag. "I don't think I have," she continues. "Please don't tell me that you've lost one child already."

She's underqualified. She's also still here.

"Are you familiar with the seven stages of grief?" she asks.

I'm done with her. She needs to go. "Seven stages of grief? That's bullshit. Let me tell you what grief is. It's like a controlling drug. It has no stages. It has at least one hundred side effects, including raising a mother's mortality rate by 133 percent in the first five years following the loss of a child. It keeps you awake at night. Grief sends you to the ER with a panic attack because you broke down in a grocery store over a memory you had with your child planning Thanksgiving dinner. It makes you feel crazy when you're not.

"Losing a child is crazy. It makes you angry at God, yourself, medical staff, and it makes you question everything. I could give you ninety-five more examples of what losing a child feels like, but keep your pamphlet. There are no seven stages."

"I've never heard it explained that way," she replies "Would you like to talk to me about your son? When did he pass away?"

What doesn't she understand? "Please don't come in this room looking for me again."

I walk out and find a restroom, lock it, lean into the door. My daughter is not dead, but I need to be the fuck out of palliative care. People die here. Someone probably died in Carol's bed. We've been here for two hours, and I don't want this experience. We are all holding on loosely to Carol's life, volleying each other's pain around from one person to the next. It's a good time to leave and get Carol's magazines. I run to the bookstore while Carol's friends spend time with her. They try to help her FaceTime on her iPad with her boys, but she falls asleep.

When I get back, I ask Max if Carol talked about death, her fears—anything? He tells me it was like a business meeting. She told him,

> One: please do not move. Stay in our house for one year. The boys need to be close to their neighborhood friends. You need the support also.
>
> Two: hire an au pair immediately, someone who can take care of the house and the boys when you are out of town. Give her the entire top floor as her apartment.
>
> Three: keep them at their school. Please do not take them away from their teachers or friends. I

> want them to stay there the first year I'm gone, so life is as stable as possible.
>
> Four: you are a great husband and father. It's important at some point for you to find another partner. I want you to do that. I don't want you to be alone, and I trust that you will choose a woman who loves our boys.
>
> Five: I also want you to tell everyone that I lived a happy life.

Max says she showed no emotions, no fear—nothing. She presented it all quickly and thoroughly, like an assignment. Once she said what she needed to say, it was never brought up again. Carol does not want to talk about death or how much time she has left, not with Max, not with the doctors, not with me. Max also tells me that she wants her mother to stay with her all night. It's what I do. I'm in the hospital for the next thirty-one hours…by her bedside.

Max worries she could die right here in this hospital and never go home. I believe the radiation treatments will work. It will stop the vomiting. She will be able to eat again, go home, get to another oncologist, and extend her life more than three months, maybe a year, maybe two. My daughter will not drift away. Darkness has invaded my soul with a small flicker of light.

It's after 11:00 p.m. It's she and I. She's been sleeping for a few hours, but I haven't let go of her hand or arm.

Day eleven: March 7, Tuesday

Carol wakes up screaming at 3:00 a.m., "Avery! Avery! Avery!" She pushes me, pulls out her IV, kicks at her covers, and yells, "Why did you put me in this classroom? I want out! Get me out of this classroom!" She stands and punches me in the gut. She is angry and delusional.

She's kicking and moaning, so I call for a nurse. Carol's eyes are wide with fear. We settle her down, and she falls back to sleep but wakes up forty-five minutes later and yells again, "Why is O. J. Simpson in my class?"

I call her but she doesn't recognize her name. She gives me a piercing stare, blaming me for bringing her into this classroom. Two nurses calm her down and call the doctor. She now gets a booster shot every hour along with two milligrams of hydromorphone every three hours. An hour later, she's asleep again. Another hour later she wakes up, grabs water, spills it. It takes us forever to change everything, and she blames Avery—me—for throwing water at her.

This is not the night I wanted. I'd hoped we would have real mother-daughter time, a chance to be present with each other. Instead, I have witnessed the loss of Carol's memory, her identity, her beautiful, brilliant mind. She doesn't know me, and I'm scared shitless to wander into this new phase of intolerable hell. I sat here and watched my daughter's mind slip away.

While I wait for her return from her radiation treatment, I lie on the couch by the window. I've had two hours sleep in the last forty. The therapist walks in again, so I pretend I'm sleeping. Max returns and says, "She couldn't do it. She asked me to make them stop. I couldn't ignore her. I told them we will try again tomorrow." Max believes she's too sick for radiation.

We have all watched her consciousness and memory come and go. By 7:00 p.m., I'm not functioning well and probably shouldn't drive, but I need to leave. I've been awake for almost three days, and it shows. I can barely see street signs, and I miss an exit. I pass out on the grief chair until the next morning, still in clothes I've worn for two days. I'm afraid Carol may never get to Boston or Houston for treatment. She may never return home to read a bedtime story to her boys. She may never laugh with them again. She may never hold them on her lap.

My daughter and I started this journey in July of 2015 with her breast cancer diagnosis. I'm not stopping now. She's in the lead, and I will give her what she needs.

Day twelve: March 8, Wednesday

Some of Carol's sentences don't make sense. She sleeps more, moans, seems annoyed with the oxygen tube, and keeps removing it. We all take turns being with her while there are brief snippets of conversation and moments of deafening silence.

Radiation is cancelled. Max asks if we could all give him private time with his wife. He wants to lie next to her, hold her, take a nap, be with her for a while in bed. He stays with her for a couple of hours and returns to the waiting room crying.

Day thirteen: March 9, Thursday

I shower quickly, catch up on calls while driving, and get my coffee at the hospital. When I reach Carol's room, I hear whistling noises followed by loud moans. She is nonresponsive. Her eyes stay closed. The reverence in Carol's room is palpable. No one talks. Her condition is worse, with shallower breathing, moans, and noises in the back of her throat that are unbearable to hear. It continues all day long.

People come and go. I don't want to leave, but then Laura tells me, "Debra, I've seen patients like this. It's only going to be a couple of days. Maybe you should get some rest tonight and come back in the morning with what you'll need to stick around."

Her first best friend, Amy, wants to spend the night with her. Max is coming too, and I wait for him. Once he arrives, it's eleven thirty, and the parking garage closes at midnight. For a minute, I think of staying. Then I remember when I come back, I will be here at least two days. Amy is sitting by her side every minute. Her first best friend from third grade stays with my daughter. What a brave soul and the best of what a best friend can give. The courage to sit with her while she dies.

I kiss Carol's hand, her forehead, her cheek and rub her arm. I tell her, "I love you, my girl."

At home, I fall into the chair, clicking on the TV. The strength to rise above psoriasis! Ask you dermatologist about Humira. TV off.

I pack for the next day. Clothes, meds, toiletries, plenty of personal items to last four or five days. If Laura says Carol has two days, Carol has a week. I set the alarm for 7:00 a.m., take sleep meds, lie down, chasing moment after moment, wide awake. Fuck miracles! I place four pillows around me and wait until I can return to my daughter.

Day fourteen: March 10, Friday

At 1:38 a.m., my phone rings. I jump up. It's a Richmond area code. "Hello, is this Debra?"

"Yes. Who is this?"

"It's Lucy." One of the nurses.

My tongue and lips turn to lead.

"Debra?"

No, no, no, don't tell me.

"Debra, please answer me. Are you there?"

"Yes."

"I'm so, so sorry. Carol just passed away. Debra? Did you hear me?"

"Yes."

I hang up the phone and call Max. I want to come to the hospital, but I took sleeping meds and can't drive. He's staying with Carol. We'll meet at the house in the morning to tell the boys.

I fall back into bed because sitting or standing is too hard. I don't know what to do or how to feel. Carol's face is floating all over the room. I see her at ten minutes old, age two, six, fifteen—every age up to thirty-nine. It makes no sense to call twenty people at two twenty in the morning. I deal with this alone in the dark. I choose to spend time alone because I need silence. My dear daughter is dead. All I want is for the noise in my head to stop. I need this time to accept that the end result of this is that my daughter lost half of her adult life.

An hour later, I feel at peace almost to the point of feeling guilty. Carol is at peace. She doesn't feel any more cancer. She doesn't have to worry about her boys anymore. It's her peaceful spirit that I feel.

She is free, and that makes my heart lighter. I'm not thinking about what I have lost. I'm thinking about what she has gained. My girl is cancer-free. I feel as if we have connected in spirit, and I'm somehow with her. I can feel her everywhere in the room. What a beautiful difference one life made, forty-one years ago, in my life. From beginning to end, Carol made me proud, filled me with honor, and lifted me up from every piece of dirt that was thrown at me. She was there. She was always there for me. I'm not crying.

I know the grief will be insane. At 6:00 a.m., I start making phone calls. Thus begins my new reality, and yes, oh yes, I am crying.

Before I leave for Max's, I grab a piece of paper and write, "I'm so sorry, Carol. I'm so sorry this happened to you."

While I'm driving, the tears keep falling. My connection to my daughter is unexplainable. I feel nothing but absolute terror in my soul. I feel like I'm going to lose my mind. I will never miss anyone like this again. My daughter was my first lifeline after rape. I raised her myself. She is my pride, my reason to heal. I gave her everything inside of me. She took it all and built many towers in life. She's the kindest woman I know.

March 17, Friday

The memorial service is held at the Cathedral of the Sacred Heart in Richmond. Over a thousand people attend. It's standing room only. I stand and speak in her honor the way I spoke for Ryan. "Carol left kindness as her legacy." I speak about being her mother, about her kindness, and about her soul. I share with those I know who are hurting, "We grieve because we love. No matter what happens to any of us, know that love is stronger than any suffering life throws at us. It's the most powerful force in life. It will withstand the death of someone you love. Love wins over fear. Love is the reason we can begin a new journey without our beloved Carol." I speak without a tear or a crack in my voice because Carol would have wanted me to.

"She was loved and will be remembered by hundreds of humans. God bless my girl. May we all remember her with peace."

There were at least two hundred family and friends who gathered at Carol's home after the service. I was one of the last to arrive. The reality of her death is knocking me out. I pull over into a parking lot. For a few minutes, I shut the car off, laid my head back, and wondered how in the name of God our Father, am I going to live without my only daughter, the death of a second adult child? Slowly, the images of her life dying and life living all diminished into one energy, and I knew this moment was the same moment I had with Ryan. I have to carry this for the rest of my life.

No, no, no, no, no, no, no, no, no. I can't carry two dead children. I need my mother right now. It feels like mother has been dead my entire life. Where does a mother go when she loses her daughter? She goes straight back to the life she had when her daughter was alive. The video in my head plays over and over and over as I journey through the memory of the most important woman in my life, the one who forced me to grow up right alongside of her, *my dear daughter*.

Chapter 23

IN CLOSING

2021

In the spirit of celebration, I would love to deliver a hard-won and beautiful happy ending, but what is true for me is I am okay. Many days, I'm better than okay. I live only in the day. I realize that grief will forever be a companion. Life moves on while the mother who lost a child learns to carry her sadness for a lifetime. We carry it with as much grace we have to honor that our children existed. Love, whether on earth or at soul level, is the water of life.

For two years after Carol died, I was exhausted from emotional pain, agitated by the sound of my TV and phone, restless, on edge, paranoid, incapable of a complex thought, and barely able to take care of myself. When I lay down to sleep at night, all I could see was the two dead faces of my children. There were many times I could not get more than a couple of hours of sleep. Tossing, turning up and down, wrestling with four pillows, staring out the window, watching the clock, turning the blue screen on then off, and wide awake in deep thoughts of all the hows and whys. I went to the doctor's office or drove to the fire department to have my vital signs checked, went through stress tests to assess my heart, and stayed for months in therapy that wasn't working.

Grief made me physically feel sick with two back-to-back processes of my children. It was impossible for me to accept—after coming through sexual assault and other tragedies earlier in my life, after the transformation that came with my mental health diagnosis, and after a successful escape from the grips of alcoholism—that life went on to rob me of two of my children. I was stuck too deep in grief for tears.

One night, I stared at bottles of medication, picked them up, and tried to figure out how much I needed to take to die. Then I thought of Brock, my nine grandchildren, Flap, my best buds, my readers, my cat, my strong inner circle and knew they were all my reasons to stay alive. It's times like this when the soul expands when there is human suffering. There's a point where suffering transcends into understanding that grief is only sustainable if we face it, all of it. Let it move through us and feel the pain.

We can't heal intense sadness by hiding it. You sit with it. Stay with it. You create space for it. This is some hard stuff, but I promise you, life will come back, and you will find your purpose. Give grief the attention it deserves. Unexpressed emotions show up uninvited and destroy healthy relationships. It's a side effect of unhealed pain. Only through feeling it do we know we are alive.

So much of this intense sadness is done on our own…alone. So much of my life has been walking through tragedy after tragedy with an *invisible limp*. My hope in telling my story is for someone to see the invisible me and make it visible.

One month after Carol died, I returned to my book and finished it. It required me to work again to pay for a professional editor. I woke up at 3:45 a.m. to report to work by 5:00 a.m. At the end of all this, am I a badass? Yes, there's a fire in me to kick some serious ass. I had to fight my way through it all. You can't try new things, feel things differently, change your thoughts with or without fear without staying in your arena and showing up every day. I grew faith in my fear and moved forward with it. Today, I have not only continued with my sobriety, lost all of my stress weight, I let people take pictures of me now. The only real lingering anxiety is being in the back seat with an Uber driver. Not sure back-seat driving will ever not trigger *that* night when I lost my identity.

Victor Havel wrote, "Hope is not the conviction that something will turn out well, but the certainty that something IS worth doing no matter how it turns out." Gradually, somewhat like breaking a wild horse, I worked to tame my mind. I directed my focus more toward immediate steps, steps, steps to begin healing and end suffering rather than some future outcome. Day by day, I began treading the thought pathways worth deepening in the arduous journey from grief to healing. I press the pause button of grief and yell out loud, "Stop," to restore the feeling of contentment.

It works to practice mindfulness, and no yoga mat is needed to meditate. We can meditate while cooking dinner, during long drives with music, walking, bird-watching. Prayer is my form of highest meditation. I've learned when to let my grief *be* and when it needs to *pause*. Doing the work with real trauma ignites resilience. We are not free on the inside until we reach a place within where we have nothing to prove to anyone but ourselves. After years of healing, my grief no longer feels like an emotional purgatory. And my healing is always, *always* a daily conscious choice.

Once again, I face the fact that my life was changed by circumstances beyond my control. My daughter's doctorate could not stop the cancer that killed her. Ryan and Carol's five young children, ages two to seven, could not keep their parent alive long enough to raise them. Death is an inescapable law of God.

I had to let go of the suckiness of guilt, intense sadness, and fear that came with losing my first and second-born children. Let go of the feeling of being responsible on any level for the death of Ryan or Carol. I was not the cause of their deaths. I was the reason how beautifully they lived. I gave them life. They are two birds on my shoulders, two beautifully unfinished poems.

It's August 2021, and I filled up a twenty-foot truck and drove my *sixty-nine-year-old* self from Richmond, Virginia, to Winter Garden, Florida, to live six miles from my only living child, my son Brock. He has four children. It was important for me to have a family back. Ryan's children live in Florida, and I felt this was a beautiful way to show up, bring our family back together, and keep making memories. The move to Florida felt right. It was right. Then it suddenly felt different, and I'm okay with that too.

The feeling I moved here for was no longer available. How did I manage that? I said the Serenity Prayer a few times a day. There's a godhead within me that keeps going. My life needs a mission, and I found it in books and writing. And on and on and on I write, and on and on and on I keep moving forward. God keeps me digging until I dig deep enough to find gold. How does God talk, and who does he/she talk with? The God of my understanding speaks to me with feelings. There's a soul language between God and I. It goes beyond any religion.

I've never felt one moment of shame about my diagnosis of a mental illness. On the other hand, what I have endured from people close to me has sometimes been harsher than the actual illness. I didn't choose this illness, which comes with consequences, complications, and medications that work and stop working. I choose to be public about it because our culture could better understand that the behaviors of a person diagnosed with bipolar disorder do not define their character. I was born with a hardwired brain that needs medication to think, talk, and focus. The highs and lows can be mentally and physically exhausting. I have a disability not so different from that of a person in a wheelchair.

All disabilities are complex. Some are visible. Others are invisible. Either can mean a hard fight for an individual to receive respect or understanding from others. Many mornings, I wake up and see the sad insanity in my own eyes, but I am not my disability. I'm a mother, grandmother, friend, sister, aunt, writer, and someone who has a deep tenderness for humanity. I try to be a decent person despite all my dark, chaotic moods.

If I have learned anything from this disability, it is that every survival story is somewhat miraculous. I have loved and lived and grown under the worst of circumstances. I'm not ashamed of who I am today because when it comes to humanity and mental illness, opinions don't matter from those who do not suffer from a brain that on some mornings wants you locked down in bed with another part of your brain screaming, "Get up, move, snap out of this emotional cave, and take a shower, make tea, read!" I don't care what anyone thinks of my mood swings and creative bomb bursts. It's now all a big bloody "I don't care," and I live my life by my own standards. All expectations shifted, and I evolved out of decades of a fog into a reality that I could accept and respect.

It's now five years after the death of my daughter. I'm inspired by the women of the world who experience trauma, grief, violence, and despair yet take their pain and put it to work. I call them my army of wounded healers. That's how I wrote this book. I created a vessel for my pain and the universe responded. I climbed a mountain with humans who were bold, fearless, and had the guts to climb it together. That's what we do. We climb together.

My soul has grappled with the darkness long enough. It's time to give myself another chance at life. How many chances do we get? As many as we take. Is it possible to begin life over in the eighth decade? I'm ready to make that happen, and I will advocate for those coping with mental illness and for the grief community until the day I die. My work on this planet has just begun anew. God and I are not done yet. Love and healing and I are not done yet. What I learned about healing while writing this book is we don't heal and begin loving ourselves. We love ourselves and heal. Grab life each morning with a big dose of hope with your coffee. It beats the alternative. Hope is real, and it's found in rock bottom places.

Carol, at age twenty, wrote a short piece while a student at the University of Virginia titled "I Am the World. Can I Get a Piece of It?" She wrote about three hundred words, and one passage sticks with me: "I kind of believe there is a general rhythm of kindness in this world to which we each can contribute." She goes on to describe… the "Why bother?" mentality: "I abhor this attitude that people sometimes have about helping other people. ALWAYS BOTHER."

I believe Carol was right. There is a body-mind-soul rhythm of kindness in our world today. Be a part of it. Remember to get a piece of it. *Always bother.*

Transformation from trauma after trauma needs change. Change can only happen when we consciously decide to let go of the mute button and start somewhere small. Make your bed every day. Walk ten minutes. Set boundaries. Take magnesium. Eat apples. Pray. Read. Go to a park and walk. Try to do something that scares you. Love the *becoming* of your higher self. Nurture it. Surround yourself with people who care about you. Change also needs acceptance. Rest. It's a massive stretch from victim consciousness to human consciousness, fear to faith, anger to forgiveness, sadness to contentment, living dirt-poor to learning how to make money that feels comfortable, suffering to serenity, grief to gratitude. It's not a bridge out of your reach if you begin to put yourself first. Baby steps, inch by inch, day by day, being aware of what you're doing every single hour—it requires you to pay attention to your thoughts. It calls you to give a shit about yourself, all of you, everything. Life is not worth losing. Do you hear me? Life is one precious, unfathomable gift.

If you want to change your life, take the journey that calls you inward. All happiness is sustainable when our thoughts and feelings capture our energy where there is some universal flow. When there's enough wisdom in our bones to understand our highest thought and feeling is total acceptance of who you are in the day. Time—it takes time. In real life, it all takes time. Wisdom comes from both a higher and deeper source. My writing of the book is like delivering my fourth child. It feels like Marion Woodman's book *The Pregnant Virgin.*

"The one who is virgin, one in herself, does what she does not for power or out of the desire to please anyone, but because what she does is true." My transformation began with this book, this quote, decades ago. I gave birth to my highest self on this journey. To get this far it required me to understand that my life was not created to feel destroyed. It is given to know myself with each experience and that there is no limit to what I can become. I stood with my *truth*. I respect and love myself through the writing of this story. It's my story. It's my life. The gift is survival. I made it. I'm here. I'm not miserable. I want to live again. I sit with another sort of light. I survived an identity transformation. My soul is shining out for those to see it, feel it like they are looking through clear glass.

I will honor the divinity in me. I will honor it in you. Our deep essence is made much of the same. All of us come here to love. We come to heal and throw an oar out to those that are drifting. Deep water in the river is quieter. The deeper we go within ourselves, the more peace we will experience. Why? Only one reason: God lives there, and God—he/she, Holy Spirit—is the kingdom that brings darkness into light. Ask anyone who is dying if there's any such thing as a false God. We can call it whatever we want, but there is an invisible force of nature that is visible when we bravely show the world our wounds. There is one flicker that lights another flicker and another and another until the flame is so bright that the heat produces binding energy. It has been generous to be loved. I feel it every new day. My writing the end of this book is *home*.

My life has changed forever. So can yours. Now go create dreams you wanted all your life. Fall in love. Risk everything for love. Get the degree you want, the job you want, the pet you want. Bless others. Eat dessert first. Stop procrastinating. Your dreams are real. Don't you know, if you give up on the dream, your spirit dies?

I hope my story does some damage to your kingdom of darkness. Dare yourself to go higher. Live life your way. I hope you find that silence is holy, mercy is essential for healing, grace shows up last, and inner peace is the highest accomplishment in life. I hope you know that my open door, exposing everything without shame or guilt, my courage to be vulnerable, will open your doors that have been slammed shut. I hope you make a choice to get what you deserve out of life. And grow a huge heart to give a voice to all the beautiful tiny things deep inside you. I did.

Finally, at seventy years old, I bravely transformed my entire being. I never gave up hope with my wildly energetic spirit. I wake up praying, not because I believe there is a being out there who is listening. Prayer helps me remember how deeply grateful I am still alive. It helps me keep one foot in front of the other doing the next best thing. A part of me is still that girl on the Ferris wheel with an inexhaustible voice.

I hope you remember my story, not for the tragedies and suffering but for the courage it took to relive these events, moments, write my story, and choose *love* over fear, trauma and grief. Thank you. Thank you. Thank you. My walk with personal integrity today comes out of how many hundreds of times I've fallen. I'm truly sorry for everyone who lost their inner magic due to those who have treated you as someone with no value. I promise you, there are millions who see through a spiritual lens who care about you. Our deepest wounds grow layers of wisdom. Let the world hear you. No matter how you arrived here at the final page, dig deep, my friends. Dig really deep.

God is love, and the seeds are in you to heal, evolve, connect, vibrate, rebirth, transform. God is whatever lifts your face out of the dirt, telling you to rise! Rise!

Love is larger than any horror the universe drops in our lap. Love yourself and others like it's the last day of your life. Please make kindness your legacy, *then wait for the miracle to happen.*

ABOUT THE AUTHOR

Debra Mak has a high school education. She's worked forty-plus jobs.

Debra is the mother of two deceased children and one living child. She has nine grandchildren, a brother, a niece, and nephew. She currently lives in Winter Garden, Florida.

Printed in the USA
CPSIA information can be obtained
at www.ICGtesting.com
LVHW041221111223
766048LV00001B/68